Chicken Soup
for the
Indian Soul®
Celebrating
Brothers & Sisters

Chicken Soup
for the
Indian Soul®

Celebrating
Brothers & Sisters

101 Stories of Love, Laughter and Changing Relationships

Jack Canfield,
Mark Victor Hansen,
Baisali Chatterjee Dutt

westland

We would like to acknowledge the following publishers and individuals for permission to reprint the following material. (Note: the stories that were penned anonymously or that are public domain are not included in this listing.)

Eating People. Reprinted by permission of Amrita Rajan. © 2012 Amrita Rajan.

No Hitting. Reprinted by permission of Amrita Rajan. © 2012 Amrita Rajan.

My Brother and I. Reprinted by permission of Bali D. Sanghvi. © 2012 Bali D. Sanghvi.

(continued on page 367)

westland ltd
Venkat Towers, 165, P.H. Road, Maduravoyal, Chennai 600 095
No. 38/10 (New No. 5), Raghava Nagar, New Timber Yard Layout, Bangalore 560 026
Survey No. A-9, II Floor, Moula Ali Industrial Area, Moula Ali, Hyderabad 500 040
23/181, Anand Nagar, Nehru Road, Santacruz East, Mumbai 400 055
4322/3, Ansari Road, Daryaganj, New Delhi 110 002

ISBN: 978-93-81626-12-2

Inside book formatting and typesetting by Ram Das Lal

Printed at Gopsons Papers Ltd., Noida

Contents

4. BROTHERLY BONDINGS

5. COOL COUSINS

6. BONDED BY THE HEART

Introduction

It's not the easiest job in the world, being a sibling. We are often not wanted; many a-time resented; occasionally pounded; and frequently taken for granted.

Those of us who have been blessed with a younger sibling know what an irritating pest s/he can be. These mamma's and papa's babies, usurpers of love and attention, chocolate thieves, t-shirt 'borrowers' and nosey parkers who listen in on telephone conversations and read our personal diaries, have had many of us berating our parents for not having used their better sense of judgement to bring home a puppy instead.

Those of us who have the great, good, benefit of an elder sibling in our lives, know what an insufferable pain s/he can be. Parent's first love, know-it-all, paragon of perfection, moral police and dispenser of swift (and often painful) judgement; they have many of us whining to our parents that with them in the picture, Life will always gift us hand-me-downs.

And for those of us who have quite a few in the mix, well then, it's just one big free-for-all, isn't it?

Except, it isn't. Not by half. Not even by a quarter, because the joys of having a sibling far outweigh these minor, niggling little bothers. Because, suddenly, we grow up. And we are compatriots, compadres, forever friends. With the occasional tale-tattling to Mom, of course. That last one just goes with the territory.

To have a sibling is a guarantee that you will always have a witness to your past, a keeper of your secrets, a custodian of your dreams and a corner of home no matter where in the world you may be. A sibling is that invisible thread that binds us to our memories, to where we came from and the people we once used to be. A sibling is the sign on the highway, telling us where we had planned to go and how we can get there. A sibling is also the night watchman, shining that beacon of light to guide our footsteps back home when we get lost in the dark.

A sibling may sometimes be your worst critic, but s/he is always your fiercest protector. While we can fight with them, run them down, tease them and play pranks on them, may there be safe hiding places in the remotest corners of the earth available for anyone else who dares.

They are the pillars of strength, the arms of comfort when we're up against a hard wall. They are the patient ears we need when we have to rant and rave against the brutalities and unfair ways of the world. They are our fellow soldiers in solidarity when our parents are on our case — after all, they're the ones who'll truly understand.

Reading the wonderful stories about brothers and sisters that my writers have shared, just reinforced everything I already believe about this relationship. Heart-warming stories about distance and duty; funny stories about making peace with a sibling that's born the 'wrong' gender; cute stories about those carefree days of childhood; crushing stories about the one who now lives on only in memory...

We all have them, don't we? Stories about the big brothers who used to bully us at home when we were little, but turned playground protector and bodyguard outside. Stories about the big elder sister who'd never spare us the lecture whenever the situation arose (which they made sure was often enough!), and yet they were always the silent, sympathetic listener whenever we needed someone to whom we could unburden ourselves. Stories about little brothers who pulled our pigtails and revelled in irritating us, but then suddenly grew up to amaze us with their magnificent sense of responsibility. The little sister who'd never stop with the whining and reported our every move to Mom, and yet who was always the best cheerleader to have.

And these aren't the only stories that we star in. There are more stories that go all the way back to our childhood; stories that bloom during the summer vacations spent at our grandparents' house; or stories that would be waiting for us during special weekend trips to visit aunts and uncles; sometimes stories brought to us by special house guests who come and live with us for a while. Cousins. They're part of our story. They're the special people in our lives without whom life would not only be unimaginable, but also incomplete.

And then of course there are those people who are not bound to us by blood, but they are by soul. The brothers and sisters we choose to make our own and it's because we can't help it, we are connected by heartstrings and soul songs. They make water equivalent to blood. They make us wonder about our past lives and karmic connections. So what if we're not related in this life? We obviously were in another one.

Brothers and sisters. Cousins. Siblings. Heartstrings. The people who make our lives richer. Better. And incredible.

One of my favourite sibling stories perfectly exemplifies the honest-to-goodness warmth and beauty of this tremendous bond and I'd like to share it with you: I remember last year, on the eve of her wedding, a friend put up a status message on Facebook that went something like this: 'Oh my God! My brother's FB status just made me cry.'

And what was it that my friend's little brother had written? 'My best friend's wedding.'

It's perfect, don't you think? I cannot think of a better way to capture in one sentence, the entire essence of this forever relationship. In those four words, my friend's brother had defined their entire life together. And it even managed to convey those three important words without actually saying them: I love you.

We've got to hand it to our parents. They didn't just provide us with siblings; they provided us with friends for life.

Baisali Chatterjee Dutt

1

WE ARE FAMILY

You don't choose your family. They are God's gift to you, as you are to them.

–Desmond Tutu

Eating People

The world is full of people who like to snigger at those of us who have a hard time planning a party. *What's so difficult about it?* they ask. You invite a bunch of people, make sure they're well fed and watered and then send them home.

Yup. That sounds about right, and when you have a father who is a master planner of parties, as a confident young child you begin to have delusions that this is something you could do just as well. I was perhaps seven when I decided the time had come to put this to the test. Sadly, that is my one unforgettable dinner party.

My favourite restaurant at the time was an intimate little Chinese one that, for reasons that are currently unclear to me, I was convinced was a revolving restaurant. I think there actually was such a restaurant very near the Chinese one, but it had shut down a few years previously. Anyway, I had it fixed in my head that if you sat down in the Chinese restaurant and closed your eyes, you could feel it slowly moving round and round. I was probably anaemic.

It certainly wasn't the cuisine that drew me there. I liked

precisely two things on the menu, both staples of the well-stocked Indian Chinese restaurant: sweet corn chicken soup (I liked this because my aunt liked it and I liked my aunt) and crispy shredded lamb (leathery bits of mutton that they didn't know what to do with so they deep fried it — I liked this one because my brother said it was good and I thought if I did what he did, it would automatically make me a grown-up). Left to myself, I would have haunted the ice cream place, but my brother implied this was because I was greedy, so I left it strictly alone.

So when our cousin came to visit, I decided I had the perfect treat in store for him. I would take him and my brother to the revolving Chinese restaurant and it would be a cousins-only date — no adults allowed. What fun!

I chose my outfit for this marvellous event with great care: a denim mini skirt, a white cotton tank top that laced at my shoulders and my beloved snakeskin high-heeled sandals that I had blackmailed my horrified mother into purchasing by threatening to put on a ten-alarm tantrum in the middle of Connaught Place no matter what the consequences thereafter to my person might be. My ideal self-image was apparently that of a hooker, but I thought I looked fly. And self-confidence matters.

I sashayed into the restaurant with my two long-suffering brothers in tow at five in the evening (my curfew was six o'clock and my parents were disinclined to relax it this once even if I strongly felt it was the acme of my social life) and took a seat at the best table in the thoroughly empty restaurant that was just setting up for the evening crowd.

I would like to express here, my intense love for my brothers.

I like to (rightly) give them a great deal of grief for the many horrors they perpetrated against my childhood dignity, but I'll hand them one thing — they never laughed in my face when I made a fool of myself. They'd always wait until they'd made a fool of me so it didn't hurt my feelings, only my ego. There can't be a lot of teenagers/twenty-somethings who would willingly indulge their pesky little sister's nutty desires when they have a good idea of the horrors in store for them. Like Chinese food at five in the evening. Make that: Chinese food *they absolutely did not want* at five in the evening.

Cousin (reading menu): What shall we eat then?

Me (magnanimously patting tiny back pocket of miniskirt): Anything you want.

Brother: I like the XYZ here.

Me (even more magnanimously): Eat the sweet corn chicken soup!

Cousin: Sweet corn chicken soup? Oh, I didn't want any soup. Is it good?

Me: It's excellent! Right?

Brother (rolling eyes): It's soup.

Me (getting upset): But you like soup! You eat it with crispy shredded lamb!

Brother (looking hunted as he recognises the telltale signs of my fraying temper): Yes. Alright.

Cousin: Is that what you want?

Me (peace restored): Only if you want.

We finally share one bowl of soup and one plate of crispy shredded lamb between the three of us. Then I advise them to shut their eyes at the conclusion of the meal so they can feel the restaurant spin. Waiter grins like a fool the entire time. I decide to leave him a tip even if he doesn't deserve it because that's the grown-up thing to do. Cousin thanks me by putting me in a fireman's lift over his shoulder and walking me back home, flashing my panties to the world. I vow eternal vengeance even though I secretly had a good time.

It all took me a while to process, but you can bet I no longer invite people to my favourite Chinese restaurant to eat what I want them to eat. And I make damn sure nobody even *thinks* of spinning after a meal.

Amrita Rajan

No Hitting

The problem with a younger sibling is that there are so many rules about causing him/her damage. It makes kids rather tetchy about playing with them. I speak from personal experience: when you're three and even the cousin nearest your age is a lordly six, you're not exactly Miss Popular at the rowdy game of the hour. They have to wait for you to run and catch up, help you up the tree, bowl underhand as you try to wield a cricket bat that's roughly your height, and stay constantly vigilant in case they permanently maim you by accident and end up having to face a long line of furious adults who happen to be fans of corporal punishment. You are, in short, a nuisance; a loud, curly-haired nuisance in a pretty frock.

This was back in the days of long, long ago when kids went out to play because our television sets were full of advice for farmers and our phones were large contraptions that could barely handle making a call. For entertainment, we had backyards and open fields where we did things like hunt for tiny fish that the monsoon clouds collected off the sea to pour into muddy puddles, and search for shiny marbles left over from carelessly stored construction materials. I suppose the modern child would see this as a deprived existence, but from my vantage point as the perennial short-legged tag-along, my brother and the assorted cousins who cluttered up my grandmother's house every summer certainly seemed to have a great time.

They'd do exciting things like sneak into the attic and shimmy out the window so they could tippy toe onto the mango tree that wearily leaned its fruit-laden branches against the side of the house. These were special mangoes that tasted watery and fibrous when consumed in normal fashion but were somehow transformed into delicious manna when eaten twenty feet in the air against your mother's very strict orders.

They'd do fun things like turn the kitchen upside down pickling gooseberries in brine over the squawking protests of the horrified great aunt who ran the household. Three days later, the 'pickling' done, we'd spend a whole afternoon happily accumulating a stomach ache, deriving enormous pleasure from the unshakeable conviction that we were getting away with something. What exactly, I don't know — but it was *something* and it was good. The gooseberries were proof. Hard, crunchy, salty little things that tortured the nerve endings of your teeth with every sour bite — but oh my God, I can still taste the joyous summer of their memory.

They'd do ... um, educational things like teach the dogs to 'break dance' to Michael Jackson's *Bad*. It was the '80s, after all. FYI, Boxers are much better dancers than Dobermans. And German Shepherds are basically your dad, standing in a corner and watching the goings-on with a faintly puzzled yet encouraging air. Pomeranians are the worst — very eager but absolutely useless; can't remember a step to save their tails.

Naturally, I wanted in on the action.

'Me!' I said. 'I want to play!'

They expressed disinterest. It was nothing personal, you understand, but at my tender age I was much better suited, they felt, for adult company. Let the grown-ups play with their living, breathing dress-up doll; the kids were far too busy to take care of a toddler.

'But I want to play!' I screamed.

They simply ran off and left me to my tantrum.

It is at this juncture of their lives, dear reader, that every younger sibling must choose one of two paths:

a) accept that biology and fate have already determined that you're forever too late to join the cool crowd

b) fight for your share of coolth.

I've always been a fighter. Next up, therefore, I tried stealth. I spied on their every move, straining my ears to overhear confidential plans of parentally disapproved activities and trying my best to slip along uninvited. Every moment I was awake, I was certain that somewhere in the house fun was being had in my absence. Unfortunately, owing to certain deficiencies in planning and resources, my early efforts at shiftiness came to nothing: I was defeated by my mother's systematic use of afternoon naps as a method of behaviour-control and my own tiny body that couldn't run fast enough to catch up with the rest when they refused to heed my cries to *wait for me!*

So then came manipulation. I attached myself to my female cousin — a gentle, maternally-inclined soul eight years my senior who was the only one happy to play with me. Since she was also my brother's best friend, I figured I could swim in her wake when they were off on one of their adventures. I reckoned without my brother, the hard-hearted villain, who had no problem whatsoever in summarily booting me off despite her tender-hearted protests.

Finally, I struck gold. I complained to my mother. Now, I know this is a method that is held in some contempt by a lot of people, but I would like to stand up for sneaks everywhere by pointing out a simple truth: It Works.

The next time they played a game of cricket, guess who got to participate? Me. Not only did they invite me to join in, but I was a very important part of the game.

I was The Wicket. Not the wicketkeeper, you understand — that's an inferior person who stands around waiting to catch the ball, my brother explained. I was The Wicket. I got to stand behind the batsman the whole time and if you hit me, you were out.

Amrita Rajan

My Brother and I

I often think about my childhood, and every time I do, I cannot help but smile at the silly things I did, the toys I would play with, the tantrums I would throw and, most importantly, the fun, secure relationship I shared (and still do) with my elder brother, Abhisekh, whom I fondly call 'Bhai'.

Some people are surprised at how close we are, probably because my brother and I are totally opposites: in thoughts, in behaviour, in looks. In fact, in all aspects. But there's something that connects us very strongly even today.

I remember Mom talking about the time when I was born. Of everyone in the family, she says, my brother was the happiest. She said he could not wait to take me in his arms and would get angry if he was not allowed to do so. His little mind did not understand that I was too tiny for him to hold and play with. He was always extremely possessive about me. He would not let anyone touch me, and if anyone wanted to play with me, it had to be done under his watchful eye. When Mom would feed me Cerelac, he would get all his toys and sit and play there. I would eat without any fuss then. When my mother would bathe me, he would help her soap me, and when she would dress me, he would hand her the powder, the oil, the cream, the diaper, one by one. Everyone would tell my mother that, with Bhai around, she would not have to worry about anything.

I remember an incident when my parents, brother and I were in the Toys 'r' Us store in Singapore. My brother and I were at the age when we wanted every single toy we saw. While I was the shy one, my brother knew how to get things done his way. At the store, he said he wanted a particular toy. When our father said no, my brother threw the biggest tantrum ever. He lay down on the floor and started howling and screaming. My dad tried to lift him up, but suddenly, he was stronger than He-Man! Finally, our poor, flustered father gave in. Bhai looked at me, raised his toy, winked and mouthed the words, 'For us.' Everything was for us, never for him or me. It was always US.

We would spend hours and hours playing with our toys. It did not matter whether the toys were supposedly for a girl or a boy. Together, we created a huge house for Barbie, Ken and their babies; we collected each and every figure of He-Man and got a special showcase made to stock all of them. We have a huge garden, and one area was filled with sand and stones. There, we created a whole battlefield with our GI-Joe toys. We also had the whole collection of Hot-Wheels cars and, together, Bhai and I would 'drive' around the whole house and hold Grand-Prix tournaments. In the evenings, sometimes, we would take out our colouring books or sit on the swing and read. Whenever I fell ill, he would always get a gift for me and take care of me. We never felt the need for a friend as we were more than enough for each other.

At school, while I was a good student, my brother struggled and faced the wrath of my dad every night. Sometimes, my dad would forbid him to even have water till he finished studying a particular chapter. My mother and I would sneak in and, while I distracted Dad, Mom would give Bhai water to drink. The three of us were always a team.

From the innocent days of childhood to school, finally, we reached the age of young adulthood. My brother decided to join work at an early age while I had just entered college. Things moved on and then came the big day — Bhai's wedding. I could not believe that he was getting married! While a part of me was extremely happy and excited about the whole thing, one part of me was scared because, with Bhai's marriage, I thought my anchor would be broken. I knew that, soon after, my father would start looking for prospective grooms for me too.

Before that could happen, tragedy struck. My brother's marriage was slowly falling apart and, eventually, small fights and differences led to the involvement of parents and a very messy divorce. Bhai blamed himself for everything, and I tried my best to prevent him from going to pieces. We would talk way into the night about life and its lessons. Bhai had become vulnerable. He would cry. Sometimes he would come to my room in the middle of the night, wake me up and just break down. I tried my best to be there for him and make him see the brighter side of things. I knew that I was the only person he could depend on and I made sure that, come what may, I would stand up for him. I went with him for the legal meetings and to our relatives' homes. I also went with him to court.

They say time heals all wounds; slowly, life returned to normal. Five years after my brother's divorce, I got married.

More than my parents, it was Bhai who was incredibly happy for me. At some level, I think, he had felt all this time that I wasn't getting married because he was a divorcee. He made sure that my wedding was everything I'd dreamt it would be. We would sit in the office together and label the wedding cards, we shopped together, we hung out a lot with my fiancé Darshan, who got along well with my brother. On the day of our engagement, my brother wrote the most beautiful letter to Darshan, pouring out his heart and expressing his deepest emotions.

And then, five years after my marriage, Bhai got married again to one of the sweetest persons I know. Today, life has come full circle for us. He's happily married and madly in love with his wife who loves and respects him equally, and I'm a new mother to twin boys. Bhai is already the devoted 'mamu' and looking forward to playing with them. In fact, he's thrilled that he can finally dust off our old toys that he had lovingly and carefully kept away ... for the next generation.

Bali D. Sanghvi

Quality Time

Help your brother's boat across and your own will reach the shore.

–Hindu proverb

When my father called me from Chennai with the news, I was shocked. 'Turn on your television, the World Trade Centre in New York has gone down!' It was September 11, 2001 — a day that continues to haunt the world even today. I didn't have a TV then, so I rushed to my neighbour's house. My brother was in Washington DC that very day. Only when I heard those words, 'He's fine', a few hours later, did I realise that I had been holding my breath. Despite the distance and the too infrequent calls, I realised how much my brother meant to me.

My earliest recollections of my brother are tied in with exercise and Maths. It seems an unlikely combination, but he was passionate about both. His rapid-fire questions when he got home from his hostel would make me sulk and weep alternately. 'Did you stretch and do push-ups?' he would ask, and then, 'How about working out a page of Math problems?' Nevertheless, I looked forward to his visits with excitement. Being eight years older than me, he treated me like a child, and I lapped up the attention. He would listen to me patiently, teach me songs on the guitar and play indoor games with me. At the same time, he would chastise me for not working hard on my studies or engaging in any physical activity for my age.

By the time I became a teenager, he had already left the country to pursue higher studies. We started writing to each other then. Being prolific writers, the momentum was strong. His letters helped me tide over my teen years, our moves to different cities thanks to my father's transferable job, and the absence of not having someone to share my anxieties at home. At times, when I was despondent, the letters were the antidote. I would read them all over again and feel rejuvenated. My childish scrawls soon gave way to superior cursive writing as I learnt from one of the best. Every Saturday I would rush to the mail box for that first glimpse of the aerogram. If there was an envelope I would tear the stamps off and add it to my collection.

His letters brimmed with news. Whether it was about meeting with friends, going out for pizza, visiting places, or events in the campus, his letter would read like a story and make it all come alive for me. I also sensed the loneliness behind his missives and caught my mother surreptitiously wiping her tears at times. When photos arrived with the letters, they were the icing on the cake. I could see the changes in him and sometimes feared that he had become a stranger. Who was this adult with a moustache?

Siblings are a blessing. When I share my childhood memories with my own children now they roll their eyes. They give me

a perplexed look and remark. 'But you hardly spent time with
your brother!' My stock reply to them: 'It's the quality of time
and not quantity that matters, isn't it?'

Chitra Srikrishna

Because of This Bond

I remember that horrible sight oh-so-well. I was six and my brother two when one day we heard these heart-wrenching sobs coming from somewhere. We rushed up the stairs with our father to find our mother sitting on the floor crying uncontrollably. I stood there unsure of what I should do, my father's hands gently gripping my shoulders. My brother climbed onto my mother's lap and wiped her tears away.

Being so young we hadn't been told much. In fact, we hadn't been told anything. I had just gathered from the hushed conversations around the house over the past few days that one of my mother's brothers, back in India, had passed away from renal failure. He was not yet twenty-five.

To rub salt into everyone's wound, a letter from the American consulate addressed to my uncle reached his address a few months after his passing. Inside that envelope was his visa approval, granting him sanction to come and visit us in New York.

My mom's heart broke a little bit more.

My uncle's tragic death changed our lives forever.

It acted as the catalyst for our return to India. My mother said that was the last time she was ever going to be so far away from her family in their time of need. She never wanted to be so many continents, time zones and expensive flight tickets away from her parents, brothers and sisters again, and so she was going to bridge the gap created by the Atlantic Ocean by coming home. Or as near to home as possible.

And so, four years later, my mother, two reluctant kids in tow, came to India and settled down in Bangalore. Yes, so, it wasn't Calcutta. But, at least it wasn't New York either.

Of course there were a few other issues that contributed to the move, but the sibling pull factored as one of the top reasons.

My mother comes from a large family: she is the third child, with six others after her. So her maternal instincts kicked in rather early. The elder children were responsible for the younger ones and the younger ones made sure their big brothers and sisters always had their hands full. From sharing rooms to clothes to food to books to friends, the bond between the Chakraborty siblings was cemented at an early age. So many events shaped and moulded the siblings, because of their bond.

It was because of this bond that my eldest aunt flew all the way to the States to be with my mother right after I was born, since my grandmother could not make it.

It was because of this bond that my mother, while listening to a popular Bengali song, *Shey Aamaar Chhoto Bon* (she is my little sister), decided to take the next available flight to India to be present for her elder brother's wedding — an event that she had originally thought she would not be able to attend due to financial constraints. It was because of this bond, and for the same wedding, that my eldest aunt cut short her dream Europe tour, so that she could celebrate with her brothers and sisters (she never did get to see the places she missed). It was also because of this bond that my uncle, the groom-to-be, made sure he was at the airport in the wee hours of the morning waiting for her flight to land ... despite knowing that he would have no time to catch up on his sleep, as the wedding rituals were due to kick off at the crack of dawn.

It was because of this bond, that each and every sibling wanted to get tested and donate a kidney to their sick brother.

It was because of this bond that the three youngest brothers, despite having next-to-nil house-keeping and kitchen skills, encouraged their mother to pack up and go to Delhi to be with their eldest sister, because she needed help to look after her newborn baby girls. That entire month, the three strapping young men basically got by on boiled rice and eggs, and mercifully, they did not burn the house down!

It was because of this bond that, though drowning in their own sorrow at the loss of their mother, my youngest aunt and my mother were able to put their grief aside to make sure that the brother who was most attached to their mother, was not overcome by anguish.

It is because of this bond, that no matter where they are, they try and get together at least once a year during Diwali, to celebrate Kali Puja, an event that is intrinsically linked to each and every one of their first memories. And it is because of this bond that the Chakrborty siblings share, that we, their children, look forward to the yearly gathering as well. We cousins love watching our parents indulge in all-night sessions of catching up, singing and warm-hearted merry-making.

As my mother says, 'We may not have grown up with much, but we did grow up with a lot of love.'

To see them together, is to know just how true that sentiment is.

Baisali Chatterjee Dutt

'We're Getting a Boy Baby!'

'We're getting a boy baby!'

You, a little three-year-old girl, announced to an open-mouthed extended family. We had just broken the big news to them that we planned to adopt our second child. They were hoping to dissuade us from what seemed like an unwise decision to them.

And then you, Mili, turned around, from watching that scene playing on their TV, the one from *Hum Tum*, where the boy baby in the hospital nursery is admiring Saif Ali Khan's precious girl baby. And you said, 'We're getting a baby for my Anna (Daddy), just like that one. Because my mother has a girl, so now Anna will have a boy.'

The startled silence spoke a million words. I was grinning inwardly, because that was when they realised we were serious, and accepted our decision. You did it for us Mili!

And of course afterward everyone roared with laughter because you thought this boy baby was in Anna's tummy. We didn't know then, that your innocent words had started off a cascade of life-changing experiences for our family, that brought tears of laughter and enriched our lives with events, things and people we'd only dreamed of having in our lives.

So it was perfectly meant to be that just four days before your fourth birthday you, Mili, were the first to hold your brother Hunny, not us. He was yours first. All of two months old, he looked at you so curiously. You got upset when we couldn't bring him home immediately. You picked out his name in the few days that we waited, readying your old crib, toys, stroller and clothes for him.

I have this picture where we've just arrived home with Pud baby, exhausted but triumphant, and he is lying on the bed next to you. Both of you look so tired, but content. He's gazing up at you with this priceless wicked look, 'Oh, I'm gonna be your quintessential pesky lil' brother, just you wait, Sis!'

I wonder if this letter to you can express how I feel about you and Hunny, my two blessings. Your story has just begun, and I want to see how it unfolds.

From day one, you both got along like a house on fire. You held him on your lap and fed him his bottles. He crawled into your tent and broke your childhood toys that you'd carefully preserved. Heck, he broke *my* childhood toys that you'd carefully preserved! You boasted in school about your new baby brother, which resulted in many four-year-olds going home from school and demanding that their mommies bring home a sibling for them too! I remember the exasperated calls from those mothers!

Hunny's exuberant antics and gleeful giggles were a perfect foil to your quiet, serious nature. He got you moving and going. He snuggled up to you, sulked when you went to school and knew when you came home, even if you were quiet as a mouse. Actually you've never been quiet when you come home! You *will* wake him up to coochie-coo with him.

You coo over him when he's asleep and we giggle at his antics and cuteness together. He looks up to you big-time, and copies everything you do. He just can't wait to be as big as you are, and chafes at the age gap between the two of you. Equality with you is his birthright, or so he believes!

You think he's a pest, but you start fretting when he's not around for a while. He can't live without you either. The day he joined you at your 'big' school, I cried at the gate as I watched you walk in, hand-in-hand. You've introduced him to all your friends at school as 'MY brother'.

You set right a friend who insisted that a 'real' brother had to come from the same mummy's tummy. You, a little four-year-old kid, towered over that seven-year-old boy with your indignation. 'GOD said he is my brother. In front of God, the priest said he is ours. Do you think God is wrong?' And that boy retired, vanquished!

He didn't like the rakhi you'd tied for him as a baby and toddler; probably it irritated his soft skin. He now wears it proudly to school, and he wanted to know why he couldn't tie a rakhi on you, thinking it's a friendship band. Suits me fine; brothers and sisters *should* be friends.

Next year, you both can tie rakhis on each other. Why should only girls tie a rakhi for a brother's protection? I think you can take care of yourself just fine! You're growing a tough skin outside your super-sensitive core. Maybe Hunny has helped toughen you up? The way you scream at each other one minute and gurgle with laughter in a tumbling heap of arms and legs the next, is teaching you about conflict resolution and coexistence. Maybe that's what protection really means.

Not a one-time incident when he fights off people who attack you, but a long process where you both learn to fight back for yourselves and to not take everything so very seriously.

We struggle to give you both equal attention and time, a real challenge with your different ages, needs, temperaments and even gender! We introspect like crazy if something we do or say will later cause you'll to nurse grudges against each other. Nursing grudges against us and ganging up against us is okay. It's the sweetest thing I ever experienced, because I'm an only child. Every interaction between the two of you, whether acrimonious or adoring is so very precious to me.

Your brother completed our family. You started it. If not for him, we would've been this gloomy, over-serious trio that couldn't see the funnier side of things, that couldn't let the small stuff slide. You would've been the only child of an only child ... really lonely. If not for you, he would've missed out on some heavy-duty nurturing. Some clueless people say we saved him by adopting him. I think he saved us from ourselves!

I don't know what your relationship will be like when you grow up. I never take sides. As long as I'm around I'm going to make sure you'll are able to work out your differences and treasure what's wonderful about your relationship. I think I have all the answers to prevent those wretched adult sibling feuds. Maybe I don't. But I'll certainly try.

It's like you said the other day. 'Amma, when Hunny smiles his starry smile, I feel like the whole world lights up.' Yes it does, Hunny and Mili. You both light up my life. May you be there for each other all your lives.

Nayantara Mallya

Pilgrimages of Love

'Next time we won't visit our relatives as if it's a pilgrimage,' my mom says. 'We'll go to some different places. Everyone else comes here and travels around, but all we end up doing is going is Gorakhpur, Nagpur and Lucknow.'

She says that on the last day every time she visits India. My dad keeps quiet, I giggle and my sister supports my mom. When we were younger, we would also say, 'Yes, next time we will go to the Taj Mahal.'

My dad moved out of India twenty-seven years ago. He is a professor and he is currently in Kenya. When we were kids, we would visit India once every two or four years, with bags all stuffed and a wish list in hand, which usually consisted of Hindi audio cassettes, watching the latest movies and clothes. Our trips were straight out of the scenes in Jhumpa Lahiri's *The Namesake* when Ashoke Ganguli brings his family to India.

Those days, we did not have a place of our own in India. Our trip would start at Mumbai and then we would go to Pune, Nagpur, Lucknow, Dehradun, Gorakhpur, Bahriach and Faizabad — places where my parents' relatives live. We would travel in trains, buses and the local transport available in each city, like cycle rickshaws, auto rickshaws, local mini buses and our relatives' scooters and bikes. And after each trip, on the last day at the airport, my mom would say the same thing about the 'teerth yatra'.

Over time, my sister and I moved to India for studies, and then we stayed on and started working.

Last week, my mom called up and said they'd booked their tickets to India and that they would arrive soon. The following day, my dad's e-mail arrived with a list of train tickets to book.

My dad has four brothers and four sisters. When he visits them, it takes him all over India. He spends a day or two with each one of them and they all look forward to his visit. He is the youngest of the brood. They pick him up and then his brothers' wives and now their daughters-in-law all cook his favourite meals. I don't think they can catch up on the one-two year gap, but they laugh and make the most of the little time they have together. The size 38/39 shirts he used to get for them have been replaced by kids'-size clothes for their grandchildren. His sisters still get a shirt for him and my mom still makes sure my father has a sari to give each of them! Without fail, when it's time to say goodbye, they have a pooja thali ready, to wish him a traditional farewell, and along with that, an envelope with some money to give him. They bless him, say prayers for a safe journey and hope to see him again.

My mom has three sisters and three brothers, with her being the middle one. Her brothers stay in a huge farm. My mom also always has something for her brothers, and her brothers get the best rice, fish and chicken for her. They pick us up from the bus stand and lavish us with love and attention. My mom's sisters stay in Pune and they are also always happy to see their younger sister.

Over the years, as I've grown, I have come to understand a thing or two about relationships, family dynamics and the love that blossoms and grows from these 'pilgrimages'. The hours that my parents spend with their brothers and sisters, I believe, is as good as spending time at any holy place, because at each of these places, they are showered with lots of love and blessings.

Prashant Kumar

The Four of Us

There were four of us — Anwar, Tasnim, me and Tarique, in that order — and this is a slice of our childhood. We were away at our boarding schools in Nainital for nine long months, but come December and the house would lose its calm and tranquility with the four of us turning everything topsy-turvy.

First thing in the morning, even before brushing our teeth, we would rush to the front veranda to see how many snakes had shed their skins the night before. Bahadur, our night chowkidar, would line up the moulds on the front steps for us to see. They were so astonishingly pretty, with the most intricate geometrical patterns, that it was difficult to associate them with the venom-spewing reptiles. Bahadur would tell us how to recognise the ones that belonged to the poisonous snakes.

We would then go racing to the back veranda of our house where Amma would have scattered seeds and grains for the birds and placed little troughs of water that served as bird baths. There we would sit quietly, watching the birds pecking greedily, often squabbling and pushing each other out of the way.

Anwar was the 'good boy'. Handsome, intelligent, always at the top of his class, always obedient, never in a fight and everyone's pet. He was also the caroms champion in school, even as he garnered the most number of gold cards for excellence in academics.

Tasnim was a born leader. She was also fiercely protective of the rest of us. She could beat, bite, kick and thrash an 'enemy' to pulp if necessary. At other times she would write comic strips for Tarique and me. The one I liked best was about the girl who went to Mars in a flying saucer. She also played the meanest of tricks on us. One day she decided to swindle Tarique and me of our share of the Shab-e-Barat halwa. This is how she did it:

'Want to see me perform magic?'

'You actually can?'

'Yes! See, I'll eat a piece of your halwa. It'll be in my mouth but you'll get the taste.'

'Wow!'

Many bites later...

'Mmmm! Can you taste it?'

'Not yet,' Tarique and I looked at our disappearing share with some trepidation.

'Oh, you'll get it. Just be patient.'

After the last piece had been munched up, 'Still haven't got the taste in your mouth?'

'No!' we both yelled in frustration.

'Hmmm ... then something must be wrong with your taste buds,' and so saying, the 'magician' dusted her hands and walked away, licking her lips, leaving us to stare at our empty boxes.

Tarique was my baby brother. 'He'll play with you when

he's bigger,' Dadi had promised me the day Amma brought him home from the hospital. We would be playmates for many childhood years, but little did I know that the participation would be very one-sided. Tarique would sit in our toy car and I would spend hours pushing him from one end of the veranda to the other. He would sit on the swing and I would push it as high as I could. When it was my turn he would run off on some pretext.

Tarique always decided on the game we would play, his favourite being sailing our rubber slippers in the garden tank. One time he leaned in too far and slipped right in. Deep into the murky water went my little brother and there was no one around. I was petrified. Then he came up to the surface gasping for breath. I grabbed his hair and clung on for life, screaming my lungs out at the same time. My screams of fear finally brought the gardener to our rescue.

Those were the wonder years. And then we grew up. School, college, jobs, marriage, children … life carried us forward and away from one another. But never too far away.

In March last year Anwar was diagnosed with cancer of the liver. Our lives shattered. Tasnim left her home to be with Anwar during his entire stay at the hospital. She was once again his little sister who protected him from bullies in the school bus. This time she would remain at his side protecting him from depression and defeat, filling his last days with love and laughter and tender care. She was a pillar of strength for Anwar and his wife.

Anwar left us soon after in June. His passing brought us closer. We're united now in caring for one another, for our mother and all the children in the family, because life has taught us to appreciate and enjoy the company of loved ones while we still have them around.

My mother passed away in November this year, having lived a full and fruitful life. She was ninety-one.

It's now just the three of us. And even though there's a big gap left behind by Anwar, we still make a great team.

Rehana Ali

Same-Same, But Different

Nagaland is a place that I call my second home and it is not just because of the beauty of the place and the peace I feel when I am there. I share an intense connection with the land, because I found a family there — people who began as strangers have now become my very own.

Of all the amazing stories that I can share about this newfound family of mine, the story of my two 'brothers' is one I cherish greatly. Let me call them A1 and A2.

I met A1 two years ago. His mad energy as well as his willingness to go out his way to help a non-Naga, single female traveller like me told me volumes about his character. I just knew that he would be my absolutely first Naga friend. Seemingly happy-go-lucky, he is ever willing to make everyone else around him smile, laugh and embrace life. Being a college drop-out didn't stop him from working hard and becoming the youngest entrepreneur in a beautiful district of Nagaland. His ambitions and hardworking nature propelled him there.

Over the next few weeks, he was my guide and soon became

a fast friend. He made me promise to keep in touch and to meet him when I was next there for work and I happily agreed. So, when I did go back a few months later, A1 was right there waiting for me. We had gotten to know each other very well by now, but I could tell that he carried a great sadness in his heart — one that he wasn't ready to share with me. He drank much too much, didn't pay much attention to his business, and when he wasn't talking, he'd have this faraway look in his eyes, filled with an incredible melancholy.

He took me over to meet his parents and they lovingly welcomed me into their family. They wanted to know about my travel plans and when I mentioned I needed to go to Kohima, they said that their younger son, who was pursuing a Master's degree in History at Kohima University, would be happy to show me around. My jaw dropped. Younger son? I turned to A1 and asked him why he hadn't told me he had a younger brother, and he just laughed it off.

When I finally met A2, we hit it off just as easily and fabulously. Yet, I couldn't help but notice that the relationship between the brothers was not easy. A1 seemed to be too eager to please while A2 seemed a little guarded. In front of me they laughed and joked, but the laughter seemed a little forced. They behaved in a similar manner, yet their behaviour was markedly dissimilar. I couldn't really put my finger on it; there was just something different. I searched in their faces, smiles, walk, hands, eyes ... but there was nothing remotely alike in that regard either! When I mentioned it the first time, they laughed and said, 'Same-same, but different.' They couldn't have put it more perfectly, because that is how I felt about them too, 'Same-same, but different'.

I grew very close to both of them in a short span of time and they both decided, separately, to 'adopt' me as their sister.

One evening, when the sky was a patchwork of grey and blue, and the silence surrounding us was like a blanket of calm, A1 bared his soul to me.

This is his story...

A1 was to be born into a rich family, but the young parents-to-be were trapped in an extremely difficult and unhappy marriage. They decided to part ways when A1 was just a mere eight-months-old in his mother's womb. However, so as not to do their child an injustice, they decided to find him a family that would take care of him. Once A1 was born, he was given away to a poor family and his birth parents went their separate ways.

His adopted family lavished him with love and attention and yet his favourite childhood memories are those of the monthly visits from his favourite uncle. Little did he know that the 'uncle' was his biological father!

When he was finally told the truth by his grandmother, his world came crashing down around him.

So his mom was not his own! Neither was his father, nor his brother! He had always wondered why his parents had had another baby within a year of his birth. No wonder he could never solve the mystery of the age gap!

He was devastated ... everything his parents did for him seemed like a duty and everything he did for his family seemed like repayment and acts of gratitude. He questioned the love. He questioned loyalties. He questioned reality and truth.

A2 knew nothing of it all and silently watched his brother destroying himself. He wanted to help, but felt helpless. He wanted to give hope, but felt hopeless. What was happening to his big brother whom he loved so much? What was eating up his best friend that he seemed hell-bent on wrecking himself?

Finally, his mother told him the family secret and he slipped into silence. Many thoughts spun around his head like a tornado.... So that bundle of ruined energy was actually not his brother. So the love that was only supposed to be his was being shared unnecessarily. How dare he scream at *my* mom and *my* dad! How dare he demand anything from them? How dare he have a room to himself? My mom, my blanket, my father, my walls, my wood, my pork, my clothes, my dog, my cat, my home ... my everything! The unfairness of it all seemed to drown him in a pool of angry, seething silence.

And ever since the secret came out in the open, the two brothers grew apart. A1 felt guilty; A2 felt cheated. Yet, to their parents, it was so simple, so straightforward — they had enough love and more for both of them.

Then the parents told A2 that I also knew the truth and that the situation was not a big deal to me at all. Somehow, that got A2 to wondering, was he over-thinking it all in his head? He started on his own soul-searching....

And then, one day, he looked over at A1, drooped over in his own private hell, sinking in his own quagmire of misery at thoughts of being abandoned, unloved and unwanted.

A2 looked back on the life that they had had together and realised that his life would have been so incomplete and empty without A1. *Of course* A1 was loved and wanted! A1 was wanted by their mother and father! A1 was wanted by him — his brother!

A2 got up, walked over to A1 and hugged him. The

floodgates flew open and a deluge of pent-up emotions, fears and thoughts came tumbling out.

They were brothers. Always had been and forever would be. Just let anybody try and take that away from them! Today, they are like the best friends they once used to be when they were little boys; they discuss their girlfriends, drink together, go for picnics together, laugh, exchange dirty jokes, dance, sing, fight, punch, yell, look out for the other and take care of the other's needs. A1 is determined to see his younger brother become an officer. A2 wants his brother to quit drinking and get his life back on track. Who cared about the differences, little and big? They were brothers, same-same, but different!

And now, they have me in the mix too. Their sister. So different, but very same-same!

Ritika Mittal Nair

Full House ... Full of Love

'You're *expecting*?' Granny asked Mum, darting a quick look in my direction to check if I had heard her surprised reaction. As a bursting-with-curiosity thirteen-year-old, *of course* I had caught what she had said.

Seated at our dining-cum-study table just a few feet away from Granny and Mum in the tiny room that served as our living room by day and bedroom by night, I had been engrossed in my homework. But now my mind was no longer on my studies. How could it be? When things were on an even keel in my little world, Mum's revelation had shattered the peace like a tornado.

'So when is the baby due?' Granny asked Mum, a wan smile taking the edge off the concern reflected in her eyes.

'In May,' answered Mum, briefly looking up from her task of making hemming marks on one of the dresses I had outgrown. She was altering the frock to fit my younger, ten-year-old sister, Vera. Third in the pecking order was my six-year-old brother, Gladwyn.

And soon, there was going to be a fourth child!

I kept up the pretence of studying till Granny left, surreptitiously stealing glances at her and Mum every few minutes. Ears cocked to one side, I followed their hushed conversation while feelings of disbelief, confusion and resentment welled up inside me, almost choking me.

Our modest two-room accommodation was cramped for sure, but despite its limitations, it was a place we were happy in. And now, a new brother or sister was going to disturb the established order of things? I squeezed my eyes shut in disgust. We barely had enough floor space to accommodate the five of us at night. Where was the room for one more sibling? I was so furious I couldn't concentrate on anything else that day.

But a few months later, when I held my newly-born sibling, Cynthia, in my arms, I did a complete 180-degree turn! Utterly smitten by the cherubic new entrant into our family, I helped Mum bathe her, whip up her cereal for her, and feed her. I even changed her diapers. Not just that, almost every week I brought a few school friends home so I could show off my cute baby sister to them.

Now, decades later, I can see that while it was smooth going with Cynthia from the start, things were different with Vera. I was just three when she was born and I guess I had looked at her as a bothersome competitor.

I remember how I resented the way my parents called Vera 'baby' even after she had started going to school. 'She's *not* a baby,' I would say fiercely. In fact, their 'baby' was a smart cookie. She often evaded rolling away her bedding the way Mum had taught us to by scampering off to brush her teeth immediately after waking up. And then Mum would insist that I put away Vera's bedding along with mine. Smarting at the injustice of it all, I would protest, 'Doesn't she have hands? Why should *I* do this for her?' Mum's no-nonsense reply would invariably be a firm 'She's your sister, that's why.'

On the other hand, I did have a few, loving big-sister moments too. I remember one day, during the summer holidays, when I was around six or seven, Dad took Vera and me to the Circarama show in town which was pulling in huge crowds every day. We had shuffled along for an hour or so in the long winding queue, inching closer to the entrance of the giant-sized Circarama dome, when suddenly, we discovered to our dismay that Vera was missing. Apparently, having failed to keep pace with us as we moved ahead she had got lost in the swirling crowds. The horror of what had happened beginning to sink in, I started weeping hysterically.

Fortunately, Dad found Vera and our evening out didn't end in a Bollywood-style siblings-separated-in-a-mela type of disaster. Once inside the crowded dome, we were treated to awesome visuals of the Niagara Falls, the Grand Canyon and other places as we watched *America the Beautiful* projected on the circular screen surrounding us on all sides. The show was spellbinding, but I was alert enough to hold Vera's hand tight till it ended.

Moving on to Gladwyn, I was seven years old when Mummy came back from the hospital on a rainy day in July with her first baby boy. It was just a matter of time before history began to repeat itself all over again in our little home. This time round, it was Vera and I ganging up against our kid brother, protesting that our parents were favouring him over us two.

Mum was very strict about clothes, books and toys being put away in their proper places. So, after school, whenever

Gladwyn forgot to hang up his uniform in his eagerness to run off outdoors and play with his friends, and Mum asked me or Vera to pick it up, we would balk at her suggestion. 'Why should I?' we would retort.

'Because he's your brother,' Mum would tell us patiently.

At times like this, it seemed to us that Mum was being unfair, when she was in fact sowing the seeds of family bonding in our hearts, encouraging us to show our love for one another. But, too young to understand what Mum was doing, we would sometimes holler in a fit of fury, 'You're soft on Gladwyn because he's your S-U-N sun!' Instead of flying into a rage, Mum would deal with our juvenile outbursts sensibly and with immense tolerance. Going by her own experiences of growing up, she knew these were only tiny bumps on the road to maturity and we would be way past them in no time.

It was not long before Mum was proved right. All it took was Gladwyn's bout of paratyphoid when he was in high school. One day, when his fever shot up dangerously to 104 degrees, the doctor had us strip him to his underwear and instructed us to sponge him with ice water till the fever dropped below 101 degrees. Our neighbours then chipped in by cranking up their refrigerators so we could have an uninterrupted supply of ice for the next few hours.

I was already out of college, but I wept like a baby watching Gladwyn lying on the couch in his briefs, shivering uncontrollably as he endured the agonising ice water bath. I could see from the grim expressions on their faces that Mum and Dad were equally scared. Visibly tired, their fingers stiff from the freezing cold water they were handling, they kept on with the sponging. Vera, who was pursuing a degree in nursing then, was the calmest of us all. Emotions well under control, she diligently followed the doctor's orders, taking and recording Gladwyn's temperature every fifteen minutes till he turned the corner.

Today, my siblings have flown across the high seas to settle in different continents, and we are miles apart. But bonds of love and shared memories keep us close.

In retrospect, I can see that despite the ruffling of feathers during our own *Wonder Years*, love held us siblings together even then. Only, just as the stars shine brightest in the darkest nights, our lurking-beneath-the-surface bonds of love would be most evident in times of crisis when we were kids. Thankfully, not any more. And if ever we have to fight, we're on the same side. For now, we're a team.

Veena Gomes-Patwardhan

The Baby

We stared at the tiny creature in our mother's arms, bundled up and cradled in the crook of her elbow. 'This is your new sister,' she'd said. The Baby, as we had almost instantly christened it, was fast asleep and held our rapt attention for exactly five seconds, and then we were off, doing what was most important to us at that point — bringing the house down.

We were three siblings before the arrival of The Baby: my elder brother was six, I was four and my younger sister was two. For any homemaker, kids of these ages mean trouble, but kids of these ages thrown together 24/7, spell doom! I still wonder how my mother managed, especially when The Baby came along and disrupted our existence.

My brother had just started school and had suddenly transformed into the responsible kid, but my sister Sana and I had all the time in the world to be our unruly selves at home. We ran up and down the hallway. We jumped on laundry piles. We climbed up the terrace wall and on top of the roof. We played with our dog. We played hide and seek. We invented new games imitating our mother's kitty parties. We used her starchy sarees to make tents, regardless of how expensive they were. All that mattered to us was that they made good tents. We basically owned the place, when suddenly, out of the blue, there were rules!

We despised these rules. Don't leave your dolls and toys lying around. Don't run inside the room. Don't watch cartoons so much. Keep the volume down. Don't talk loudly. Don't experiment with The Baby. Afternoons were torturous, because at a time when we would all park ourselves in front of the television to watch the latest episode of *Spiderman*, we had to actually draw the curtains, whisper around the house and pretend that it was night-time. The Baby slept all day, and our lives slept with it. Suddenly, from being high-voltage-kids we had become the boring kids whose high point of the day was playing with Barbie. We had never played with Barbie before.

We hated The Baby and so we boycotted her. The elders had named her Amna, but to us, she was just 'The Baby' for a very long time. Over the years, she grew up alone and aloof from the rest of us, cranky and irritable. She played with the plants and made her shadows her best friends; and we never acknowledged her existence. She was perpetually sick and thus perpetually in bed and hence perpetually with Mom! She was Mom's favourite and we both accepted and loathed that ugly truth. She would get away with any misbehaviour because she 'was sick' or 'the youngest in the family'; she would get the first choice in all gifts, which I felt was my birthright being the eldest sister; and we *still* had to vacate the television room for her every afternoon.

We were not alone in our hatred; she was jointly hated by all
our cousins too. Everyone had gotten into trouble at least once
because of her, and she always had this bad habit of ratting us
out. She was Mummy's spy, and a very good one at that. In
return, we tortured her whenever we got the opportunity. Sana
and I had convinced her one time that she was born a boy and
her name was actually Aman; another time we told her that
she turns into a bird each night and we swore we could see her
beak and feathers; and many, many, many times that she was
adopted and everyone hated her.

One night, we all decided to take revenge. As kids, we were
never allowed to watch horror shows which were all the rage
in India in the '90s, but we still somehow managed to catch a
few episodes here and there. On one such show that we had
all watched, a girl committed suicide by hanging herself in
her room and subsequently continued to haunt the girls of her
hostel who had ragged her and led her to the deed, for eternity.
The scariest scene in the show was when her friends walked
into the room and switched on the lights and fan to see her
body hanging.

Now, I had a life-sized doll and a skipping rope and my
cousin Ozair had this brilliant idea of recreating this scene and
scaring Amna for all the times she had tattled on us. We were
young and didn't realise the consequences; we were just very
excited. We had a plan to execute!

Ozair bhaiya and I set up the scene, covered the doll in a robe
and tied her to the fan using my skipping rope. We decided to
do this in the afternoon because all the elders would be asleep.
My brother Athar was supposed to lead her to the scene under
some pretext and someone had to switch on the fan from

outside the room (the switchboard was next to the window) and then we had to leave her alone and run away.

The time had come. Our excitement was palpable. Everything went as planned and we got her to the room while we watched from our hiding places. The fan was switched-on on cue and she was left alone.

She turned around and all hell broke loose. She bawled and howled and stared at the doll tied to the fan in shock and couldn't move out of fear. It didn't even take us a split second to realise how bad an idea this was. It took all of two minutes for everybody to come rushing in from every room in the house and take her away. That day, all of us kids got the biggest lecture of our lives and the concept of death was introduced to us. We were made to understand how stupidly we had acted, and how this prank could have led to a cardiac arrest in a child so young.

After that incident, we all kept our distance. We neither teased nor spoke to her, out of fear of what we had done, but we had a weird kind of truce. She forgave us and that in turn humbled us to civility.

When she was four, she caught the chicken pox, and that was unfortunately the time we decided to befriend her. So, in the summer of '97, the Undisputable Trio of Nida, Sana and Amna was born, worst-enemies-turned-best-friends-for-life! And all of us spent that summer in bed, with chicken pox, driving Mom wild, and bonding over chicken soup.

Nida Karim

2

BROTHERS & SISTERS

Siblings are the people we practice on, the people who teach us about fairness and cooperation and kindness and caring — quite often the hard way.
                                        –Pamela Dugdale

Unity in Adversity

I was born in mid-transition India when 'equal rights for the girl child' was not yet fashionable. When mom's gynaecologist came out of the delivery room with his head drooped in apology, my maternal grandparents almost thought it was a stillbirth. It wasn't. The doctor was sorry to convey the news that a baby girl was born. It was an atmosphere of contrast that season — while my maternal relatives rejoiced and celebrated, there was stoic indifference in my father's family. This indifference to my existence continued till my brother was born on the same day, six years later. All of a sudden, I began witnessing the kind of loving and caring behaviour my paternal family was capable of, as they pampered my little brother silly. Thus began a silent battle of bitter hatred between me and my brother, Samrat.

Till then I was accustomed to the family's forever negligent behaviour and naturally expected them to mete out a similar treatment to Samrat too, when he was born. But he was closely looked after and attended to. As a child of six, I was a baby myself, too young to understand the psychology behind anyone's actions, yet mature enough to know that I was being discriminated against. The family reasoned that Samrat needed the attention he was showered with because he was still a toddler and dependant on others for survival. They urged me to take care of him similarly, raising me to the status of Didi, the yet small 'elder' sister. Somewhat convinced, I succumbed to their reasoning. But as a couple of years passed, I observed that their excuses kept changing. Now Samrat wasn't a toddler anymore but it was me who had grown up and was presumably ineligible to deserve their attention. The hostility grew within me gradually and surely, though there was precious little that a child could do against an army of girl-child haters in the family. What I *could* do was avenge their animosity onto this little soul who placed himself with implicit trust in the hands of his dear Didi.

I turned wicked during that period. I would look out for those rare occasions when the two of us would be alone and deliberately scare Samrat with stories of the monster toys I knew he was afraid of. I used to turn the room lights off for a few seconds on random nights to make him cry. Yet every time, after getting scared, my little bro would invariably run into my arms and hug me tight to feel secure again. Admittedly, I began feeling ashamed of myself. Being sidelined from the start, I had learnt to reserve for myself whatever little joys came my way. But Samrat, though so young, learned to share because of the love extended towards him. He would often take a tiny morsel from his plate and put it in my mouth before starting his meals. In no time, his innocent ways made me introspect. I had been punishing this sinless soul for the misdoings of others. It didn't take me long to realise that Samrat was possibly the only person in our family who genuinely loved me.

But good times, as they say, don't last forever. My father, who worked abroad, secured a family accommodation license in his next term contract. My parents took Samrat along with them, leaving me behind in India at the mercy of fate and my relatives. I was told that I was being left back so that my education wouldn't be hampered. Yet another lie. My brother attended an American school overseas, while I struggled between studies and household chores back here in India. By now, I had learned to differentiate between the beneficiaries and the benefited. I had stopped blaming Samrat for the privileges bestowed upon him by destiny. More than anything else, this line of thought helped keep me sane and strong. For all the years that followed, I waited for my kid brother to return, so that I could apologise and compensate for whatever wrong I had done to him in my childishness.

When he did come to India eventually, he was a grown-up kid — mature, wise and very intelligent. He had strikingly similar interests and thinking as mine, despite our six-year age gap and the fact that we were raised continents apart. He had grown up inspired by my academic and personal achievements; I was his role model! 'If Aamrapali becomes a doctor, he will build a hospital; if she runs a garage, he'll become a mechanic,' the family would say, a little sarcastically. Perhaps we had stopped just short of becoming another Ram and Lakshman … because here, Ram was born female.

And true to my word, on numerous occasions I asked him to forgive me for my childhood jealousy towards him, and each time he would lovingly claim that he could not recall any of the episodes. Forgetting is another name for forgiveness.

Today, I am thirty-one and he's twenty-five years old. Conditions in the family are still the same, except that they were forced to acknowledge the resilient feminine power when I started my own successful architecture firm eight years back. As if in a case of fact replicating fictional humour, Samrat is an architect today. Though we both maintain our own individual businesses, we run to each other first for any solace that we need ... be it for work or life.

Aamrapali Bhogle Sonawane

The Buddy

Having celebrated my thirteenth birthday recently, I could not help but thank my mother for the sweetest birthday present that I had ever got. The bundle arrived in October, swaddled in a clean white sheet and won my heart immediately. With Diwali lights all around, it seemed that the whole city was celebrating with us, the arrival of my little baby brother, Ashutosh.

Life suddenly changed. My sister and I were now extremely excited to get back home from school each day to play with him. On weekends we'd watch our mom and sometimes even help her give him a massage and bath. We were amazed at how little a baby is. As he crossed one little milestone after another, we'd find ourselves in a constant celebration mode. From the first time he rolled over, to the time he sat up and the first time he crawled — it was excitement and cheers all round. When I think back now, I realise that to my sister and me, he was more like a doll ... an adorable doll that had emotions, whose eyes would light up each time we entered the room.

As we grew older, we got busy with our studies, but we always had more than enough time to play with him. A toddler now, he would potter about from one room to another. In each room he found something to engage himself. My books, pens, clips and his favourites ... all my shoes to chew! Mom was happy to see the three of us playing together endlessly, as long as we did fine at school and were not over-indulging the little boy and turning him into a whiney monster.

In time, we sisters saw ourselves through the eyes of our little baby brother. It happened when he turned four. He made it amply clear to the family that my sister (who is four years younger) was his 'buddy' and he would not call her Didi. He had a few nicknames for her and used only them to address her! And she loved it! 'Ashu and I are buddies you see, I don't want him calling me Didi,' she'd say, half-defending him and half-thrilled about being given such a fun status. As for me ... I was the *older* one, and was called and am still called Didi. Not having much choice I reconciled to my boring status while envying their camaraderie.

Soon after, I moved to a hostel for higher studies. Returning home was always such a delight as my little brother would run all over the house screaming, 'Aarti didi is here! Aarti didi is here!' He would then tell me little things about his nursery school, his toys and about many things around the home that he knew I would have missed out on while I was away. He'd share his fears and his wishes. I'd try and help him as best I could. One day I took him out for a cartoon film and I remember having the best time of our lives. He invited all of his friends and I ended up sitting amongst fifteen little boys! It was amusing watching him and his friends squeal with laughter each time something crazy happened in the movie. Among lots of cold drinks, snacks and chatter, we all had a great time.

Would he always remain the same for me ... a baby brother? I wondered.

I must have been eighteen years old and my brother about five and I was back home from the hostel. I don't remember why, but that one day I was upset about something and was crying. Obviously not wanting to cry in front my parents or siblings, I had retreated to my own room. I was browsing through a magazine, sitting on the floor. I didn't think my brother, being just a little boy, would notice anything was wrong if I hid my face from him. But I was wrong and he immediately knew that I was upset. I heard him walking up to me and I looked up. He gently stroked my hair and said, 'Don't worry Didi, everything will be all right soon.'

I looked at the tiny person in front of me, amazed and touched. When did the roles reverse? How did he know? And how can someone so young be so caring? He smiled and ran away. Concern and warmth expressed by someone so young can drive anyone's blues away. When he ran out that day, he took away with him my worry as well! I immediately forgot whatever was worrying me and went out to join my family.

My brother does not remember this incident today, but I do and will always cherish it. That baby boy is now almost through with his teens. He called up some days back to tell me about his 'options' for his 'future' post the twelfth board exams. And we had a long chat about it all. As much fun as it used to be, to listen to him talk about the little things in his life when he was a toddler, it was wonderful as well to hear him talking about 'what he wants to do'. I sensed hints of both fear and excitement as he spoke about his step into the threshold of adulthood.

Watching him play with my little kids takes me back all those years when I was a teenager playing with him. He breaks my reverie when he offers casually, 'Didi why don't you and Jiju catch a movie? I'll watch the kids. I know you both have not been out by yourselves in ages.' I look at him dumbstruck. He's not kidding! 'I am serious Didi! You guys just go!'

I look at the young man in front of me. Is this really the little white bundle that I held eighteen years ago? Who is this new person with whom I share my closest thoughts now and whose company I enjoy so much?

It's my new buddy!

Aarti Katoch Pathak

Touching Wood

Life was pretty much normal for the almost seven-year-old. She went to school, played with her friends and did her homework before she slept. Then one day, she noticed that her mother was getting bigger. Just the tummy really, and then they told her she was going to have a baby brother or sister to play with. She was very excited. She hoped it would be a boy. She wanted a brother's wrist to tie a rakhi on and to get gifts on Bhai Dooj.

Suddenly, one day, her mother was in the hospital, and she was there too, eagerly waiting with her grandmother. Sometime later, she noted a flurry of activity and it was only afterwards that someone took pity on the little girl who kept asking everyone who passed by, 'What happened? What happened?' Her prayers had been answered!

She went to see the baby. Her *own* brother. She was amazed at how tiny he was. Wearing a pointy-eared cap, he looked like a bunny rabbit. Her mother made her sit on the bed and put him on her lap. She held him as if he were something extremely fragile and precious as she let her fingers gingerly stroke his soft skin.

But this love affair was short-lived. She quickly lost interest in the baby: he did little more than sleep and drink milk. She just did not know what to do with him. As they grew older, she found that she was filled with paradoxical emotions. She was protective about him — she could kill anyone who bothered him; and yet, she was also a bit of a bully and not exactly the best big sister one could have! She felt a little resentful that everyone's attention was now divided between her and her brother, but on the other hand, she was probably the person who was most proud of his achievements. She shed tears when he missed out on getting things he should have just by a whisker.

And then, one day, it was like a barrier was broken. Whether it was her brother's precocious nature or just a question of age, she still does not know, but she cannot thank her stars enough for the day that the great divide was crossed. Suddenly they were cracking jokes, making fun of each other, ganging up against their parents and discussing movies. They made up their own language and drove everyone around them nuts! They knew that in each other, they had a strong shoulder of support and an ever-ready ear for listening. Always.

The brother always claimed that he would be happy to be rid of her when she got married. He would finally get some extra space in the house for his stuff. She bet that he would cry. When it turned out that she was right after all, she did not do her normal victory dance at having won a bet. But later, after all concerned pairs of eyes had been dried and the tears had turned to smiles, she never let go a single opportunity to tease him about it. There was even some photographic evidence!

She was the one he called in the middle of the night to share the news of his internship and then his job. It was with her that he plotted to surprise their parents by flying down from across the seas when they were least expecting it. She was not in the same town, but the excitement was infectious. She itched to call her parents and ask her brother what their faces had looked like when they saw him standing at their doorstep at an ungodly hour.

Soon, he graduated and went abroad to study some more. They both hugged and cried again before he left. But before he went away, he got to see his nephew. She loved seeing them together. She felt like there was some kind of an instant connection between them. She was proven right. Her son and her brother met only once a year, yet her son jumped up to his uncle as if he had known him forever, and it always warmed the cockles of her heart to see the love between them. It broke a little too because they lived so far apart, but mostly she was just happy. Make that very happy.

This time when he came back, he had two kids to pamper. His sister had given birth to a daughter. He came loaded with gifts for all of them and yet again she was struck by how much her little brother had grown up. The vernacular 'Didi' was now replaced by a more hep 'Sis', but it sounded as good. He had picked up such perfect gifts for everyone. He was even looking rather mature with his French beard, but it took just one childhood memory to unleash those bouts of merciless teasing! Her son watched his mother and his uncle indulging in fist-fights with a wide-eyed wonder that she will never forget.

This time she saw her daughter, who was only around forty-five days old, take to him like a child takes to cotton candy. He, as always, amazed her by being superbly comfortable handling such a tiny baby and having actual conversations with her. Her son was still under his spell and she once again breathed in the perfection of the moment and her hand reached out to the nearest piece of wood.

And now, as she looks at her son and daughter, she is swept up in the emotions of it all. She remembers her son holding on tenderly to his little sister when she was put in his lap for the first time. She notices how he runs to her cradle every time she cries and how she has eyes for no one but him when he is around. She sees the occasional resentment and anger too. She gets a little worried and then smiles. She knows how this is going to turn out eventually. At least she hopes she knows. She says a little prayer thanking God for this sight, asking Him to bless them with an equally special relationship and once again reaches for that piece of wood....

Sometimes it's a good thing that we cannot pick our relatives!

Abha Atitkar Jain

A Suitable Boy

'Why can't you be more like your brother?' she asks.

We've all been there. At some point in our lives, one or the other parent looks at us and realises that there is definitely room for improvement here. Maybe the neighbour has been especially unbearable about his mole-like daughter's exceptional grades; perhaps that annoying second cousin has once again been calling everyone long distance to humbly brag about his robot son's rapid rise through the ranks of a Fortune 500 company. But there eventually comes a day when we hear that dreaded phrase implying we aren't quite what our parents ordered from the stork.

When my mother says this to me, however, she's not so much worried about my shortcomings as she is concerned that *she* must have gone wrong somewhere. You see, over the years she's somehow managed to raise a daughter who refuses to wear jewellery or learn to make proper sambar, but has a son who cleans his bathroom with a toothbrush and handles his laundry like he's bathing a newborn infant.

He might be big, strong and scary on dark nights, but

there's no denying the fact that my brother has all the makings of a fantastic daughter-in-law in him. There is a certain type of man in this world who is rather proud to admit that he's never stepped foot in a kitchen; my brother is emphatically not one of these. His chicken curry is justifiably famous, his crème caramel is better than Mom's, and he's always experimenting with the grill. Then there's his talent with the brush — vivid landscapes, rich with miniature detail in painstaking watercolours. Even the simple sketches in his biology notebooks were works of art. He plays the guitar and is the only one in our family with a singing voice. And what nature did not blossom, education brought to fruit. First, the good Fathers who ran the boarding school he attended as a child drilled excellent company manners into him with the liberal aid of the library cane. Next, the feminist principal of his high school insisted that Home Economics classes be a strictly gender-blind affair and by the end of the school year my brother's complicated cross-stitch patterns were putting his female classmates to shame.

Meanwhile, there I sit, the girl who once famously managed to turn chocolate inedible with the cunning use of Cadbury Gems (don't ask me how — I'll never tell!). An unsociable lump with no discernable talent other than a willingness to eat whatever is placed in front of me while emitting appreciative grunts at appropriate intervals. Strictly speaking, Mom had done her job by successfully raising the perfect Indian woman and the average cosseted Indian male — it's just my brother and me that got a little confused about who was supposed to be which.

'Why can't you be more like your brother?' Mom asks.

It's the only thing she can ask because nobody in their right mind would want my brother to be more like me. I mean, he's lovely but God's honest truth, he'd look frightful in a dress.

Amrita Rajan

A Letter to My Brother

Dear Bhaiya,

Both of us know that there are no Rakshabandhan-like stories in our relationship. In fact, I find it ironic and yet fitting that we don't even celebrate this event! However, I am writing this letter to tell you all that I haven't been able to say, simply because we were too caught up in pleasing our cousins and ignoring each other.

There are five big reasons why I love, adore and respect you; reasons that have shaped my love for you to what it is today:

Do you remember at age nine, when I ran away from home? Well, the truth was that I was fed up of our constant fights and thought you valued our cousins more than me. It was quite a scandal of course, but when I got back home that night, I remember you coming to my bed, tucking me in and murmuring a silent prayer. I saw you through my half-closed eyes … tears were rolling down your fat cheeks. I know I broke your heart and everybody was ready to blame you. But a look into your eyes and I knew I had been wrong, that you really

really loved me and cherished me. I am sorry for that phase of awkwardness, Bhaiya.

The second incident is when we moved to Mumbai and you had to take me for my classes by train. Although you outwardly loathed having to do so, you made sure I learned the ropes and never let me fail. You were my constant guide and made me street smart.

When I cleared my Class 10 Board exams, you were away on vacation, but you were over the moon with my results. Well, it was *your* hard work paying off, for had it not been for your constant encouragement and words of wisdom, I wouldn't have been motivated to do my best. Bhaiya you were my strength then and even now.

Mumbai life is fast-paced and hectic, but you always made it a smooth ride for me. Although I was in college, our parents refused to give me the freedom fit for a grad student. I remember you used to cringe at the thought of taking your lil' sis to pubs and rock concerts, but nevertheless, you did! And you did it because you knew that was the only way I was going to get to taste the fabled 'Mumbai college life'. I thank you for not making me feel like a pile-on and treating me like an equal. You made sure that I wasn't left out of the good times.

The last incident is obviously the darkest one; the one where you discovered that I had been abused by a close cousin during our childhood. Bhaiya, you couldn't have done anything … I didn't even understand what was happening. I know it shattered you and amidst your devastation, I still remember the tender look in your eyes, asking for my forgiveness for failing to protect me. But Bhaiya I don't blame you, far from it! Just let go of that memory and let's just look up to bigger, brighter things....

Yes, our relationship was rocky earlier, but that is our past. I guess those milestones have been instrumental in shaping this beautiful bond that we share today. I don't need any sacred thread to tell you how much you mean to me. I just know it in my heart that I couldn't have asked for a better brother than you.

You simply are the best!

I don't say this too often; but Bhaiya — I love you!

Your loving sister.

Anonymous

A Sister Remembers

It rained that day in '84 ...
the day Ma made
Mohun bhog at home.
Remember the fierce Westerlies?
They almost washed away the alpana
I had so carefully etched out
on the mosaic veranda floor.
Yes, it was years ago
but the smell of damp earth
still lingers in the sinuses of my memory.
For years I tied on your wrist our umbilical
bond from the womb.
Saving every paisa to
get the brightest hues.
So Hari could never say
his didi's was better.
You loved the big orange ones with
their yellow flowers and their green spongy leaves.
I remember how I'd soak them in Ma's perfumes

before they were ready for your tiny hand.
And for days after
you would run it under everyone's nose
proudly proclaiming the
colourful whiff of sibling love
You were the little brother I loved so much.
So much.

And then suddenly you were gone…
miles and miles away from me.
To a land of stethoscopes,
where under the Westminster
the famed river flows.
A land we so often discussed
after eating Ma's mohun bhog…
on the very same mosaic veranda,
where you recited Wordsworth,
while the misty Westerlies blew.

So Bhai, oh Bhai, tell me….
Would you spare a thought for warm Ganga this day,
there in the land where the icy Thames flows?
Because she is worried about the alpana
that will not be painted on your polished oaken floors.
*(This poem was written on the occasion of Bhai Phonta, the Bengali
variation of Bhai Dooj. I wrote this when I saw how much my wife
was missing her brother who now lives in London.)*

Arthur Cardozo

A Sister's Prayers

'*Bhai er kopaale dilaam phonta...*' It was the occasion of Bhai Phonta, a day when Bengali women prayed for their brothers' long life and celebrated the sibling bond. Gouri, my wife, had been chanting this mantra ever since she was old enough to talk. When she was young, she used to put the sandalwood paste tilak on her brother's forehead, just the way her mother had taught her. Then her brother left home, to join the army, and was rarely home when the festival came around. So she learnt, again from her mother, to place the tilak on a wall or on a door frame while chanting the mantra that was meant to invoke the gods to bless her brother with good luck and a long life.

As she chanted the mantra, her mind began to wander. Kashmir was in the news once again for the terrorist attacks and the army was busy warding off the invaders at the border. Encased in the warmth and comfort of her home, she felt uneasy thinking about what her brother might be going through right then. Her elder brother, she teasingly called him Major saab, had been posted in the strife-torn valley of

Kashmir for the past one year. As life went on at its usual pace and Gouri remained busy in managing her family, once in a while her mind wandered to the icy mountain ranges where the army was busy fighting insurgents and terrorists bent on disrupting normal life all the time. At such times, she would lift her head up towards the sky and murmur a silent prayer for her brother's well-being. Every morning, she would be the first to rush towards the door to pick up the newspaper and scan it for any news related to the Kashmir valley. The previous Friday she had visited a new temple that she had heard so much about. The deity there was said to be all-powerful and answered the prayers of those who went there for fourteen consecutive Fridays.

Months later, with the family gathered round the dinner table, Major saab was the guest of honour of the evening. He had come home for his annual leave and my mother-in-law as well as my wife were relieved that his field posting had finally come to an end. The next three years of home postings would be relatively peaceful unless a war broke out again, which was unlikely so soon. Very naturally the discussions drifted towards the war.

'So Dada, you have been busy fighting off the terrorists all the time?'

'Not always, but we did have our hands full most of the time. The operations not only involved warding them off but also trying to keep track of the various sympathisers that they have on this side of the border.'

Gouri playfully extended her fist, pretending to hit her brother. 'Have you killed quite a few?' she asked teasingly.

'Oh, that's something I cannot reveal. But let me show

you something; I got it from the pocket of an insurgent who was killed.'

With that Major saab got up, opened his suitcase and brought out an envelope. The envelope was addressed to one Havaldaar Majid Khan and bore the stamp of Lahore, indicating that it had come from Pakistan. Inside the envelope was a letter written in Urdu, which Major saab translated for the benefit of all of us.

It was a letter written by a sister to her younger brother asking him about his well-being. Apparently, another sister, across the border, had not been very lucky. The lump in Gouri's throat, seemed to make it difficult for her to breathe as she desperately fought back tears. She was lucky, she realised, she was so very lucky.

Goutam Dutta

I Will Fix You

I sought my soul, but my soul I could not see.
I sought my God, but my God eluded me.
I sought my brother and I found all three.

When I was fifteen I came across this quote for the first time in a Chicken Soup for the Soul title. I related to it a lot because it summed up how I felt about my brother.

I am amongst those lucky people who has a sibling so perfect, that even if I spend the rest of my life trying to be as good as he is, the pursuit, even if not successful, will at least refine me as a person. My brother Ankit is my Dalai Lama, and has been since childhood. He has a way with words. It's not the style, but rather his uncomplicated way of speaking after calm and logical deliberation that makes everyone respect him.

I remember once we went to get the deflated tyres of our bicycles repaired. As always, being a brat, I said I wanted mine done first. As soon as my bicycle was repaired, I began to ride it. Circling around him I said, 'I am leaving! I am leaving! See you later!' And my twelve-year-old brother just calmly said, 'You are so selfish, Juhi. I waited while your bicycle was getting repaired, and you do this.' Thoroughly ashamed, I stopped immediately, his words hitting home.

As we made our way back home, it became very dark. We were not allowed to play after seven, so I tried to persuade him to tell Mom that another friend was with us and that is why we got late. He responded with the calm of a saint. 'Look Juhi, if we lie to them, it may save us once, but it will make us liars forever. Instead let's tell them the truth, I am sure they will forgive us. We don't have to lie to our parents, they love us, they will understand.' Can you believe these were the words of a twelve-year-old? I'm sure that, had my mother been there, she would have had tears in her eyes in true Bollywood style!

These small lessons that came from a sibling, who is just one-and-a-half-years older than me, changed me in permanent ways. Over the years we grew into the best of friends; we only fought over TV, and that only when there was an excess of cricket.

When I was twenty-one, I felt that Ankit and I were no longer particularly close, because we had stopped partying together. He and I had different friends. At the time, I was going through the blues of splitting with someone I was very close to. I sent a message to Ankit, saying that I was shattered and felt like a clown headed nowhere in life. To which he responded, 'I see you as an extraordinary human being, for whom anything is possible. You deserve the best and love will find you. I am always there for you.' After reading this, I felt a little better, but the message he sent me after that filled me with so much confidence that I soon found myself back on the dance floor, boogying those blues away.

I always used to fight with my mother, maintaining that she loved Ankit more than me and that he was her favourite, but that night I discovered that I am his.

So whatever it is you are fighting with your sibling over, be it the better bed, room, table, TV remote, it's all good. Enjoy the ride, remember the wrestles and quarrels. Because when we are beaten emotionally by the world, these are the arms that you will cry in and in these arms you will find all the love that you need to heal.

Here is the text Ankit sent that night: I later discovered he had borrowed from a song.

When you try your best, but you don't succeed
When you get what you want, but not what you need
When you feel so tired, but you can't sleep
Stuck in reverse
And the tears come streaming down your face
When you lose something you can't replace
When you love someone, but it goes to waste
Could it be worse?
Lights will guide you home
And ignite your bones And I will try to fix you.

Juhi Rai Farmania

Hanging On to the Good Times

It is just a year-and-a-half that separates my brother and me. He is some 444 days older to me — well, give or take a couple of hours. I'm told that he was a protective young man even at the tender age of a year plus. The minute his baby sister would start crying or showed the slightest sign of distress, he would run as fast as his little legs could carry him to my mother and somehow convey to her the urgency of the situation. Barely able to speak a sentence, he would manage something like 'baby cry' accompanied by the most alarmed expression to make up for lack of articulation. That was my little but strong elder brother, carrying out his responsibilities with heart-warming devotion.

As those wonder years rolled on, life with an older sibling was an adventure of rough-and-tumble games interspersed with quiet hours spent in happy companionship. Life was good, as he had to shoulder the blame of every mishap or accident, make all the sacrifices and share life's goodies with his younger sister.

Then somewhere this fairy tale of the two happy siblings

morphed into a Sturm und Drang story of two dysfunctional siblings. The 444 days separating us in age slowly started to stretch like the chewing gum we loved to pull out of our mouths as kids. The distance grew till we seemed to be light years away from each other at an emotional level. The physical world we inhabited seemed to have become too small and suffocating, and we were always too close for comfort, always in each other's hair, me in his crew cut and he in my odd pageboy-styled locks. I felt like a garbage truck bumping along life's lanes as he cruised alongside on his cool wheels. Simply put, I felt unwanted, like that ugly, bumbling, foul-smelling municipal trash transporter next to you on the road, the one you want to lose in a hurry.

I longed to have my brother back, but the chewing gum difference between us now seemed to be stretched to its utmost elastic limits. It had stretched till it had become almost invisible, as if he too wanted to simply disappear from my world. Worse still, maybe just spit it out and lose both the gum and that awful stinky garbage truck in the avatar of his little sister. I was terrified that our fragile bond would snap any time.

Then somewhere, somehow, almost imperceptibly the chewing gum transformed itself into a wondergum, soft yet tough and everlasting with wonderful flavours of childhood, of rain and sun and florid orange Kissan squash and ice and roasted peanuts. It was a magical gum that you could chew and stretch forever. He was once again my rock and anchor even as his own boat rocked perilously amidst stormy waves. Those hands, that had picked me up as I stumbled taking my first baby steps, once again helping me find my bearings in a brave new adult world. Even as his dreams lay crushed in a place we both did not want to visit, he made sure I lived mine.

He has not had an opportunity to display conventional acts of heroic courage and bravery. But with the most simple yet profound and quietly touching gestures, he has done much more. Our father passed away suddenly, and though his health had been failing for some time, even he as a doctor did not think the end was so close. And when it came, my brother quietly and bravely strove to make it as easy and painless as possible for me.

As my father fought a hopeless battle, my brother spent that dreadfully dark night alone in a cold sterile hospital, 101% sanitised, with all feeling and emotions scrubbed away along with the germs. The grim darkness in his heart uncannily intensified in the cold white light of the hospital tube lights at every step. Someone told me later that he should have perhaps called that night, but I understood his wisdom instinctively and that he did what he thought was right. I was two train journeys and a long flight away from home, alone with my three-year-old twins, my husband away at a field posting.

Finally, when despite all efforts by the doctors, it was all over, he called and told me in the saddest little-boy voice, the lump in his throat beating a dirge-like tattoo. 'Come whenever it is practical, I want you to remember only the good times we had with Daddy and how lucky we were to have him as a father. I do not want you to see him like this.' He could not go running to my mother this time as I stood hurting and trying to somehow make sense of it all, but with his own unique wisdom and touching tenderness, he was shielding me and protecting me once again just as he had done as a little boy.

Some may doubt this logic, but I understood it perfectly. I know he did not want to keep me away from Daddy in those final moments or during the heartbreaking process of the last rites. He just wanted to protect me. I was awestruck at his strength, knowing how long and lonely that last night must have been for him, as he paced up and down the corridor outside the ICU, looking at our father calmly and speaking reassuringly without betraying his own fears and sense of helplessness.

Last year, I witnessed my mother struggle bravely with first her sense of pain and helplessness and then grief as her brother fought cancer in a battle that was pre-decided by destiny. He too was in an ICU, in another city, she was too old and not in the best of health to be able to make the journey, to be with him even for even an hour to say, 'Goodbye and thank you and I love you Bhaiya'. I remembered my own father's passing away and how completely bereft his brother felt and the role that my brother had played at that time. Then quietly it came home to me, this inevitability that we would face one day.

We may or may not be able to be there beside each other in our final moments, to say thanks, to say goodbye, to hug and hold hands. The time for all that is now, to catch up on the years in between, choking with laughter while waving photographs of us in bell bottoms and dog collar shirts, sporting Sadhana cuts and Amitabh Bachchan hairstyles; recounting stories from gawky growing-up years. Say a hundred 'See you agains' before you say that final 'Goodbye'. Chances are you may not be there with your sibling when the time comes, and when the time does come and when it has passed, just remember the good times, as my brother asked me to some eleven years ago.

Jyoti Kalapa

Forks and Fish-Bones

'... and then they served us the most awesome seafood, paired with the crispest white wine ever...'

I listened with a smile, to my visiting-from-America 'baby' brother hold forth on all things seafood, wine and fine dining related. No wonder really since he works at one of the best seafood restaurants in Virginia and also since he's been working hard to get a degree in wine appreciation. The boy who wanted to be a pilot was now serious about becoming a sommelier.

My husband listened intently to all the 'spirit'-ual bits, soaking up all the info like a sponge. Next, my brother started talking about how tables were laid, cutlery placed and about the right kind of glasses for various drinks and cocktails. My eyes widened with amusement as a certain memory popped into my head, and as if on cue, my brother turned towards me to note my reaction. He caught my smile, gave me that boyish grin of his that I love so much and turned back to my husband.

'You know, Da, I really have my sister to thank for all of this.'

My husband laughed, 'Yes, well I have your sister to thank for a lot of things as well!'

But Boomz, as I fondly call my baby bro, was serious now. 'No. Seriously. I remember being in awe of her when she used to eat her fish curry with a fork while I used my hands. She used to pick out the fish-bones with her fork and for some reason I thought that was the ultimate in cool and I wanted to be that cool!'

I laughed and chimed in with another memory. 'Remember when we went out for lunch with my friends once? You were sitting at the far end of the table. I had just taught you how to use a knife with a fork and you were still a bit shaky about how to hold what and with which hand. I remember being deep in conversation with a buddy when I suddenly heard this voice urgently trying to get my attention, "Didi, Didi, Didi..." It took me a few seconds to register that it was you calling out to me. I looked up and across the table at you, you just directed my vision towards your plate with a jerk of your head and raised your eyebrows questioningly, silently asking me whether you were holding the fork and knife correctly! I felt all gooey and mush-mush inside! God, I remember that so vividly!'

We all laughed and my husband chimed in with a memory of him and his younger brother. My mother joined in with a few stories of her own. And the night aged gently as we indulged in great food, heady cocktails and trips down memory lane.

It was a lovely evening which sparked off a million memories in my head. Being almost five years older than my baby bro, I was very protective about him. Adding to that streak of protectiveness was the fact that our father worked in the US while Mom bustled about in Bangalore trying to bring up two kids. So it was always just him and me. We didn't try to gouge each other's eyes out, nor did we try to break each other's bones. I marvelled at his boundless energy, while he wondered at my ability to read books from morning till night. We shared our food, our school stories and yes, even the TV remote! And of course, we'd gang up against our hapless mother at times too!

The next day, at my Mom's, I woke up and went to the dining room. I saw my brother standing behind my elder son, bent over his head, guiding his hands as he helped my little boy slice an omelette in half, '...you see, because you've pinned this end down with the fork, now you can cut it smoothly with your knife.'

My younger son, who had been watching the whole scene with intense concentration, looked up at his uncle and said, 'Mamu, now my turn?'

My brother caught my eye and once again gave me that boyish grin of his, and then he turned to his two little nephews and started off on a story. 'Do you boys know who taught me how to use a knife and fork?'

I smiled and sat down with the newspaper. The cycle continues....

Baisali Chatterjee Dutt

After All...

Raj and Diya were two mischief-makers who were born, it seemed, to shatter their parents' peaceful existence. They had some really bad records, like breaking a piece of crockery every two days; dismembering a piece of furniture, weekly; and monthly complaints from neighbourhood kids who had been beaten up by either one of them. And as if all this was not enough, they fought with each other too ... violently!

One fine day, when they returned home from school, they found that their mother was feeling rather ill. Flushed with fever, she warned them to have their lunch quietly and stay out of trouble so that she could take a nap.

Now, Diya was thirteen and Raj was fourteen, and while they had lost all their milk teeth, they certainly hadn't lost their penchant for getting into trouble.

As soon as they entered the kitchen, Raj started stuffing his mouth with food. Disgusted, Diya said, 'Take a plate and eat properly, you pig.' Raj pulled her ponytails. 'You pig-tailed donkey, mind your own business!' Diya, without a second's thought, took a rolling pin and flung it at Raj — bull's eye! It found its mark on Raj's back. Furious, Raj picked up the blue, porcelain teapot on the table and threw it at her. Alas, she was too quick and he missed his shot. But the pot broke and the noise brought their poor, tired mother into the kitchen. Just one look at the shattered piece of crockery and it took her a second to come to a decision.

'Raj, you will stay out on the veranda till the evening!' she said as she pulled him out of the kitchen by his elbow, shutting the door firmly when he was out.

'Amma, I'm hungry...' he wailed.

'Well, you should have thought of that before breaking the teapot.' Then she turned to Diya, 'Insensitive brats! I have a high fever and you kids can't even bother to stay quiet and give me some peace for a few minutes. Now hurry up and finish your food, then go to your room and lie down.' Looking out at Raj, she continued, 'One peep out of either one of you and I will...' Her voice faded as she moved towards her room. For a moment, Raj and Diya looked daggers at each other. Then Diya took her plate, sat down at the table and was about to have her first bite, when she stopped. Her brother's plaintive 'I'm hungry...' rang in her ears.

She picked up her plate, went to the kitchen window and offered it to him. Initially he was reluctant, but then the sight of food overcame his sulk. There, at the window, they started eating from the same plate and within minutes they were talking about their day at school, their friends and the cats in their colony. Gradually their murmurs got louder and louder and their high decibel levels reached such a point that it brought their worried mother hurrying back into the kitchen.

'Diya, what are you doing at the window?'

'Amma, he was hungry,' she said. It really was as simple as that.

'I am the one who is a fool to interfere in your fights. Weren't you both hell-bent on cracking open each other's skulls just ten minutes back?' she asked.

'He is my brother after all...' Diya said, and they both smiled shyly.

And their helpless mother had no option but to smile back and let Raj in and fill his growling tummy.

Mudra Rawal

Surprise Birthday Celebrations

I was quite nervous when I got back from school. My brother had just undergone multiple surgeries, and I was going to visit him in the hospital. He had been operated in the morning, to remove fluid from his brain, for hernia and ear problems, and I had no clue as to how it had gone. His past surgeries had all been quite risky.

On the way back home, biting my nails, I recalled that the doctors had said he would be administered anaesthesia yet again, and that they didn't know how his body would react to this. Suffering from Hunter's Syndrome, the success rate of the operation couldn't be predicted. The doctor assured us he would be fine, but he'd added that it might or might not make a big difference; it all depended how his body would react.

I reached home and got ready to go to the hospital. My sisters and my grandmother accompanied me. When I entered the room, I went up to my brother, and the sight of him made me cry — stitches on his head and stomach, tubes attached to his body, his hands tied (for the glucose drips — the needle had to stay intact).... I started sobbing silently.

I couldn't fathom the pain he was going through. My aunt hugged me and asked me not to cry. I went out of the room to wipe my tears and calm myself.

When I went back in, right on the table was a cake, and everyone wished me happy birthday. Amidst the tears, I managed to cut the cake and feed everyone. I was sitting next to my brother on his bed, and he hugged me and kissed me on my cheek. And the next second, I don't know why, but he started smiling and laughing. Nothing had happened, but he was smiling. I looked at him: was this the guy, who had just undergone multiple surgeries a few hours back, which had required cutting through the skull? He was in so much pain, yet he was smiling, for me, just for me — it was his sister's birthday, and he didn't want me to be upset. His strength, courage — it was something worth learning. He taught me an important lesson that day: no matter how much we undergo in life, always keep smiling; it keeps you happy, as well as the people around you too. Through his pain, he kept smiling and never let the pain win over him. Years have gone by, and I never got a birthday like that one, and will never do so. It shall remain the best birthday of my life.

Palak Surana

Little Steps

It was a Sunday afternoon and I was waiting for my boyfriend at a local market place. Delhi's scorching heat was making me feel irritated and dehydrated, and all I wanted was to get out of there and sit in the cool environs of a movie hall. I mentally started ticking off my boyfriend for making me wait in the heat.

Suddenly, my reverie was interrupted by a childish chuckle; it was like a breath of fresh air. I looked towards my right and saw a sweet little girl and a young lad around nine, holding her in his lap. The little girl had a dusky complexion, cute dimples, and lovely big black eyes. She was wearing a cotton top with short pants and was barefoot. The little boy wasn't fancily dressed either; he was wearing khaki shorts with a shirt that had definitely seen better days. It was obvious that these two children didn't have the basic comforts in life that so many of us take for granted.

And yet, there they were, smiling, giggling and enjoying each other's company without even noticing the heat.

The little boy kissed the baby on her cheek and put her down on the floor. He took a few steps back and opened his arms wide and said, 'Come baby, walk up to your elder brother!'

The little one stood up, smiled with a charming innocence, and daringly took a couple of steps towards her brother, her arms wide open, but, oops … she fell down on her fourth step! Her brother ran towards her, picked her up, cuddled her, dusted her clothes, asked over and over again whether she was hurt or not, before finally setting her down and encouraging her again. This time the little one was more confident. She managed to take a few more steps than the last time. With each step of hers, the little boy's smile grew wider and wider. He held out his hand, she grabbed it and they took a little walk around the free space of the market area. When they were done, the little boy planted a sweet kiss on his sister's forehead.

Watching all this brought a lump to my throat and made me feel terribly sentimental. I couldn't stop myself from approaching them and talking to the little siblings. I patted the baby's cheek and remarked how sweet she was. The little boy puffed up with pride. I asked him about their parents. He said they were orphans: their mother had died giving birth to the sister and a couple of months back, their father had died in an accident in the factory where he worked. They were staying with their uncle and aunt, and the little boy worked in a small restaurant as a helper and cleaner. 'Didi,' he said, addressing me, 'I want to give my sister everything; she will go to school when she is bigger, unlike me, who had to drop out so that I can work. She is my princess!' His voice quivered with emotion, conviction and … love.

I could barely hold back the tears pricking my eyelids. I pinched their cheeks and bought them some chocolates, chips and biscuits and wished them well.

My phone rang just then. It was Rahul, my boyfriend, calling to tell me that he had arrived. So I bid goodbye to the little ones and went to meet him.

I was lost in my own thoughts, so touched was I by the deep love that I had just witnessed between the little siblings that Rahul had to ask me whether I was okay or not!

When I got back home later that evening, I was still in a contemplative mood. I took out some old albums that had just been sitting in my trunk for ages and started going through my family photographs. Pictures of my birthdays, festivals, family outings and trips. I saw my brother and I smiling together, having fun and making funny faces. We used to be up to all sorts of mischief and were partners in crime!

He was the one who taught me how to cycle when I was eight. When I fell off my bicycle the first time we tried, he bought me a big teddy bear to bring a smile to my face.

My elder brother. Elder to me by just three years and yet how protective he was, how sensitive and caring. We were really thick and such best friends.

But lately, we had gotten so involved in our own lives that we hardly got the time to talk except for the usual, 'Hello and how are you' type of impersonal conversations! It was as if life had suddenly gotten in the way and we had no time for each other.

But that day, seeing that little boy with his younger sister, something happened to me.

So blinking back my tears, I sat down in front of my computer and started typing out an e-mail.

It was to my brother.

Poornima Dhiman

My Big Brother

It's a strange relationship. Siblings. Can't live with them, can't live without them. Nature serves you one, or two, or maybe more (shudder), and you spend an entire lifetime manoeuvring your way across the family chessboard. They fight with you, you yell at them. They complain that you always get better clothes; you know in your heart that they get a better allowance than you do. You have food fights, pillow fights, 'I am not talking to you ever again' fights, and 'How dare you tell on me' fights. They are infuriating. You wish you were an only child. But then again, you don't.

I have an elder brother. And he was born with the Godfather complex. He could be very patronising — and I am being kind with words here. When all the other girls my age began dating, I felt like the most unattractive girl in the city. No one ever wanted to date me. It was years later that I found out that a simple threat involving broken necks and powdered bones had stood between me and dating heaven. When other girls my age were busy poring over fashion magazines, acquiring and polishing their 'personal style', I was busy attacking a home-made kicking bag and learning break dance moves with talcum powder thrown on the floor to make it smooth and slippery. When other girls were learning Indian classical dance, I was preparing to represent my state in an all-India karate championship. I had nothing girl-like in me. How could I? I had an elder brother.

My childhood and teenage years were coloured in dark, masculine shades of 'tomboy'. I worshipped Bruce Lee, sang Elvis songs, and watched gory action movies. I wore my hair shorter than most girls, cut my brother's pants into shorts for myself, and thought that denims were the coolest invention ever. I wasn't hooked on to Barbie, and found Ken to be a bit of a candy-ball sissy. I did not walk, I swaggered. I stood straight. I believed I could be anyone, do whatever I wanted, and spent hours weight training to improve my muscle mass. I loved horse-riding. I hated cooking. Can you believe that? A little girl growing up into a woman, not realising that boys and girls were different! Can you believe how lucky I was?

In fact, I myself did not know how lucky I was. I did not realise that my elder brother was colouring the pages of my life. That he was bringing up a younger sibling and not a younger sister. He could not tell the difference, so I never learned the difference. I grew up to know that Barbie was a cultural monstrosity. I grew up to know that Bruce Lee was a better role model than Madonna. I grew up atypical. Of course, like all good things, this was to come to an end. My brother left the country for higher studies, and I became a girl. Femininity took hold of me with a severe vengeance. I grew my hair. My wardrobe included long, flowing dresses. I acquired beautiful, sequin-studded gowns, and started making appearances in local pageants. And I became like any other young woman. Not that I have anything against all the other young women. It's just that I did not realise then that having an elder sibling of the opposite gender had given me a unique personality, which I lost in an instant.

Fortunately, some of what my brother unknowingly brought into my life has stayed with me. It has seen me through the kind of upheavals in my life that would have left anyone else broken. I still walk straight, am accused of a swagger, and the need to appear in control has helped me remain in control of my life. Which is a lot to say, because mine isn't the kind of life that stays stuck in second gear. I live on the race track of life. And I would have been road kill, if I did not have an elder brother.

So, well, siblings. Can't live with them, can't live without them. Life gave me an elder brother, and if I could go back and rewrite my destiny, I would change many things. But one thing would remain unchanged. I would have an elder brother.

Pratishtha Durga

Siblings Without Rivalry

Hermione Granger reminds me a lot of my daughter, who is six. She is a stickler for rules, almost always at the top of her class, bright, smart and like Hermione, if it is in a book, she can learn it! A teacher's dream student, to put it more simply. She rarely forgets to take anything that the teacher has said must be brought to class, even if the teacher herself has forgotten!

The school my children go to is a stickler for rules and is very strict about the dress code, among a lot of other things. They have a winter uniform, the tie and blazer being mandatory, apart from the school belt and school ID card that each child has to compulsorily wear. If any child is seen without any of these, they are labelled defaulters.

This morning, long after the children left for school, I discovered to my horror that my daughter had forgotten to wear her blazer. The school does not allow parents into the premises once the assembly bell rings, so there was no way I could reach it to her. I felt bad when I discovered it, as it meant she would be punished as she had a special school assembly that day. She hates being punished, and in her books, being pulled up at school is the ultimate disaster, loss of face, end of the world. She's not the type of child to take it lightly.

There was nothing I could do except wait for her and her elder brother to come back from school. I was certain there would be huge tears rolling down her face, and I would have to comfort her and hug her for at least forty-five minutes before she calmed down, the time required expertly calculated from years of parenting!

I was wrong. They both came back from school, my daughter with a big smile on her face and wearing an oversized blazer — her brother's! I was dumbstruck.

Apparently, after they'd boarded the bus to go to school, my son (he just turned ten) realised she didn't have her blazer and would get punished. So he took off his blazer and made her wear it. She was not caught — he was. He said he was a defaulter and owned up. I wondered what must have gone through his mind when he did that. I was so proud of him for protecting his younger sister. I was moved too, by his selfless act.

On some days, when they fight, it seems as if they hate each other and would kill each other if they could. Those are the days I wonder where I went wrong in raising them.

But today is one of those days when I'm going to bed with a happy-warm feeling, knowing that I must be doing something right!

Preeti Shenoy

Love

'Congratulations! It's a boy.'

The midwife swaddled the baby and handed him to Raj. Despite her exhaustion, Nayana was excited. After four years of trying to conceive, she couldn't wait another moment to hold her firstborn.

'He's perfect,' she whispered almost to herself as she gazed at her son.

Her husband nodded and kissed her on the forehead. 'Just like you.'

Jay, as the little boy was named, was the spark Nayana and Raj's life needed. Work, the repeated attempts and subsequent failures at trying to conceive, and constant bickering had begun to drive them apart.

But Jay came along to mend their relationship. They were the perfect parents and also the perfect partners. Between them they made sure Jay had all he needed and more.

Jay on his part made sure he kept his parents on their toes. A healthy toddler, he was quite active and was growing up to be quite a restless young boy. 'This boy is so full of energy, he is draining mine!' Nayana joked to her husband, as she flopped on the sofa after an hour-long session of running after Jay.

Raj of course was convinced his son was a genius. By age three, Jay could already add and subtract two-digit numbers. So when Nayana complained about Jay's extreme naughtiness, Raj would laugh it off. Even his son's lack of affection towards his parents did not seem to bother him. 'Boys, eh. I am sure he will come around,' Raj consoled Nayana, who was a little concerned by her son's aloof behaviour.

When Nayana became pregnant the second time, Jay was four. His behaviour had gone from bad to worse. He was given to loud temper tantrums, disobedience and disruptive behaviour at school. The parents weren't sure how Jay would take to the new addition. When Mira was born eight months later, Raj and Nayana became busy with the newborn's needs and Jay became even more withdrawn.

'I think Jay is feeling lonely; I feel so guilty about leaving him alone,' Nayana despaired. She tried spending more time with Jay; tried helping him know his younger sibling better. Jay was not moved. To Nayana's dismay, he shunned her touch completely. His only companions seemed to be his math books, abacus and all activities related to numbers.

'We need to take him to a child psychologist, Raj. Maybe she will be able to coax something out of him; help him adjust better!' Even Raj had to admit that Jay's behaviour needed professional attention.

Dr Anita Fernandez was Raj's boss' wife. She had offered to help when Nayana had mentioned Jay's erratic behaviour to her at a dinner they had together. After a session with the young boy, she called his parents to her office.

'I want to know more about his behaviour at home. Give me as many details as you can. How he spends his day, how he reacts if taken off a routine, his numeric abilities etc.' Nayana and Raj tried to fill in the picture for her, detailing Jay's mathematical prowess, his behaviour, his inability to connect. 'Hmmm… Nayana, Raj what I am going to tell you is not easy and I need you to stay calm…. I think Jay is on the Autism Spectrum.'

Nayana's sobs broke the stunned silence.

'What are you saying? I know he is disruptive … but are you sure?' Raj stuttered. It couldn't be happening to them. Their son was perfect. He had to be. He was the sunshine that filled their lives!

'Please calm down. I understand how distressing this is. But things are not so bad!'

'So you can cure it, right!'

'It is not a condition that can be cured Raj. But I can help to ensure that Jay has the best shot at leading a healthy life. Please believe me.'

'Will … is … Mira…' Nayana asked through her tears.

'We can't say till she is a bit older.'

Life changed for the family of four from then on. Jay's parents now understood that their son was not merely naughty but had special needs. They tried to come to terms with his aloofness, learnt not to take it personally.

Mira adored her older brother. It didn't matter to her whether he pushed her away or ignored her. She followed him everywhere.

As she grew up to talk and become more aware of things and people around her, she began noticing the difference between Jay and her friends and cousins. 'Why does Bhai not play with my other friends,' she would ask her parents. They weren't sure if their daughter could understand the nature of Jay's condition. 'That's because he has his own way of having fun,' Nayana told the four-year-old.

However, Mira was not one to give up. She kept trying, though in vain, to help Jay engage with her friends. Bit by bit she understood that her approach would always come to naught.

Life fell into a routine for the small family; Jay was coping well with school and friends. He was calmer but still aloof. His family learnt not to take it to heart. Mira, however, could not understand. As the years passed, her attitude towards Jay turned sour. She would get upset with her older brother, at times reducing him to tears. Nayana was worried that her daughter was turning into a bully. Punishments did not seem to deter the now seven-year-old girl.

They tried talking to Mira. 'Sweetheart, you need to realise that Jay is different from your friends. Just like you like certain things he has his own preferences.' The little girl was confused. Her cousins, who were also Jay's age, were not different from her.

Then one day she came up to Nayana and asked her, 'Mom is Bhai like Christopher?'

'Who?' a confused Nayana asked.

'The boy in this book,' Mira pointed to the book in her hand. Part of her course work, *The Curious Incident of the Dog in the Night-Time* was Mira's favourite piece of fiction. She was a big fan of Christopher, the hero of the whodunit. He was so smart and determined, and a super whiz at math, though he seemed awkward around people. He seemed so much like Jay.

Nayana looked at the book and understood. 'Yes, Mira, Bhai is something like Christopher.'

'Okay,' Mira replied, and walked away.

Nayana let her go to make sense of her discovery.

After a couple of hours, she peeped into the children's bedroom.

Jay was bent over a math problem as Mira was busy running around telling him the story she had read and how she was sure the book was based on her brilliant brother.

Nayana shut the door quietly behind her. A tear rolled down her face even as a smile lit it up. Sunshine had touched their lives again.

Prerna Uppal

Being a Big Brother

Sisters are these nasty little girls who live in the same house as you, feel like they're entitled to your things, steal your share of chocolates from the fridge, complain to Mom and Dad about everything you do that they (your sisters) don't approve of, and insist that you vamoose from the house when their friends come in. They are nothing but a series of fights from the day they are born. It's bad when they are elder; it's worse when they are younger, Leo, dominating and completely self-assured. Or that's what you think when you are young.

In the year 2000, I left home, glad to escape from my only sister, three years my junior. I had just turned twenty then (and was still trying to hang on to nineteen). I had finished college and joined the Indian Institute of Science in Bangalore where I was to do my Master's.

A few months went by and I was struggling to manage by myself. There were so many things for which there was no Mom or Dad in the background to handle. Clothes piled up, demanding I wash them. Dust swirled on the floor, demanding I sweep it. The bank passbook often peeked out from the pile of papers, insisting that I balance my finances. Every time I entered my room, I would plunge into a sea of guilt. Classes actually seemed an escape from the mess. And then my sister arrived for a holiday.

She was to stay with my aunt, who lived at the other end of the city. But feeding and entertaining her were my responsibilities. Up to the time I met her at the station, I was full of plans. I had chalked out an elaborate itinerary. We would take Karnataka Tourism-organised tours to Mysore, Coorg and the Shravanabelagola-Belur-Halebid circuit. I had bought the tickets, studied the brochures and read all the e-guides I could find on the Net. My aunt and cousins came along on the trips to Mysore and Coorg, so they went smoothly. The third trip was a series of disasters.

It was just as the bus left Bangalore that I realised we hadn't brought water. There was no chance of picking up a bottle till Shravanabelagola, the first stop, so we'd have nothing to drink till noon. And that was only the start of my problems.

The moment we were off the bus, we splurged on colas. And that was when I realised the second problem. There was barely any cash left after I had paid for the colas. The trip was to include food and ticket charges, but I hadn't taken into consideration extra expenditure. The idea of carrying extra money for emergencies wasn't something that had penetrated my skull.

There was of course enough money for a cola, but not for worst-case scenarios — like the bus breaking down midway, either my sister or I falling sick. And that was what the remaining two hundred rupees in my wallet were screaming about.

The sun in summer in south India can be counted on to be strong — and it was. Shravanabelagola is famous for its enormous Jain statue erected on a hill. We had to take off our footwear at the base of the hill and climb about 650 steps to reach the shrine. We took off our sandals and began the climb. We were back to the shoe-stand in a trice. The heat of the bare rock was unbearable.

There were people there who were selling cotton socks. This seemed to make sense. Our feet would be protected on the climb, so they would be mildly scalded, not scorched. The price of course, made no sense whatever. Twenty-five rupees for a pair of socks, for exactly one use? But there was no bargaining on the price; the foreigners who crowded the bus (we were among the rare natives) were paying without bargaining.

I looked at my wallet, then at my sister. Would she mind foregoing the socks? We could do the steps a few at a time, pause to rest, and climb again. Come on, the ancient pilgrims didn't mind the heat. And if we are going to a religious place, we should not think of our comforts. Besides, what will we do with these socks later? A waste of money.

The look in her eyes threatened rain. She was a tourist, she said, not a pilgrim. It was my idea to come here, not hers. And what kind of brother was I, to think of my wallet and not her comfort. And who told me not to carry extra cash? Didn't I know she was coming?

It was a big struggle in my small head over the money. I had to keep some cash till the end of the journey; who knew what further disasters lay ahead. And yet if I was cruel to my sister (in her opinion), I would never hear the end of it when our parents found out. Luckily, she didn't have a cell phone those days, to immediately place the complaint. The struggle was short — I gave in.

And so we went up the hill. She, in a pair of flimsy cotton socks that she didn't tire complaining about; I, in my bare feet, praying for mercy from the sun. And so we went up, saw the statue, offered our obeisance, descended, had another round of colas (mine turned to ashes in the mouth) and clambered into the bus.

So that was what it meant to be Big Brother in real life. You are Responsible. You make sacrifices. Of course, big brothers are always making sacrifices from the day their younger sibling is born, but now you actually *decide* to make them. No mom or dad to tell you to. You bear the scorching heat, and you can only blame yourself. And you suddenly learn the real worth of twenty-five-rupee cotton socks. In fact, you learn the worth of everything.

And your sister is still this little girl who lives in the same house as you, feels like she's entitled to your things, steals your share of chocolates from the fridge, complains to Mom and Dad about everything you do that she doesn't approve of … only now, you decide that you wouldn't have it any other way, or anyone else for a sister.

Raamesh Gowri Raghavan

The Turning Point

Waiting outside the ICU, I could hear his screams. It was then that I realised how much I loved him. I was in Class 4 and he in Class 1, and I could not think of one day that had passed without us fighting. We would fight over TV programmes, stationary, the window seat in the school bus, the upper place on the bunk bed, our parents' affection, the music teacher's attention and every other conceivable thing.

Another shriek from the ICU and I just shut my eyes. The whole sequence of events played out in my head like a horror movie.

My brother, Ishaan, had been playing outside in the porch with a cousin while the rest of us were inside. We'd all collected for Bhai Dooj. We heard his screams and before we could react, the cousin came running inside the house, screaming, 'Monkey! Monkey!'

We rushed outside to find a huge monkey clawing at Ishaan's back. Seeing us, the monkey ran away. Suddenly free of the monkey's grip, Ishaan ran to Ma, clinging to her legs. He was shaking with fear. The back of his shirt and pants were stained with blood. When the monkey had attacked him from behind, our cousin mumbled incoherently, she had seen Ishaan unzip his jacket so he could remove it and run away. But he had been unable to do that, for the monkey had bitten his legs and hands. Blood was oozing from his wounds. His shirt was torn below the collar, the blood patch on it growing large. My brother, just seven, had been wearing his best clothes, his favourite shirt and jacket, for the festival. His large innocent eyes, usually so expressive, were now shut with pain.

My parents put him in the back seat of the car with me and we left for the hospital. He sat with his bleeding back away from the backrest, his wounded legs hanging. He was wincing with the pain. I carefully put my arm near his waist. He turned and clung to me, sobbing. I ran my fingers through his hair.

'Didi,' he said, cringing, grinding his teeth in pain, hugging me tighter. Tears welled up in my eyes. His blood dripped onto the seat of the car. 'That's it ... we are almost there. The doctor will bandage it and it will stop hurting. You are a brave boy, aren't you?' I said, not allowing my tears to fall. He nodded, his head resting against my shoulder. Each time he flinched, his little body shook against mine.

His hair smelled of Keo Karpin, as he held onto me, his elder sister. My little brother was suffering so miserably and I couldn't do anything to help him.

Our family had a history of allergic responses to medication and so the doctors chose to administer the injections in the ICU. They were going to inject the medicine directly near the affected areas and he was not going to be sedated. My parents told me what that meant. They were going to prick needles all around his wounds, without making him numb to the pain.

When they were taking him inside, I kissed his cheek and said, 'You are a *very* brave boy. Remember that.' My legs were shaking.

I stood outside, hearing his screams. With my tears came the realisation of how dear he was to me. I promised myself that I would never fight with him again. I knew now that he really was my little brother and I did not have to compete with him for anything. I loved him.

The accident changed us all. There was a marked difference in the way I looked at and out for my baby brother. Of course we still fought and bickered after that, but the fights weren't of the out-and-out-scream-fests and I'm-going to cause-you-pain variety. I guess the incident caused me to be more caring, that horrible possibility of 'What if?' always at the back of my mind.

Yes. The incident definitely changed us. My love grew deeper and our bond grew stronger.

Rasagya Kabra

Being Each Other's Strength

The strength of a butterfly lies in its fragility and the memory of its own past. A beautiful butterfly is always a diffident caterpillar when it first arrives in the world, and so are human beings.

Human beings are not born perfect; but we aspire to be the best that we can be. We start off having rough edges, and we go through our own life trajectories before we find out who we are and what we want from life. What often help us in realising our dreams are the people who are the wind beneath our wings.

My brother Rudra is one such individual. When I came into the world, Rudra was already eleven years old. At the age of six, I remember my seventeen-year-old brother towering over me. I was blissfully unaware that not all brothers are 6 feet 5 inches tall. In my head, all brothers carried their sisters on their shoulders, and all sisters had to be careful lest their heads bumped against the ceiling, leading to colourful bruises. And yet, my brother never intimidated me. I affectionately pulled his cheeks, painted on his starched clothes and even scolded him when he did not eat right. He never once complained. Everything was forgiven with the twinkle of an eye and a bright smile.

Rudra always taught me to think independently. He never took decisions for me, but helped me to come up with my own ideas. If I ever needed his advice or his support, all I would ever have to do is ask. And he'd be right there.

Before long, all my seniors in school had a huge crush on my brother. It didn't take me long to come up with a very convenient barter system. The 'big Didis' in school would have to buy me the choicest ice creams, and in return, they could come over anytime they wanted. My parents, although slightly surprised at first, put down my having so many older friends to the fact that I was a precocious young kid who preferred hanging out with those much older than me. Little did they suspect that they were coming in droves to catch a glimpse of my brother!

Once, when I was about fourteen, I was at my swimming club, drinking a large mug of orange squash after a tough competition, when a boy came up to me and started chatting me up. I wasn't even in the least bit interested and politely asked him to go away. He did not listen but persisted and that too in a bullying fashion. Suddenly my brother appeared from nowhere and muttered the unforgettable words, 'Leave my sister alone. Otherwise I will distort your face sooooo much that even your parents will not be able to recognise you.' While I was extremely scared for the boy, I was proud that my brother had stood up for me.

My brother was always my hero. For me, he was better than Superman. Or even Batman. Nothing could touch him. Or scare him. Until one day, it did.

My mother had gone for a routine check-up to the doctor's when the family discovered that she had a tumour in her breast. What was even worse was that it had a high chance of being malignant. It was our mother herself who broke the news to us and my brother was the epitome of calm ... in front of her. When Ma left the room to get herself a glass of water, Rudra signalled towards me and we went upstairs to my room. He locked the door, sat down next to me and shed silent, uncontrollable tears. It was the first time I had ever seen him cry. At that moment, I understood that it was my turn to protect him. My brother had protected me all my life. My brother had let no one hurt me. And here he was, crushed and struck with so much grief that for a second I did not know what to do. I hugged him and told him that everything would be alright and that we both needed to be strong for our mother. He cheered up a little bit and we began to think of ways to keep our mother positive during these dark hours.

If I was to pick out one incident that changed my life forever, it was seeing my brother crying like that. Apart from feeling intense pain in a very visceral way, I realised that vulnerability is enmeshed with resilience and you are strong only when you have the strength to reveal your weaknesses. My brother taught me that there is innate strength in loving and being loved, and in giving without any expectation.

The tumour turned out not to be malignant. All of us heaved a sigh of relief and my brother was back to being his cheery, ever-helpful self.

Many years later, when I was applying to different universities, I decided to apply to smaller colleges because I did not have enough faith in myself. I did not ever think I would get into the London School of Economics. It was my brother who insisted I apply, and wonder of wonders, in came the acceptance letter one fine morning. He taught me to dream, to fight for my rights and to never give up hope.

I write this from a faraway land and this is the first Bhai Phonta that I am spending away from home. I hate being away from my brother on this day, but I can't thank God enough for giving me an adorable, humorous and wonderful elder brother and hope that in the years to come, all our Raksha Bandhans and Bhai Phontas are spent together.

Reeti Roy

Hang On!

A far better swimmer than I, my younger brother always took pleasure in challenging me to races, giving me half a length lead and then reaching the other end before me and gloating over his victory. When he wasn't doing that, he'd swim up under me, hold my legs and drag me down, while I'd wail, flay my arms about in desperation, and swallow litres of water. By the time he'd let go of my legs, and I'd managed to frantically kick my way up, gulp in oxygen, swim to the side and look for him, he'd already have swum away to the deeper end, leaving me fuming and frustrated.

However, it wasn't any of these troublesome incidents that caused me my greatest embarrassment. *That* happened on a day my brother was trying to be helpful and teach me to jump from the highest board of the club pool. The board was a high board, and my brother easily ran up the ladder and jumped in, and swam out, climbed the ladder, jumped in and repeated the process several times. I watched, fascinated. Though I could swim lengths and I knew four strokes, I didn't have his confidence. I watched from the side as he waved to me and jumped straight in, waved to me and twisted and jumped into the water, waved to me and jumped backwards into the pool. It seemed like he was having all the fun while I was a boring spectator.

Charged by how effortless he made it appear and his repeated assurances of how easy it was, I decided to jump from the high board. We climbed together and stood side by side. 'Don't think, just jump,' he advised me. But that's not how I am made. So instead of listening to him I stood up there and stared. Suddenly the water seemed very far away, suddenly the pool seemed very deep, and suddenly I couldn't feel my legs anymore. I held on to the handle to stop myself from collapsing. My brother, who was in a helpful mood, decided to jump and show me how simple it was, so he casually walked off the board, into the water. I watched from above as he pierced the surface and disappeared deep inside, resurfaced a moment later, and then returned to my side.

But I was still not convinced. So my brother tried another approach. 'You want to walk down the diving board steps after having climbed up?' he asked, making it sound like the most heinous crime he could expect me to commit. '*Nobody* walks back down, Richa.' That was true. In all the years I'd swum in the pool, I'd never seen anyone climb down the steps. That left me with just one option: to spend the rest of my life squatting on the diving board. By then my brother's patience had thinned substantially and his interest in trying to get me to jump was waning. He tried one last time. 'Let's hold hands and jump,' he suggested. But that was unthinkable. What if he used his hand to pull me down further? I may never see the light of day again. I refused.

So then he did what he thought was the only option left to him. While I was standing at the edge, almost in tears, trying to coax myself into taking that leap, he silently crept up behind me and said 'Boo!' My feet slipped and I fell. But my survival instinct was strong and I held on to the edge of the diving board, dangling from it above the club pool.

I think I forgot to mention that this happened to be summer, when the pool was crowded with several gaping swimmers. I was mortified!

Fear turned to anger and I began cursing and fuming while I hung from the board. My brother realised the seriousness of what he'd done, so he crouched on the board, his face white, and very unhelpfully tried to pull me up by grabbing my arm. Obviously he couldn't. We were roughly the same size and I was just plain dead weight hanging mid-air. 'I'm sorry,' he said, 'but don't tell Mom, please, don't tell Mom.' Don't tell Mom? Was that his biggest concern right then? Didn't he realise what I was doing to my reputation, dangling like a pendulum from a diving board, with my brother tugging at my arm and a pool full of people shouting advice and instructions. *Of course* I'd tell Mom!

The swimming coach finally decided to intervene. Upon his instruction my brother finally let go of my arm. The coach placed himself in the deep end of the pool and asked me to let go. By then my arms had begun to ache, and all hope of pulling myself back to safety had vanished. The option of squatting on the diving board was lost forever. I really did have only one option. I let go.

I fell into the water, my face barely a few inches away from the wall. Any closer and I would have had a smashed face to accompany my aching arms and bruised ego. But the fall didn't seem that frightening. And the whole process of letting go, sinking deep inside the water and resurfacing lasted only a few seconds.

My brother ran to me, happy to see me alive and in one piece, more for his sake than mine. When I saw the fear on his face that day, I realised that if anything had happened to me, my brother would have been shattered. Hmmm, my tormentor *did* love me after all! The incident perfectly captures the essence of our relationship; his ceaseless and often merciless teasing, yet his overriding concern for my safety and well-being.

However, it has to be said that when he repeated his, 'I'm-sooooo-sorry-please-don't-tell-Ma' speech, I just glared at him. There was no way I was going to forgo that opportunity!

Richa Wahi

A Natural Bond

Gall stones were inconvenient at that juncture. Vikram was not yet two and Vinita, hardly four weeks old. Apart from medication and diet restrictions, the specialists had advised me to avoid lifting anything heavy, including the children. My maternal aunt took care of the kids till Vinita was four months old. When we moved to Pune, Ayi (my mother-in-law) came to live with us to help look after Vikram. Mama and Mami (my uncle and aunt), who had no children of their own, offered to take Vinita to Bombay and to care for her for as long as I needed.

My nights were spent weeping into the pillow. How would the kids get to know each other and bond? My army officer husband, Ramesh, was practical. He said the sooner I got rid of my gall stones the sooner we could bring Vinita to Pune. So I concentrated on growing stronger. Bombay, after all, was not too far off to visit once a month.

'Bonding comes naturally. You see how gentle he is with her?' Ramesh observed while in Bombay. He was right. For though Vikky was overactive, he was extremely careful not to hurt his sister in any way. Then, a year-and-a-half later, Ramesh said he had his posting orders for Ambala in the north, *miles* away from Bombay. I panicked.

My husband tried to reassure me. 'Easy ... easy. I have everything planned. Ayi will be with us anyway, and maybe we could have someone to look after Vinita in Ambala. The immediate problem is getting the little one used to the idea of living with us; and convincing Vikky that she's part of the family.'

Mama and Mami were highly cooperative, but tearful at having to part with someone who had now become a precious part of their lives. They decided to bring her to Pune and stay with us till she got used to the surroundings and to her 'new family'.

Now Vikky was a regular little livewire. He made the most of our spacious barracks at Ghorpadi in Pune, racing around, jumping about and clambering up trees. Poor Mama and Mami were on tenterhooks whenever he got too close to his sister, and tried to keep him away. He couldn't understand why, for he meant no harm. Didn't you say she was my sister? his eyes pleaded.

When Mama and Mami left, they wept uncontrollably and slunk away while she was fast asleep. I wept too, knowing how heart-breaking it must have been to be torn from her after eighteen months of attachment. The little one, getting up from her nap, looked around for the familiar faces. Not finding them, she sobbed pitifully, for her 'Amma'. I hugged her fondly and said, 'I am right here, darling,' she pushed me away, protesting, 'It is *my* Amma I want, *my* Kappimimi,' ('Kausalyamami' as I called her).

Her desperation was so pathetic that I started weeping too, and Vikky followed suit. 'Why don't you send her back to *her* parents? We can do without her, but *she* can't manage without them, can she?' I had no answer to that. A week went by and gradually the weeping subsided and she began to accept that she had to learn to live without her Kappimimi and Anna, and to adapt herself to her 'new family'. Vikky was in awe of her and did everything to keep her happy and ensure that she had her milk and meals. He became a responsible 'dada' overnight.

In Ambala, Vikky joined nursery school. He was tearful and unhappy whenever I dropped him off. It took him time to get used to the idea of school, but of course he eventually did. Soon it was time to send Vinita to play school. She shed silent tears when the rickshaw-walla came to pick them up. 'Amma, please, please, *please* let me go to college when I am as old as you are. Right now I'll study at home, I *promise*.' While the others coaxed her into the rickshaw, Vikky stood by looking miserable. When they returned on the third day, he declared, extremely upset, 'I don't think you should send her to school. Watching *her* crying, makes *me* cry too. She stops after a while, but *I* can't. I can't *bear* to see her unhappy.' And that was the turning point. Looking at his tearful face she firmly promised to stop weeping in school *from the very next day*!

My husband looked at me with an I-told-you-so smile.

They were amazingly different in many ways. He loved the outdoors while she stayed at home and looked at picture books and played with Sunila and Vanilla — her favourite dolls. One day, the two boys across the street came to ask

Vikky for his cricket set, and they all began playing cricket together in the large open area next to their bungalow. There was a sudden argument and Vikky walked towards the house with a bleeding nose, his head bowed. Vinita who had seen it all, walked swiftly to the boys and stood stiffly four feet away.

'If you don't give him a chance to bat, you can't have his cricket set, either,' she said firmly. To my amazement, Bunty and Billoo quickly laid the wickets, bat and ball at her feet and disappeared into their compound. I smiled in relief and together, we tried to make Vikky street-smart. But it wasn't easy.

'Why don't you let him be?' said my husband wisely. 'He will automatically toughen up when he grows older.'

When we moved to Nagpur, they both went to Bishop Cotton School by cycle rickshaw. At the end of the Sports Meet that year, Vikky stood cheerfully on the victory stand with his partner when the first prize was announced for the flag race. Vinita, who had stood third in the potato race, stood up after the second prize winner walked up to the stand. When she realised there was no third prize for Nursery, she sat back in her place, her face pale with disappointment. Just before prize distribution, Vikky looked at the array of cups neatly arranged on the table, and stamped his foot at the injustice of it.

'They have *so many* cups,' he grumbled. 'Why couldn't they give her *just one*?' On the way back, he made us stop at a book shop and buy a nice picture story about Billy Goat. At home, he made me write on the fly leaf: 'Awarded to Vinita Babulkar for securing Third Place in the Potato Race.' Her face brightened visibly, putting the smile back on his face.

When we were posted in Jorhat, Vikky left for the Lawrence School in Lovedale, Ooty. The following year Vinita followed him. 'It's too boring at home without Vikky. I'll go to the boarding school, too.'

My husband was right. It's a natural bond. It needs no aiding and abetting.

Savitri Babulkar

Mama-Cuddling Daredevils

November 24, 1986. It was a Tuesday and I was in school, nursery. My mother was in hospital ready to deliver my sibling. I didn't know if I was going to get a brother or sister; secretly I wished it were the latter. I was five-and-a-half years old and never understood how a brother would make a good playmate. Still, on D-day, I couldn't wait for school to finish and even nagged my class teacher to give me the yellow chrysanthemum on her desk as a present for Mommy. I reached Woodlands Hospital with my father. On the way to my mother's room I was told I'd got a brother. My face fell a bit — little did I know what a rollercoaster ride we were in for as a family. Rohan-aka-Bunty the daredevil had been born, ready to do what most infants would attempt much later in life.

Rohan was brought home and was dressed in a pink smocking frock for the first few months; he looked like an angel. But this was only for the first six months. My old cot, which my mother says I used till I was three years old, was handed down to the new arrival. As a cautious mother, she did her duties by lining it with bolsters, making sure there was no scope for her baby to get hurt. And he didn't — the bolsters were used as a stepping stone for future acts of daredevilry, and also, quite literally, as a step when my six-month-old brother used them to jump out of his cot. The first sign of Rohan's free-spirited nature.

Cue forward to Rohan at age two when he joins Harvard Montessari School. Our mother is thrilled. She's finally going to get some time for herself. Day 1 at school. A room full of children and plenty of options to keep them occupied. Before leaving him in the care of the teachers, Mama noticed bright blue and red counting rods. 'Please be careful with those, my son is very naughty, I don't want him beating up anyone,' she pleaded with the teacher. 'Oh don't worry Ma'am, that's what we are here for,' was the teacher's prompt reply.

By afternoon, the age-old theory of 'mother knows best' was proven once again. My nappy-clad little two-year-old brother, with a cheeky disposition, had turned Samurai. 'He did it,' exclaimed his teacher, almost in tears.

This wasn't the end. His acts of daredevilry went on for years, some amusing and some not. But inside him was a softie, a sensitive boy who loved a mama-cuddle every now and then.

And then, age sixteen arrived. We suffered the shockingly sudden and untimely loss of our father and life changed direction overnight. My brother was rock-solid; he never shed a tear. While other boys his age were going through teenage turmoil and angst, staging little acts of rebellion, I saw my baby brother suddenly transform into the man of the house. His focus was our mother's peace and happiness. He has been Mama's iron pillar, her errand boy, her financial consultant, her driver, her cook (most often when he is in the mood for mutton!). Through this he finished school and graduated with a degree in Commerce. Currently at his first job since the last three years, the baby boy who jumped out of his cot has been making his bosses jump out of their seat with his business acumen. He lives in another city but visits his mother and sister every now and then, when he craves another mama-cuddle or when his bosses want him to bring back home-made brownies.

Did you know that Rohan means 'ascending', and hence 'one who travels the higher path'. My baby brother's name couldn't be more apt.

Anonymous

A Sense of Sibling Love

My cousins Ishani and Vaibhav were in London at that time. Ishani had started her PhD research, and Vaibhav had joined a company soon after getting his engineering degree. Things were moving smoothly till one day when they received a phone call from their home in India.

Ishani's mother had called to inform them about their father's illness. She was in tears when she told Ishani that their father was very sick and someone had to be there beside him.

'When are you coming back to India? I feel so helpless,' she said tearfully.

'Ma, please don't worry. One of us will be there very soon,' Ishani assured her, collecting herself.

'Are you going to come tomorrow?' her mother asked innocently. 'I'll be waiting for you.'

Her mother could speak no further and Ishani had no words to console her.

The hours of that day passed with a flow of worries and contemplation about the best possible way to attend to the family emergency. When Vaibhav came back from work in the evening, Ishani told him about the serious condition of their father.

'Please don't worry, I shall go home,' Vaibhav offered almost instantly.

'Come on, Vaibhav!' Ishani interjected. 'I can understand how you are feeling, but we should be practical. You just got a job and if you decide to take leave they might ask you to quit. I have been thinking about this the whole day. I have decided to go. I will start my research work all over again next semester … it's only a year. Don't worry, Papa will be all right very soon,' Ishani said with an unusual firmness.

'What are you saying?' Vaibhav paused, as if to arrange his thoughts. 'Starting all over again after a year is no joke. You won't know whether you will get a chance to work under the same guide and obtain the facilities and above all, the project that you are working on at the moment.'

'It doesn't matter,' she said. 'What if my experiment had failed and I had to start all over again? It's something like that. It is more important to be there beside our father rather than continue the research work. I do not want any more arguments please. I'll take the first flight to India tomorrow morning.'

Vaibhav could not argue any further. He could not think of anything that might convince his elder sister to reconsider her decision. He recalled Ishani's ability to deal with obstacles with an outward calm. He felt ashamed at how he wore his nerves thin even in trivial matters. He did not want to leave his job — he considered himself lucky to be offered such a brilliant opportunity. He was proud of the fact that he worked with one of the best firms in London. But deep within he knew that he longed to see his father. He felt perturbed as he recollected how much his sister had sacrificed for him and was now about to make one more. He knew how much hard work and dedication was involved in getting admission in the PhD course, and it would not be easy to get a second chance to do research in such a reputed university.

He struggled inwardly, torn between reminiscences of his sister's unconditional love and affection for him, and the pull to achieve his selfish desires. During their childhood, she was always the one who compromised and willingly parted with her favourite possessions, giving them to him just to see him happy. He wondered how she dealt with every situation with her usual easy adaptability and always yielded to the whims and fancies of her younger brother.

Vaibhav remembered one such incident when Ishani was fourteen years old and he was ten. He had been seriously ill and it was while he was recovering that Ishani had a function in school. In that function she was to be awarded 'best student of the year'. On hearing that he would have to spend some time without her, he started crying inconsolably, clinging to her helplessly. Vaibhav still remembered how Ishani had yielded yet again to his impulsive, sudden fit of melancholy and decided not to attend the function, though she had been eagerly waiting for this special day. Vaibhav was unable to comprehend the tenderness of her boundless love and compassion and her innate ability to adjust to an adverse situation without making her disappointment evident to others.

Ishani was again making a sacrifice for him, but this time for a different cause. Perhaps this time it was love for her father and her duty towards her family that motivated her to take such a decision. But the fact that she was concerned and

protective about her brother's welfare could not be denied.
After a few hours of critical deliberation, he made his decision.
All this while, his sister had been sacrificing her desires and
now her career for the sake of her younger brother, but now it
was his turn. He wrote a small note for his sister and left for
the airport.

Sreelekha Chatterjee

The Manifold Advantages of a Big Brother

It's a cool autumn day and I'm in the doctor's office with my three-year-old daughter and nine-year-old son. It is time for the second of their semi-annual influenza vaccinations.

From the time he was three years old, I've been very upfront with my son about how shots are important to prevent illnesses and how it seems more painful than it really is if you fight it. My intention was to never hide from him the fact that he was about to get an injection. I was more afraid of him finding out that I had tricked him into something than of him being wary of a visit to the doctor.

I really did not expect the message to go over so well so quickly, and it pulled at my heart-strings when the little three-year-old child did more than I had ever wished for — when it was our turn, he let go of my hand, walked to the tiny toddler-chair, lifted his sleeve and presented his arm to a sceptical nurse. She finished giving him the shot and put on a bright, colourful band aid where the needle had gone in. He ran up out of the chair, hugged me around my legs, looked up at me and asked, 'Mama, was I a big boy?' The nurse was more than a little taken aback, I was left trying to stifle my sobs and my baby was suddenly all grown-up.

Fast forward six years later and to my daughter who's three. With her, it's a completely different story. When she was about a year old, she went through a spate of tests that involved drawing blood. The repeated visits at that age and having needles stuck in her arm each time cemented a dreadful connection in her mind — a visit to the doctor meant injections.

That association is starting to fray a bit given the numerous visits where the syringe has not made an appearance. I still stick to my philosophy about not tricking children into going to the doctor's office on the promise that there will be no injections. On this day, she knows full well why we are at the doctor's office and, as far as we can tell, seems to be holding up well.

When our turn comes, the nurse asks who will go first and my son raises his hand. He goes through the drill — gets up on the table, pulls up his sleeve, cringes a little in anticipation, and lets out a long sigh when it's all done. Then it's my daughter's turn. From experience, my son fully expects her to bawl and stands at the door to the room with his ears covered. I scoop my daughter up in my arms and sit on a chair with her on my lap. She's been watching quietly all this while and eyes the nurse and the syringe warily.

As the nurse lifts her sleeve to prep her arm, there's a sudden burst of activity at the door and all three of us turn to look at my son as he calls out to his sister. 'Look at me!' he cajoles her and proceeds to do what I never saw coming — he starts to dance a crazy little jig. His arms are flailing, his legs are turning this way and that, his face puts on silly expressions and he's making funny noises. My daughter turns to me, giggles and says, 'Look, Mom! Nanna's being silly again.' The nurse realises what's going on and seizes the opportunity to finish up her task as quickly as she can.

By the time my daughter feels the prick of the needle on her skin, she's too engrossed in her brother's antics, and much too busy giggling at his moves, to spare more than a glance at her arm. The kiddie band aid has already made an appearance.

As far as my daughter is concerned, her big brother is a major source of fun — he's great for horse rides, to watch movies with, to make puzzles with, to bounce on the bed with, to play tag with, to raid the freezer for ice cream with, to read books with and to tussle with. I hope it's not long before she wraps her mind around all the tiny ways in which he makes her life a little less hurtful.

Sujatha Bagal

The Impromptu Party

My grandfather passed away a few months before my tenth birthday. Following this, my father finally took up a job in another city. So one big loss followed hard on the heels of another. We were a close-knit bunch of cousins and my older brother and I were very attached to our extended family. Our first few months in the new city were difficult. The excitement carried us through, but when I was informed that I wouldn't be having a birthday party that year — finances were tight and we didn't know too many people there yet — I was quite heartbroken. Our grandfather used to plan these huge parties with gorgeous cakes for us, and this seemed like yet another underscoring of his loss.

My brother blithely went to school on the morning of my birthday, I less exuberantly so. The day passed in a round of classes and kindnesses, but when it was time to go home, I remember feeling quite sorry for myself. Then my brother grinned and told me that he had invited two friends to 'the party' and all self-pity flew out of the window. If anything, I was quite alarmed at the prospect of going home and explaining to my mother that we were having guests without her having invited them. However, it was too late to ask the children not to come.

We went home and after some deliberation, I told my mother what my brother had done. She, torn between annoyance and laughter, decided to put a brave face on it. My father, coming home early that night, was told to bring some snacks. She herself made a sweet dish, I think. An uncle of hers, visiting us that day, had luckily brought a cake. And promptly at five, the two boys appeared, along with a girl my age, the younger sister of one of my brother's classmates. They were a bit embarrassed at finding themselves the only guests but we ended up having a fun evening and I was sorry to see them go. The food was simple and I can't remember what we played but I do remember that it was a wonderful party, one of the best I've ever had.

Ever since, as my brother and I squabble our way through life, the memories of this party act as a touchstone for me — a reminder that underneath everything else, there lies this affection.

Sunayana Roy

Fisherprice Men

I'd forgotten about them,
those thumb-sized men
who lived for years
on our bedroom floor.
They were my brother's treasures:
the green Texan, the road-builders,
the circus ringmaster —
all hatted and moustachioed,
tunnelling out of the past
bearing the scars
of our dead dog's tooth marks.

Today, my sister's boy from America
brings the village alive again,
leading the men to camper vans
and dusty deckchairs,
giving them names
like Harvey and Stan.
My brother sits in the corner,

rocking, oblivious.
He doesn't rise to greet his childhood
spread out on the bedroom floor,
or say, *Mine, all mine,*
like he used to.
He is in a place of no time,
with no thoughts of death or fear.
Only the sound
of his beating heart,
which must tell him
that he is human,
that he too is moving somewhere.

Tishani Doshi

Night Duty on Raksha Bandhan

Doctors in India advise a three-year gap between siblings, but the age gap between my brother Rajat and me is only one year and one month. Perhaps that is why he has, as a child, treated me more as a punching bag than as a sister and I have used my claws on him with a viciousness that would put any feline creature to shame! We lived in a joint family in Delhi's Darya Gunj area, and my howling like a banshee every time Rajat hit me brought my grandfather rushing into my room, fearing that I had been murdered! Things changed drastically when we grew up. Rajat went to study medicine in Maulana Azad Medical College, which was a stone's throw away from our house, and as he stayed in the hostel, our relationship became more formal.

When Rajat passed his final year and began his internship I was thrilled. I looked forward to Raksha Bandhan as I anticipated that this time he would not give me a token amount borrowed from my parents but a substantial gift bought with his first salary. However, a day before Raksha Bandhan, Rajat came home looking glum. 'I'm sorry, but I won't be here for

Raksha Bandhan,' he murmured dejectedly. 'Why?' my three cousins and I chorused at once. 'I have night duty,' he muttered, 'you know the thirty-six hour shift.' Of course I knew all about it ... the poor, over-worked, over-stressed interns catching a snatch of sleep before rushing off to attend to some emergency or another. 'But it is Raksha Bandhan,' I argued. 'I know,' he nodded, 'but it can't be helped, duty is duty.' I mentally cursed Lok Nayak Jai Prakash Narayan Hospital where he worked for making him work on a well-deserved holiday.

The next day he returned home looking gloomy. 'What's the matter?' I asked. 'I have lost my wallet,' he muttered. 'It contained my entire salary.' He only got a stipend, not a full salary, but it was better than being dependent on one's parents for pocket money. 'Did you look in all the wards you visited?' I asked. 'Yes,' he said, 'I did.' 'Well, ask the doctor and nurses on duty if they found it,' I suggested, 'and put up a notice on the notice board.' 'I have done all that,' he said, 'but I still couldn't find it.' I looked at his face. He seemed to be hiding something. Finally I dragged the truth from him. 'Last night my friends and I went out to see a late night movie,' he confessed. 'I might have left it in the cinema hall.' I burst out laughing when I heard this. His friends and he had planned to see a late night movie and fabricated the story about night duty in order to avoid giving money to their sisters on Raksha Bandhan. But fate had deprived my brother of his entire month's earnings. Not only was this ironic, it was also poetic justice. I did not hesitate to tell him that. 'So what? Anyway I don't believe in Raksha Bandhan,' he retorted. I was deeply hurt, although I did a good job of hiding my feelings as I shrugged my shoulders and said, 'Nor do I.' Of course I continued to send him a rakhi and he sent me cash, but from that day on, it seemed forced and ritualistic.

Many years later, in 1992, I went to the UK on a Colombo Plan fellowship to do my Master's in Development Administration from the University of Birmingham. My brother had just returned to India that August after working in Guy's Hospital in London. 'Your brother has left you something for Raksha Bandhan,' said my uncle upon my arrival, and he took out a hundred pound note. A hundred pounds? It was one-fourth the stipend the British Council was paying me.

'You must be joking,' I responded. 'He must have meant to give me a hundred rupees.' My uncle merely shrugged his shoulders as I pocketed the amount gratefully. Raksha Bandhan *does* mean something to Rajat after all, I thought happily. Our sibling bond was as strong as ever.

Vandana Jena

Big Brother's Got Your Back

'I've got your back,' Bhai said and winked at me. It was the latest lingo that he had picked up and, in his desperate attempt to stay 'cool', he used it as often as he could. The usage was restricted to the dudes of the house and I convinced him that I was 'uber cool', and he could use the verbiage with me — so he did. Rakesh bhai always cracked me up. At seventy-five, he was perhaps the most energetic in the entire family.

I don't remember much of my parents. I lost both by the time I was ten. But being the only girl in five generations, and the youngest in the family, is not a bad deal. Rakesh bhai was fifteen years older, ergo almost a father figure. Even so, he was never embarrassed when I trotted around his friends with my dolly, while they were discussing the strategy for the next hockey game. My brother would do anything for me, and when he got married, my sister-in-law pampered me even more.

I was married into a staunch Rajput family — the only son among eight children. Bhai and Bhabhi were concerned. Would I be happy? Being the only daughter-in-law meant a lot of responsibility. And I also had to move away from the happening capital of the country. But they liked the boy. He seemed quite a pleasant and respectful lad. He looked good too. So with a little cajoling, I agreed to the alliance.

I settled down well, in my new home. I had seen my Bhabhi work in the kitchen, and she'd given me a crash course just before the wedding. My brother always found an excuse to visit. Either a 'business trip' was scheduled via this route, or they were planning a vacation 'somewhere close by' or they'd just lost their way to a place I had never heard of. My husband always joked that my Bhai and Bhabhi were making sudden inspection calls to see if he was treating me well.

The only time I remember being scared, was when I was expecting Rishabh. I wasn't sure I'd be able to manage. That's when Bhai sent Bhabhi over. I did not even have to ask. They had had their third son about ten months before, so it would probably be time for his first birthday around Rishabh's arrival. And first birthdays are a huge deal. But it wasn't as important as a panicky sister who was about to pop. My nephew's first birthday was very important — to me, and I knew it was for Bhai and Bhabhi as well. So I arranged for Bhai to come down. We had a small ceremony and I invited the neighbours over for a quick cake-cutting. Bhai had tears in his eyes. He stayed on and left only after Rishabh was born. Bhabhi stayed on for another three months, just to help me settle down with the stork's gift.

The worst crisis of my life however, was when Rishabh announced that he wanted to get married to a girl from his college. No, that wasn't the worst: he had to get married someday. The worst was when he announced he was getting married to a south Indian Brahmin girl. My husband lost it. He was very clear that the marriage would not happen. How could a boy of the elite warrior class marry a pandit? A vegetarian? I was in a fix. I loved my son. I loved my husband. I couldn't take sides, though admittedly I was leaning towards the senior camp.

Rishabh was quite smart in his approach. He made Bhai do the talking. He was the only person in the whole world who could convince his father. Bhai was the only person my husband blindly trusted.

'But their culture, their traditions ... everything is so different,' my husband protested. 'Traditions between one Rajput community and the next vary so much — this will be worlds apart!' Bhai tried to calm him down. 'But ... they're vegetarians!' my husband almost wailed, 'My son will end up eating grass and leaves!'

'Let the girl come into the family, we'll make her a hardcore Rajput!' Bhai joked.

When we finally saw how adamant Rishabh was, we finally set a date to meet the girl's parents. We did not even know if it was okay for the boy's parents to initiate discussions. Rishabh was useless in such matters.

Bhai did a thorough research into their traditions. Google was his best friend. We went to their house with a combination of fruits, dry fruits and jasmine. That must have impressed the lady of the house, for it was indeed part of the tradition. Bhai brought out an extra ounce of charm that day, speaking knowledgeably about their art and customs, and he even complimented her filter coffee as the best he had ever tasted. Of course it was the first he had ever tasted, but she didn't need to know that!

The marriage was finally fixed. Nothing in the ceremonies was new to Bhai. It was as if he had grown up a Tam-Brahm! He even joined a Carnatic committee in Delhi, to learn from Tamilians.

D-Day arrived. I was running helter-skelter, making sure everything was going according to schedule, the guests were being attended to and that the ceremony was taking place without a hitch. The priest suddenly asked me for the 'panchapatra udrani'. I'd be blessed if I could even pronounce the word! Just then, Bhai walked in with a silver glass and spoon — 'Don't worry. I've got your back,' he said.

Yes he did! Just like always!

As told to Vasudha Iyer

Of Cars and Cushions

My brother and I weren't really close growing up. I don't know why; perhaps it was because I'm almost five years younger than he, or perhaps we never took time to bond. As with most siblings, we had a love-hate relationship — we loved to hate each other! Bhaiya would always get his way around the house, and would generally pressurise me to do mundane tasks for him, like polishing his school shoes, or doing his arts homework. In return, he would eat my chocolates, mess up my cupboard, hide my dolls, add extra salt to my food — you name it!

One day, Bhaiya and I had a huge fight. You see, he is a big car buff. He had just bought his dream car after saving his salary diligently, right from the first month that he'd started working. In his absence, I took the car for a spin, taking along a few friends for company. Crisps and ice cream were spilled all over the newly accessorised car and Bhaiya got so mad! We fought, after which I locked myself up in my room only to eavesdrop on his conversation with my parents. He said,

'She's like my daughter only; and I irritate her to tease her. Don't worry, I would never let anything happen to her.'

'Haa!' I thought. He was obviously trying to get out of trouble for our fight by saying those things. But in due course, I realised that Bhaiya did treat me like a daughter. He has never, EVER let anything happen to me. When I look back over the years, I recall the innumerable instances when Bhaiya has been the cushion for all my falls; where he has been my friend, my mentor, my confidant.

I remember one winter, when my uncle in Mumbai fell severely ill, my parents rushed to be with him, leaving Bhaiya and me with our grandparents. I was in my final year of graduation, and exam preparations were on in full swing. Now, Kolkata winter afternoons are beautiful and you just want to be outside, soaking up the sun. I decided to take a break from studies and drive around Victoria Memorial along with my dog Coffee. My reverie was broken by a loud *bang*.

I was so lost in my thoughts, I had collided with another vehicle! I knew I would be in trouble. My immediate thought was that my car-crazy big brother would be hopping mad and my doting dad wasn't even there to save me! And while all these thoughts were running through my mind, I completely forgot to first sort matters out with the person whose car I had hit. Before I could get out of my car, a very stern looking Army man, with an impressive uniform and moustache, yelled at me, claiming that he and his colleagues would have to take me to the military headquarters!

I was so petrified that I refused to come out of the car. I thought there was no way I would let myself be hauled to the military headquarters; besides an accident is not a military offence and I mentioned this to the men around me, but just at that moment, a traffic policeman arrived on the scene! He asked me if I had a licence. I said yes, and then I realised that I'd left it at home! Sweating bricks, I called up Bhaiya. I thought he would yell at me and ask me to sort matters on my own. And I knew that once I reached home, there would be consequences. And this time, deservedly so. I'd been a negligent driver, and I'd broken the law by not carrying my licence.

Bhaiya was in a meeting and so I hurriedly told him what had happened. Without any further questions, he asked me to stay put, saying that he was on his way. I told the policemen and the military men that my brother was coming, and he would speak to them. I just sat tight in the car, the four military men hovering around me as if I was about to run away from there.

After twenty minutes of waiting, I saw my brother walking up to us. What a relief! He moved through the crowd of people, opened my car door, got me out and asked if we were hurt in any way. He gave a very stern look to a passerby who was trying to shout at me, and shut him up. He asked me to take his car and go home. Yep, the same precious dream car that I had already messed up once before. I was surprised, and relieved at the same time, as I just didn't know how to handle the situation. As instructed, I got into the car and drove home carefully.

On reaching home, I realised that I'd left Bhaiya to deal with a tough situation. I frantically began pacing up and down. I called his cell phone, but he didn't answer. Nasty thoughts started running through my head — what if they arrested him, or beat him up or punished him in some other way. I began crying inconsolably, and there was no one around as my grandparents had gone out. Bhaiya then sent an SMS saying, 'I'm handling this. I'll speak to you once home.'

I calmed down somewhat. After about six hours, Bhaiya came home. I had all sorts of explanations ready for him — as to how I'd got distracted, or how it was the other car's fault, etc. But even before I could begin, he put his hand on my head, said, 'Of all the cars in the city, how did you manage to hit a military car!' and started laughing! I couldn't believe it. I said, 'I'm really sorry Bhaiya, I promise I won't do this again!' and he replied, 'At least not with a military car! The formalities and procedures are way too long!' he joked. Then, with love and affection in his eyes, he said, 'Don't worry, I took care of it. I am just glad that nothing happened to you. Just be careful when you drive next time. And yes, I've sent the car for repairs, so Ma and Dad won't find out!'

He gave me a hug and went off laughing. He didn't even bother mentioning to me that he had to go to three police stations, explain the situation to over twenty senior officers of the Army as well as the police, and was threatened by a crowd of people who were angry that he had stepped in to save a girl who had left the scene. It was only when a copy of the police report came to us by post did I discover all this.

Bhaiya kept his word. He didn't tell anyone anything. He'd protected me. In the same way, I realised, that he'd done in the past. There had been a million situations when Bhaiya put himself in the line of fire to ensure that I was safe and comfortable. I knew that no matter how deep the fall, my brother would be the cushion to it all and ensure that I never get hurt.

Priyanka Goenka Gupta

A Brother in Need

The old clock on the wall struck eight times as Rajan entered his father's rented house in Madras. His father stood up from his reclining chair, pleasantly surprised at his son's sudden visit from Bombay. Lowering the volume of the old Philips Murphy radio set, he asked his son the reason for this unannounced visit, hoping aloud that everything was fine at work. Rajan maintained a stoic silence. In the meanwhile, his mother came in with a cup of tea and some home-made snacks and gently admonished her husband, 'Stop interrogating your son. Let him sit down and relax. He has come here after a long time.'

She then turned to him and said, 'Your sister is not home yet. Usually she returns from office by seven. It's already eight … I wonder why she's so late?' Hesitantly, Rajan answered her question, 'Veena has gone to her new home. She will not come back to this house. I got her remarried to a good man of her choice, this morning. The man loves her and will stand by her.'

His parents were shell-shocked, and when Rajan told them that the boy was a non-Brahmin, all hell broke loose. His mother started weeping and his father started yelling, 'How dare you! Who are you to get her remarried when her parents are alive? Get out of this house at once. Do not show us your face; you are no longer our son.'

Veena's first marriage in the early 1970s was an arranged one. Her husband was a bank officer from the Brahmin community. The boy's parents demanded a huge dowry and expensive wedding arrangements. Her father couldn't raise the entire funds to meet their demands, which had resulted in Veena facing much criticism and unpleasantness from her in-laws. She was verbally abused and frequently even beaten up by her husband and his parents. She would often come back to her parents' place and sob to them about her misery and pain. Unfortunately, her parents were not bold enough to confront her in-laws as they were not in a position to meet their demands. Her mother would tell her that time was a great healer and in due course everything would be alright. Veena had reached her tolerance limit and even thought of committing suicide. Her office colleagues knew she was depressed. While they empathised with her, they couldn't actively help her with a solution.

One of her office colleagues, Swami, would surround her with positive thoughts and build up her sense of self-esteem. He advised her to be brave and not succumb to pressures of life. In him, she found a friend and confidant. He was always ready to listen to her and offer words of support and wisdom.

On one occasion, Veena was severely beaten up by her in-laws and they threatened to burn her alive if she failed to arrange for the remaining dowry amount. She was asked to leave her husband's house and come back only with the balance dowry amount.

She returned to her parents' home and poured her heart out. But her parents didn't know what to do; they threw their hands up in helplessness. Hearing about the latest incident at her in-laws' home, Swami suggested that her only recourse seemed to be divorce. She stayed on with her parents and at the same time consulted a lawyer to file for divorce. Swami was her rock through her ordeal, and Veena found herself falling in love with him. She wondered whether he would reciprocate her love. Would he be inclined to marry a divorcee? When she asked, Swami's answer thrilled her ... he had wanted to propose to her too but he just wasn't sure when it would seem appropriate to ask.

When she expressed her desire to marry Swami, her orthodox Brahmin parents were enraged and threatened her with dire consequences. So Veena secretly wrote a letter to her brother Rajan in Bombay. She wrote in detail the trauma she had faced at her in-laws' hands. She then wrote about her love for Swami, asking if she didn't deserve some happiness after all that she had been through. She ended the letter with, 'If you fail to take me out of this hell, you will only see your sister's dead body.'

No sooner had he read the tear-smeared contents of the letter, Rajan was quick to act. He flew down to Madras the very next day and met his sister at her office. On seeing him, Veena broke down. Rajan comforted her and assured her that he would always be there for her. Later in the evening she introduced him to Swami. He made discreet enquiries about Swami with people in the office. He had even asked his trusted classmates to monitor Swami for some days and the reports that came back to him were glowing.

Assured of Swami's character, he decided to go ahead with his sister's choice. But there was a big problem: Swami was from a different caste; an absolute negative in the eyes of their conservative parents. So Rajan called Veena, Swami and some trusted friends and told them of his plan. He advised Veena and Swami to apply for a registered marriage. Once the date was fixed, Rajan flew back to Bombay and informed his wife about the plan and asked her to keep it close to her heart.

A day before the marriage, Rajan arrived in Madras and checked into a hotel. As per the plan, the following morning Veena left for office dressed in her every day, office attire so as not to arouse her parents' suspicion. She was asked to meet Swami and their friends, who would be standing in as witnesses, at a common point and come to the registrar's office where Rajan would be waiting. Things went according to plan. The bride and the groom signed on the registers and exchanged rose garlands. Rajan's eyes welled up when he saw the broad smile on his sister's face. The couple touched his feet to seek his blessings. He wished them a long and happy wedded life. The couple and witnesses headed to a hotel for a small party that had been arranged by Rajan.

Later that evening, Rajan escorted the couple to their new home and then went straight to his parents' home to inform them about Veena's wedding. As fate would have it, as he entered the house, he heard his father's old radio playing the Tamil song, *Malarnthumalaratha pathi malar pondru malarun* — a real tear-jerker of a song, from the megahit Sivaji Ganesan starrer, *Pasamalar*. This movie, from the '60s, had a story-line revolving around the beautiful bond of love between brother and sister. And ironically enough, with this song playing in the background, Rajan's father threw him out of the house for daring to side with his sister.

Today, both Veena and Swami are enjoying their retired life. Their children were given the liberty to choose their own life partners. Their son is a doctor and their daughter, a successful management graduate.

Even now, Veena's eyes well up with tears whenever she thinks of her loving brother who threw societal norms to the wind for his sister's happiness, not thinking twice about the consequences that he might have to face. Of course, seeing Veena and Swami so happy together, Rajan would happily do it all again.

T.S. Karthik

3

SOUL SISTERS

If you don't understand how a woman could both love her sister dearly and want to wring her neck at the same time, then you were probably an only child.

–Linda Sunshine

Through Sobs and Spoonfuls

As a kid, all I deeply wished for — as opposed to the toys and candy that all the other children around me wanted — was a younger sister. Like all my other friends who had siblings, I too wanted to share that special bond, those inside jokes and those sisterly secrets with mine.

Back then I used to live in a society with many kids close to my age and we would spend hours during the evening running around, playing and having fun. And then, everyone would head back home with their siblings and it used to sadden me to make the journey back home all alone. I'd spend hours whining to my sympathetic parents about how my life was incomplete without a sister all my own. Now sympathetic though they were, they didn't seem to do anything about it. Why didn't they just go to the hospital and pick one out already?

And then, a few months before I turned three, my mother told me that my sibling was on the way and I was ecstatic with joy. The day my sister Sanaya was born, I was so elated that I could barely get through the morning and was rushing through everything so I could go and visit my baby sister at the hospital. When I first saw her, happy as I was, I couldn't understand how that little baby could ever grow enough so as to be able to accompany me anywhere. When she finally came home, I spent every waking moment around her and it didn't take long for her to become the centre of my universe.

With time, we started having our fights and differences, but I can't remember there ever being a time when Sanaya didn't cry the moment she saw me crying or upset. Growing up, it was nice to have someone who idolised me and supported my every move. We would spend hours playing our make-believe games, eating and watching television. We used to plot and plan as to how we would achieve the utmost social power within our society or how we would get our parents to do exactly as we wished. Yes, together we were unbeatable.

My sister recently turned thirteen and I hope that I can be as helpful and understanding as she was with me during my rebellious teenage phase. I remember the many nights she stayed up waiting for me to come back home from a night out partying, so she could quietly open the door for me and I wouldn't get shouted at. Then, there have been the many fights with my parents where she has blindly backed me. One memory stands out in particular ... I had just had a huge blowout with my parents regarding my curfew. I wanted it to be extended; they thought it was fine as it was. The fight got ugly, leading to me storming away, going to my room and sitting in a corner, on the floor, sobbing hot, heavy tears of anger. Sanaya quietly came and sat down next to me ... with a jar of yummy, chocolatey Nutella in her hands. Through sobs and spoonfuls, I rambled on and on with my 'life is so unfair' tirade, while Sanaya sat there throughout, interjecting with a gentle, 'We'll talk to them Ashy,' every now and then. She had a test the next day, one that she had not studied for, but she didn't leave my side for a second, until I was finally okay. All life's unfairness was set fair in the sweet taste of that chocolate and the sweeter feeling of her unconditional support.

As we grow up and into different people with our own sets of quirks, dreams and personalities, I just pray that the special bond we share lasts a lifetime. I look forward to continuing our movie marathons and our crazy game sessions. I want to be there for her whenever she needs advice, help or just a patient ear to talk to. I hope I will always be to her, the big sister that she has idolised and loved.

I hope she knows that I will always be there for her too ... through sobs and spoonfuls.

Aishwarya Bharadia

Of Missed Calls, Plastic Bags and Love

We are as different as chalk and cheese. Yet she is the one who adds sunshine to my life. My days are incomplete without hearing her voice, but there's a catch to all our conversations — she is the queen of missed calls, a title given to her by me. I have been a victim of her missed calls for six long years!

Now let me make matters straight. This is my elder sister I am referring to; I call her Nans. She works as a senior professional in the education sector and draws a handsome salary; the global economic meltdown had no impact on her career or her salary slip. In fact, I would even say that she has prospered professionally in the last one year. So her bank balance has nothing to do with her missed calls.

Just sample this: on a hot summer evening, I hear the mobile phone ringing, and like India's golden girl P.T. Usha I run to my bedroom, but skid to a halt because it has stopped ringing. Instinctively, I know it's my sister. I don't know about her mastering any other art, but she has definitely mastered the art of giving missed calls and I, like a dutiful soldier, call her back every time.

Once after talking for little more than a minute, she said, 'I'm really busy. I don't have time to talk to you; I'll call again later.' Seething, I said, 'Hey! I called *you* up.' She replied, in a most Zen-like manner, 'Oh is that so. I thought I called you. Anyway, good that you called up ... I really want to talk to you.' And that day, we talked for forty-eight minutes!

There's another mobile mystery which I am unable to fathom. I can't understand why she switches her phone off at nine in the night, every night, without fail, as if she were following a military directive. Though her explanation is, 'Who will call me in the night?' I think she switches her phone off to save the battery, and the subsequent cost of recharging it.

In my family, we have a name for her: 'Penny wise, pound foolish'. She's the one who loves to pamper all her siblings, and even now she often sends me cheques so that I can indulge in retail therapy. Yet she's the one who very often proudly announces in our 'sister sessions' that she has never spent a single penny on a camera and music CDs. Yet, there she is in every family photograph, posing like a beauty queen with the perfect smile. According to her, the camera loves her. For a change, I must admit that I agree with her.

And then there's her inexplicable love for plastic bags. Her face lights up like a 1000 watt bulb if you give her a sari or dress material in a plastic bag. She'll take immense care in folding it and putting it away — the plastic bag, that is. She gives the plastic bag more attention than the gift that was in it! Ask her at any time of the day/night for a plastic bag and she will willingly give you one from her collection, but if you dare misplace it ... that can lead to a mini tsunami or an earthquake of 5.4 on the Richter scale! Whenever I venture out shopping during my annual visit to my hometown, she will unfailingly and lovingly hand over a water bottle in a plastic bag to me with the parting words unfailingly and lovingly being, 'Don't lose it.' Needless to say I clutch on to the plastic bag as if it were my lifeline. More often than not, my concentration on what the shopkeeper is showing me wavers, because my attention is forever on Nan's precious-as-a-diamond-studded-tiara plastic bag. I don't even give that much attention to my wallet! And it's not just me; even our neighbourhood tailor takes extra care to keep Nan's plastic bag under lock and key because she can't afford to misplace Madam's precious belonging.

But as they say, love knows no logic and blood is thicker than water; if I don't hear her voice, my day feels incomplete and so I miss her missed calls. I miss her glowing face as she takes out a bright red plastic bag from her cupboard. And I dream of growing old with her and hope that in the evening of life, we will still laugh at her profound statement, 'I have never spent a penny on a camera....'

I've already kept aside something to give her the next time I visit her, something I know my beloved Queen of Missed Calls and lover of plastic bags will love — a nice huge turquoise-blue plastic bag. I'm quite sure she doesn't have anything like it in her collection.

Whether there'll be anything in that plastic bag is something I'm still pondering over!

Deepika Sahu

The Gap

Ten years. That's the number of years between kindergarten and high school. The average time that it takes for an apple tree to grow from seed to tree.

Ten years. The age gap between my eldest sister and me. Now, that's a long time; quite a big gap. Huge, even.

While I was still struggling over multiplication tables in lower primary, my sister was already off to college. She breezed in and out of home between semesters in a flurry of excitement, shopping and Mummy's attempts to fatten up her perpetually skinny frame.

After she had my sister, my mother, it seemed, had taken a nine-year-long sabbatical from the child-rearing business. And then suddenly she woke up one day and decided to finish off with the requisite sibling business. And that resulted in two more daughters — my middle sister and finally me. We were born just eighteen months apart. Growing up, one was never without the other. One cried, the other consoled. One fussed over the food, the other helpfully offered to eat up the rest. One came up with a plan, the other executed it.

My eldest sister, on the other hand, always seemed to be a bi-annual visitor. The weeks before her arrival from hostel were peppered with a tiresome tirade of questions from us.

'Will she be home today?'

'Is today the day?'

'What time is she coming?'

The questions continued right up until the moment she arrived and was then promptly followed by a mysterious bout of shyness which left us tongue-tied for a few hours.

And then the holidays *properly* began.

I remember that we quarrelled a lot with her. Childish battles fuelled by her for her amusement and to revel in the power that any first-born or older sibling enjoys.

She seemed to find out all the little loopholes in rules that we, the younger siblings, had so ingeniously engineered. She retrieved hidden storybooks from under pillows at nap time. She kept strict tabs on the hours spent watching cartoons on TV. She reported food barters that had been agreed upon. She was the official home police sniffing out our little mischievous plots from a mile away.

By the time I was in college, and finally attaining a mental maturity to bond with her, she was juggling motherhood and a full-time job; wiping runny noses, cooking, tackling tough stains, meeting professional deadlines — the works.

And I was caught up in my own whirlwind of activities: lectures, books, exams, crushes, friends and later on, a new job.

You can see why we never quite made it to common ground — it always seemed as if, by the time I huffed and puffed my way to a station, the train had already pulled out from there.

And for her, I was always stuck in a time-warp. I forever

remained the chubby three-year-old even after I grew one head taller than her.

'Hey, bring the dirty laundry along, when you stay for the weekend. I'll wash and press the clothes for you.'

'Aww ... my baby sister. Feeling homesick? Come home. I'll prepare all your favourite foods.'

'Am I busy? Well a little. But that's okay. You come over. No problem.'

And I wonder if I took her for granted back then. I guess I might have, just a little bit.

She came to visit me when I was seven months pregnant. She decided that I absolutely could not be allowed to travel back home alone for the delivery. So she packed up her bags, booked her tickets and headed over to stay with me.

And finally we were on par. Twenty-six and thirty-six. Not so bad; two women, with a fair share of life and experiences behind them.

We spent a lot of time together. It was almost as if we were making up for all those early lost years. We shopped a lot, sometimes just pressing our noses shamelessly to shop-windows gazing at their displays; gossiped a lot; had heart-to-hearts a lot. We certainly learned a lot too, about each other.

Me: 'Do you think I can lose all this pregnancy weight?'

She: (rolling her eyes) 'Trust me. Once the baby is here, that will be the least of your concerns.'

And how right she was.

She was there beside me, all four days at the hospital after my C-section. My most vivid memory of the hospital is, surprisingly, not of my newborn son. It is an image of my sister sitting on the hospital bed, her head slumped drowsily, with my newborn in her arms doing night duty for the third day in a row. No complaints. No questions. Just plain, sisterly love.

And now, when I look back, I realise that she was always the same. I was the one who never saw it over the years.

My sister running all over town to get me that 'perfect' shade of white for my wedding gown. She refused to take me along in case I tanned too much from the sun and spoilt my complexion for the big day.

My sister saving up all those childish letters and drawings I had written to her while she was away at hostel. All of them lovingly preserved between pages of her old school diaries.

My sister reading each and every one of my blog posts (however boring) in spite of the dozen things she needed to do.

Yes, it had taken me a while. But I think I finally reached the station before the train took off from there. And you know what? Ten years doesn't seem like such a big gap anymore.

Maria Francis

Always Ahead

Elder sisters are pesky know-it-alls, annoyingly beautiful and mummy's darlings. All right, all right, no they aren't. They're just smarter than us younger siblings, and we're extremely miffed by that.

Since they have a head start (eight years, in my sister's case), and we arrive at a time when they are actually better acquainted with the world, they get to take undue advantage of our ignorance. I kid you not — if I had a rupee for every time I made a fool of myself in front of my elder sister ... sigh, I'd definitely be richer than her today!

I was always the geeky kid in primary school, reciting poems and thinking that was dandy, while she was in the school orchestra and winning awards in every event that she participated in. She was always a step ahead when it came to the Coolness Quotient. She had her own room, her own clothes, her own gang of friends, while I was the bothersome younger sibling who shared a room with her, got her clothes as hand-me-downs and followed her around like a shadow. By the time I thought basic arithmetic and sentence constructions were 'super cool', she was using cutlery on mice. And by the time I reached the age of biology dissection, cutting up animals was gruesome, not cool. My sister was already on to her next stage of coolness. She was now an elegant, working lady, earning and paying for her own high heels. By the time I reached the age when I could also make colourful presentations for a living, she was the proud mother of the most beautiful kid I have ever seen. Sigh! Always a step ahead, my sister.

But soon enough, the hand-me-downs stopped. I got my own room too, my own gang of friends and own set of awards. Then I realised that even though she was always a step ahead, she was also the reason why growing up was so much more fun, and why I turned out to become a mature woman with a good head on my shoulders.

Now my 'pesky know-it-all, annoyingly beautiful, mummy's darling' of an elder sister can laugh at that last sentence all she wants, but life definitely wouldn't have been half as wonderful had she not been ahead.

Meera Govan

Some Things Remain the Same

She stood in front of the home that had been hers. Her parents lived there with her sister now, after she had gone away to college. How, with the passage of time, perspectives change, perceptions change. Sitting on the steps at the front door, she allowed herself to reminisce.

Her thoughts went back to that evening; she had been sitting right in this spot. It had been cloudy the whole day and the overcast sky suggested that it was building up for a thunderstorm. Her heart had been hammering. She was sixteen and her sister ten. Their mother had been hospitalised the night before.

Her sister had sat down beside her and squeezed her arm.

'What's happened, Didi?'

'Nothing serious,' she lied. 'She'll be okay.'

Stifling the unspoken fear that bound them together at that moment, she forced herself to tell her sister something that had happened in school, sending her into peals of laughter. The laughter jarred the thoughts of, 'What if...?' whizzing about in her head. She wondered whether it was sacrilege for her young sister to laugh so loudly. But after all, her sister knew nothing of the gravity of their mother's illness, she reasoned. A surge of love washed over her. From that day, she vowed, she would always take care of her kid sister. All her life. Even when she went away to college. Even when she got married and had her own baby. Her sister was hers to protect and cherish.

She remembered that day when, after a whole day of labour, her mother had delivered her little sister. She had been six then and had desperately wanted to hold her sister in her arms. No one thought she was old enough though. They thought that she would drop her. Drop her little sister? The suggestion made her indignant. The nurse should have given the baby to *her* first, before anyone else! After all, Mamma had told her that the baby was for her, to play with, like a live toy. She had named her 'Fluffy'. Everyone had laughed at her, saying that it was a name suitable for a bunny or a kitten, but not a little baby. What did they know?

How she had been looking forward to the time when she would have a baby sister of her own! Yet, they did not allow her to stay over at the nursing home. Anyway, Mamma said, the baby would be asleep for twenty-two hours a day. Imagine that! And when she came back the next day to the nursing home, she could sit and put her baby sister on her lap.

On the way back home, a remark made by an aunt had cut her to the quick. She had said, 'Your sister made us wait the whole day.' Of course it was meant to be a joke, a harmless remark, but her eyes had smarted and she had wanted to retort, 'She is my sister, you could have gone home, you know.' But she had not said anything and instead looked out of the car window.

She remembered the little baby in the cradle at the nursing home, how her eyes shut tightly at the light overhead. For some strange reason, they kept the tube light on in the room. Today, she knew why. It made her smile at all those innumerable pranks she had indulged in with her kid sister and all those secrets shared at nights. She smiled like she did every time she thought of her kid sister; she felt a warm glow in her heart.

Her mother had recovered and she had gone away to another city, first for college and then when she got married. She was going to have her own baby now. But she still remembered her vow to herself, to always look after her sister.

There were some perspectives and perceptions that don't change with the passage of time.

Monika Pant

A Boon

Halloween celebrations are over. My friend and I are sitting in her living room relaxing after our bit of running around. We are chatting casually, preparing to lay the dinner in another ten-fifteen minutes when my younger one, Ananya, comes to us and complains, 'They are not letting me be with them.' 'No complaining dear,' I tell her. 'Please go and play inside the room. Both of you in there, please include her,' I simultaneously call out to my elder one, Shruti, and her friend.

There is peace for about two-three minutes and once again exactly the same dialogues are exchanged between us. This goes on for another seven-eight minutes.

Suddenly I hear Shruti screaming and crying. We rush inside to see blood streaming down her face. She's hurt her head. Her friend tells me that Ananya hit her on the head with a medal. I am in shock for a second and then without losing control or saying anything to Ananya, I rush Shruti to the washroom. While I take care of her, my husband carries Ananya outside. There are visible signs of shock on her face and her eyes well up with tears.

After an hour, everything settles down. The bleeding has stopped, the doctor has been consulted, medicines have been given and a pressure bandage is tied around Shruti's head. No major damage has taken place. It was a case of touch and go. All of us settle down for a late dinner. All the three kids are visibly disturbed. The convict, the victim and the spectator are quiet and trying to recover from what happened a while ago.

Now, let me mention their age groups. Ananya is four while Shruti and her friend are ten. Because I know my daughters too well, as any parent would, I refuse to accept the blame put on Ananya. After a lot of persuasion and talking with Shruti, I finally manage to get my facts together. Shruti and her friend were ignoring Ananya completely and even threatening her with consequences if she did not leave them alone. Then, when Shruti pointed a gun-shaped thing used to spin a top at Ananya, she swung a small bag at her. What she hadn't realised was that, in the bag was a medal, which had caused the accident.

While I thank God for listening to my instinct and for keeping Shruti safe, I try to explain things in a 'what led to what series' fashion to Shruti and her friend. I advise them never to corner anyone like this ever again or they have to face the consequences. I also try to explain to Ananya how accidents happen and never to repeat this again.

Next morning, as usual, they both play together but there is a certain change that I notice in both. While Shruti is a little reserved, Ananya is more careful, quieter and a little serious. I let time be the healing factor for both the bruised souls. Today, after almost fifteen days, no one even remembers what happened the other day. Both are back to the usual fights, patch-ups, teasing, chasing and, of course, adoring each other.

After Shruti was born, we were very clear that ours would be a family of three. Everything went on smoothly till Shruti, at four, started asking us for 'another girl in the house' so that she could have a constant companion around. We decided to fulfil her wish. She was granted her 'boon' and thus Ananya arrived. Usually Shruti is a very adoring elder sister and Ananya reciprocates with undying loyalty and ardent fan following. Sometimes in between their fights and make-ups it is difficult to say whether a ten-year-old is behaving like a four-year-old or vice-versa.

Whenever I see my girls together, I go back to my childhood days. I have a sister who is three years younger than me. Unlike other brothers and sisters, who fight with each other using their hands, feet and everything, we never had anything of that sort happen between us. In fact, whenever we had our differences, our decibel levels would go down to a level where sometimes we could not even hear each other. We never wanted to upset our parents with our fights.

We were always there for each other while growing up. When we were in the hostel, far from our family, I would look forward to Sundays. That was the day when the younger siblings from Junior School could visit their elder siblings in the Senior School, both schools being separated by a vast valley.

Once we were back with our parents, we would cycle to school together. I was in the tenth grade and she would polish my school shoes as well so that I could concentrate on my studies. She cheered for me through all my achievements, and supported me through all my setbacks.

When I got married, she was there by my side and when my kids came, she showered them with all her love and affection. Yes, she pampered me a lot. I sometimes feel that I am elder to her only in years.

But hold on, we also had our bouts of 'hating each other'. I can never forget the first time I waxed. I did it on the sly, when I was in college. I was feeling very proud that no one could find out. But she did, and announced it to everyone. I still remember the sermon I got from my mom. On many other occasions she played the spoiltsport and ruined my fun. As I probably did to her.

Today she is also married and has two kids. We've both been living in the same city for the past nine years; just five kilometres away from each other. Yes, we're very lucky; I know I'm fortunate to have someone who knows me right from the time I can remember. I find my greatest supporter in her. On days when I do not want to face the world, I find respite with her. She is the one I turn to for anything at the oddest hour and at the shortest notice. My girls adore her, sometimes I feel, more than me.

When my kids fight, I ask them, 'How would you feel if I fight with my sister?' 'Bad,' they reply in unison. They have their perfect role models in front of them. They know that sisters are always there for each other. I know it is being embedded in their psyche every single day.

When I went to her this morning, she welcomed me with a freshly baked cake and my favourite cup of tea. We poured our hearts out to each other while the cousins, aged three to ten, created a ruckus in her house. We carried on unmindful of what was happening around us.

After spending an afternoon with her, I reach home feeling lighter and better. I silently thank God and my parents for this wonderful boon. My girls get busy with each other. Looking at them, I say a silent prayer.

Need I say why?

Pragati Adhikari

The Best Gift Ever

As human beings, each and every one of us shares different kinds of relationships with different types of people. Some we treasure and others we tend to take for granted. Sometimes the most precious relationships are the ones in which we tend to fight or squabble the most. This is the charm of the bond that siblings share. We may criticise and mock their every move, but at the end of the day, we know that we have got each other and *that*, I must admit, is a very comforting thought.

Let me take you back to the year 2002, the year my little sister was born. I remember myself as a scrawny six-year-old, waiting eagerly to take on the responsibilities of being an elder sister. In fact, I now know that many of my relatives were apprehensive about how I would feel, relinquishing my spot as the only child, and having been the apple of my parents' eye for so long — but they couldn't have been more wrong! When I think about those early days, all I can remember is treating my sister like my own, personal, living and breathing doll. She would play innocently in her crib with not a care in the world. How could one not be enamoured by that bundle of cuteness? She never troubled me, never got into my hair, never cramped my style — having a little sister was a piece of chocolate cake! Why, I could still watch whatever I wanted to on TV — peacefully!

Aaah! But then she grew up and the days of having the TV to myself are now far behind me. Slowly and steadily she started forming her own opinions about different things and became one of the elder ones among all her cousins. Gradually our arguments also increased. We were two very opinionated girls not willing to let the other win on any matter. I suddenly realised I couldn't treat her like my doll anymore! She was her own individual and I needed to respect that. This realisation definitely did not dawn upon me overnight. It took a lot of arguments, fights and disagreements to help me reach that conclusion.

To everyone else, including my parents, my sister and I are two people who never get along. Very often my mother frets and worries about this. What they don't understand is that while we may not be mushy and sweet to each other all the time, it's our fights that bring us closer to each other. About a year ago we had gone on a holiday with my parents and a huge bandwagon of family friends. When there are so many children involved there are bound to be fights and disagreements. My sister was the youngest amongst all of us and wanted to be involved in everything that we did. It got extremely unnerving to include her in all the activities of a bunch of teenagers. We had a number of fights about this. The next day I heard my sister being shouted at by one of our roommates. I was appalled at the way she was being spoken to. My sister looks tough and ready to fend for herself on the outside, but I know that inside, she is an extremely sensitive girl. My sisterly fangs were out. I immediately started arguing on her behalf. Suddenly my sister and I were bound in an unspoken camaraderie. This is something I have learnt about myself over the years; I am fine with only my parents dealing with my sister strictly and if anyone else does so I become extremely protective about her.

Just a few days ago we were attending a family wedding and suddenly my sister, who has been a complete tomboy all her life, insisted on putting on make-up! This was the first time she actually thought about what she was going to wear and how she was going to look. I realised that she was growing into a young lady and in the next few years she would probably need me more than she would need our mother. I was amazed and awed at the way she dressed herself and couldn't believe that she had grown up so much.

At the end of the day, despite all our fights and altercations, my sister and I share a very strong bond that finds expression in various small gestures. We don't express it in words all the time. In fact the words we exchange would be testimony of an ongoing battle! Yet, deep down inside, both of us know that we will always be there for each other no matter what, and no argument or disagreement in the world can ever change that. When we go to sleep at night, we find an unspoken comfort in each other's presence. I know in my heart that my sister is my companion, my friend for life. She is the best gift that my mother could have given me.

Priyanjali Maitra

Three Sisters in Vienna

November is not the best month to be in Vienna, but it was not a vacation and so there we were, in that chilly month, made still more difficult by the incessant rains. My sister Suman had had a brain surgery and was not allowed to fly back for six weeks. I was with her during the last lap. I'd joined her in the second last week of her stay, along with our other sister, Priti. We moved into a cosy one-bedroom apartment in the quiet suburbs. The living room sofa had to be turned into a bed at night, our tiny kitchen would accommodate only two at a time, and the dining table seated only two. And so like the bed and the toilet, we took turns with the kitchen and the dining chairs and between all of this spent a memorable two weeks discussing our growing up years in Calcutta as we sipped green tea and gazed at the overcast sky in the historical, romantic and beautiful capital of Austria.

Due to Suman di's health, we could slot only one outing a day, which could not be for more than three hours at a stretch, and so though we were in the city for two entire weeks, we had to select our destination for the day with a lot of care and planning, keeping in mind of course our individual interests — which are as different as day and night! While Suman di wanted to try out new cafés, local cuisine and small artefact shops, Priti di had her heart set on shopping and musicals. I, on the other hand, searched for museums and palaces. One morning when the sky was heavily overcast and we knew we would be in the apartment the entire day, we actually made a call to our parents back home to reconfirm that they had not mixed any of us up at the hospital! But come a dry patch in the day and we would run out to catch whatever we could till the rains lashed again — and if any outsider were to see us clicking away at the Schönbrunn Palace or sipping cappuccino with Sacher torte (their version of chocolate cake) at a café, they would not know which was whose pick. I guess in that sense we were from the same parents!

I remember getting the front row tickets for a John Strauss opera, and I remember how bored we all were within the first twenty minutes, but were not sure of the other's reaction and so ended up sitting through the entire programme feigning attention as we clicked away on our mobiles and suppressed deep yawns not just from each other but the performers as well! I remember the laugh over home-cooked khichadi and wine at the apartment later where we confessed our love for the sitar and Kathak as against what we had just paid a fortune for!

I remember our kitchen duties, where Priti di cooked, Suman di chopped and I cleaned post meals! The one time that I put my foot down and prepared a meal, I managed to set off the fire alarm. Needless to say I was thenceforth deemed safest over the sink!

I remember how we would decide who would get priority before entering a store. Since I am a diehard fan of the brand

Promod, I would be the first to pick out stuff and only once I was done would the other two try out clothes from the ones I had not selected. Priti di called the shots at Mango, while we let Suman di pick her favourites first at her preferred boutique Staff!

But most importantly, I remember our mornings, just before breakfast, the time that all three of us did yoga together. The apartment did not have enough space for all of us to do the asanas in unison. And so we came up with an ingenious solution for that too. When I did the standing asanas (in the narrow corridor between the gate and the kitchen), Priti di would do the lying down ones in the living room and Suman di would be on the sofa, cross-legged doing pranayam. We would change places and alternate, wherein each would get twenty minutes at each position ... and yes we even chatted and giggled in between.

On the return flight to Mumbai, none of us spoke or giggled much. We immersed ourselves in the in-flight entertainment and once we landed and met a fleet of relatives, we hugged them and said how happy we were to be back home. I did not tell my sisters that I was sad that we had returned, nor did they. Our mother is a haemorrhage patient and we have long stopped bothering her with our small and big issues. We sisters have on the whole been there for each other, but somehow after that trip I have not missed having someone to whom I can report every little unhappiness if I want to. I always knew that blood bonded us; in that trip it was something more than blood that came into play ... I can't put my finger on it though. But it is not important to analyse or understand everything. Right?

Raksha Bharadia

Selected Scenes from 'Memories of a Life'

Act IV, Scene I

Remnants of dreams still linger on her eyelids. If you pat her cheeks, you'll be sure to have some glitter rub off onto your fingers. It is only when she is suddenly jolted out of her magical world that she finds herself on the floor! 'Not again,' grumbles Vedika as she pulls herself up.

On the queen-size bed lies sprawled her elder sister, Vedatri. It is as if, even in her sleep, Vedatri is making sure that Vedika knows who's the boss. Vedika grumbles to herself at the repeat performance of this daily occurrence and for a second considers calling her parents. But then the succeeding thought of how her sister would retaliate by calling out those monsters from the cupboard and under the bed at night, makes her decide against it. Instead, she just wakes her up in the politest way she knows how — by continuously poking her.

Vedatri (with bloodshot eyes): What?!

Vedika (petulantly): You kicked me out of the bed again, Didi.

Vedatri (reasoning it out for her dim-witted younger sister): Of course I didn't! You must have come across to my side and I probably pushed you while trying to save my space, so stop blaming me.

Vedika (vociferously): No Didi, see I did not cross my line; I always stick to my side... (her voice trails off as her elder sister skips to the bathroom with little regard to her complaints).

Act VII, Scene VI

The bathroom door is closed. Vedatri is inside again with the cordless phone. Vedika's ears can pick up the mumbles; it is as if she has had bionic-sound detectors implanted.

Vedika (whining, with her ears pressed against the bathroom door): Who are you talking to. Didi?'

Vedatri (irritated): No one! Go away! Why do you have to eavesdrop?

Vedika (triumphantly): Baba! Didi is talking to her boyfriend again!

And thus begins the *Mahabharata* in the Roy household, which lasts for exactly eighteen minutes as if in tribute to the great Indian epic.

Act IX, Scene II

Vedatri (reasonably): Listen, I know you are hurt but you hurt me more, so you leave my hair and we call it truce. Okay?

Vedika (in a high-pitched voice): No! You leave my hair first, because the last time I did but you didn't.

Vedatri (up to her old tricks): Okay, in three we both do it together. Okay?

After three counts, as always, they are still clinging to each other's pigtails and blaming the other person for breaking the pact, till their grandmother intervenes and forces them to call a truce.

Cut to the present

Vedika is in 'their' room. The huge bed, upon which she now sits, almost two decades later, stares back silently at her. It was an activity that both the sisters had indulged in each night in what now seems an era gone by — dividing the bed into half and marking their halves with bolsters. And then each night Vedatri would flout the rules, dump Vedika on the floor and lie sprawled like a victorious lioness. The next morning would witness dissections of the nightly game! When she finally goes to sleep that night, she lies curled up in a corner — she just can't enjoy the unending space. It feels so empty and cold without Vedatri's spread-eagled presence.

It was the same for Vedatri, when she had visited their parents a few months back. An old poster which had been torn by Vedika during a fight still clings desperately to the walls. Somehow, the torn poster of her favourite hero makes her smile much more than the intact one had done when she'd first purchased it, nearly two decades ago.

Playwright's Note

The joys of having a sibling are known only to those who have fought and made up. A child who boasts of a loving relationship with his/her sibling is guaranteed a friend, confidante and memory-keeper for life. Such is the story of Vedatri and Vedika.

To Vedatri, Vedika was the pampered one who always got

what she wanted, but then again she was also the one she could turn to when confiding her worst fears and also for help in managing a situation gone wrong. They quite literally fought their way to becoming close and yet they have defined their own space. While Vedatri was the subject for Vedika's 'My Hero' school essay, Vedika was the reason Vedatri fought all the bullies in school — after all, only she had the right to bully her sibling!

For them, being siblings never meant talking endlessly or sharing each and every bit of their lives with each other. Their interests and personalities were as different as their looks. Yet they were tied together, intrinsically, indelibly. They shared an untold pact of letting each other grow and yet being there for each other, each and every time.

Even now, when Vedatri and Vedika meet, they are not at all paragons of sweetness. Yet amidst all episodes of leg-pulling, there's a tugging of heart-strings that follows. So when one sees the other sleeping at night, still sprawled in the same manner as decades ago, and no matter how much they may have fought over the quilt before sleep took over, she snuggles up close to the sleeping one, tucks her in and says a silent prayer thanking God for making siblings and for giving their parents the wisdom to make her greatest dream come true — to be and have a sister!

Sagarika Chakraborty

When Opposites (Finally) Meet

Somewhere along the way, we lost each other. Two girls who thought they had grown up almost always together, linked by the fact that they were supposed to share everything equally and evenly, will inevitably grow apart as they grow up. So we did too.

My sister and I are opposites. People swear we can't be sisters. That is until they see the similarity in the smile or in a turn of the head, or maybe in the way we speak.

She looks like our mother, with classic south Indian features, large eyes, a double line of lashes, smooth skin, which was once called dark, but is now deemed a pretty cocoa.

I have I think a mix of my parents' features, though the cheekbones belong to my father, as do the freckles. Where the widow's peak and thin skin came from is anybody's guess, though Mom credits her father with those attributes. But the fact is we definitely, at first, second and third glance do not look like sisters. Never did.

Now less than ever. I wear my hair long, hers is short and thick, like a fur cap around her head. She keeps it a little salt and a little pepper, I change mine, ranging from burgundy to plum and before that it was naturally a kind of brown. Temperamentally too ... she is fire and I am, mostly, ice.

Talk about our leanings in books and men, well ... today she wishes she could go back in time and marry Emile Zola. While, erring on the other end of the spectrum, I had a terrible crush on John Keats many years ago, and in school wanted so much to be Dorothy Wordsworth so I could roam the lakes with William.

But through our school years, we were as if chained to one another. We wore clothes cut out of the same yardage of cloth, and if we did choose different colours, the design of the fabric and the pattern the clothes were cut from were similar if not the same. Just adjusted to size.

We were never allowed to go anywhere without each other for company. My school friends were quite accustomed to a snarling younger sister sitting around bored and angry at the parties I was invited to. And I had to watch baby movies, though being three years older, I had decided they were not quite for me anymore.

We had our fun moments of course, but I grew up believing that we were enemies from a previous birth sent to live together to fulfil a curse. I do think we believed we quite detested each other, most of the time.

Then we grew up. I got married and for the first time realised my sister, on the first steps to becoming a doctor, did not quite hate me. I was told she missed having me around! I would never have guessed it. She must be missing the fights, I told myself, not me! I of course was too busy being a married woman to miss her or anyone else, and anyway she had been too busy with her studies for me to get much time with her lately.

Then, many years down the line, she got married, and left for England.

I loved my life, but I was jealous. It was always I who had wanted to live abroad, study aboard, and here was my sister, who had professed she would never ever leave India, setting off to get her visa and her ticket, and set up house close to where Keats and Wordsworth had roamed! But I was also on to new adventures in my career, so that was that.

That was at a time when to call someone internationally, one had to wait endlessly by the phone and spend the major part of the three precious minutes yelling hello into the receiver at both ends! A few letters must have passed between us, but the inevitable was happening. We were drifting further apart, each in our own worlds.

It was only when I went visiting that she would take charge of me and try to give me a good time; take me shopping, drive me around to show me the sights, and I would see a new side to the kid I had grown up with. I kind of liked this new side, but well, there was nothing more to it.

Of course there was one stint when she was unwell during her pregnancy and I went across to look after her, and help with the cooking and other chores. I sensed in it an adventure; a chance to spend time in a country that my books and reading had caused me to love.

And it was then, I think, that we started talking intimately of things for the first time. Realising that there were points of view and vistas of our lives that we could share and learn from, could debate upon to understand life and each other a bit better. We were at last two women, not just sisters taking each other for granted.

And now, suddenly, it is as if we are really sisters, not just bound by blood, but by bonds that seem close to friendship.

It started when she decided to discover the country of her birth. She would come to spend time with our mother, who lives with me, and then we would make small trips to different parts of India.

At first it was a trip combined with something I needed to do: a visit for a show in Delhi, or a conference in Udaipur, which we would extend to explore Agra or Jaipur ... things like that.

But as we found that travelling together gave us an opportunity to talk, to share, to comment on and compare viewpoints, the trips became ends in themselves.

We now sit with the map of India spread out before us and choose places we wish to see. When I had to write a piece on Tilonia, she trotted along, tasting village life for the first time, and giving the mosquitoes there their taste of NRI blood. Other times we have chosen to visit Benaras via Lucknow, and enjoyed the traipsing around and the bits of history we imbibed. I love roughing it out, she likes the comfort of travelling easy, somewhere we find a middle ground. And even though sometimes our viewpoints clash on whether the rickshawman does indeed need to be tipped 100 rupees each time, even though he is fleecing us in fares, we manage to stay grown up enough to give each other space.

It's strange that after all these years, we know that, despite our differences, we are alike. That deep down, we believe in the same values, and the same ethics. If there are divergent aspects to our behaviour, we don't let them cross our similarities out.

And as I talk to friends, I realise that many others are doing the same thing: catching up with their siblings. Making time to gather the threads that they had let slip through their fingers, in the business of daily living.

That, I think, is what having a sibling is all about. When you turn the pages of life and what is read is thicker than what is left, it is good to know someone was, despite your not knowing, reading alongside. And will read the remaining with you!

Sathya Saran

Waging Wars

From the time my sister Poonam was born, I hated her. I was five years old and the apple of everyone's eye. Then suddenly all the attention vanished and everyone's focus shifted to my newborn sister. She was the cutest baby I had ever seen, but I resented her arrival. As we grew older, there were great times too, but more often than not we fought, in a way that would put cats and dogs to shame. In a typical spat she would pull my hair and I would scratch her with my nails, but since pulling hair didn't leave telltale signs, she would be let off and I would be punished.

My parents would despair about our relationship. They actually feared that we were liable to maim each other for life if left unsupervised (okay, that's a bit exaggerated, but trust me, it wasn't pretty!). I hated it when I was expected to let go because I was older and supposed to be the wiser one. I wasn't. I was all of eleven or fifteen or even eighteen and I was never old enough to understand why everyone sympathised with her all the time, especially when she was the one who started most of the fights. I hated my life, I hated her and I felt victimised.

Of course there were times when we would have fun too, like when I started driving. We would sneak out at night and go for a spin. Or when my parents were away we would gang up against my grandmother, the poor thing, God bless her soul. We even tried our first cigarette together. But these crazy times were very sporadic and more often than not, we had our daggers drawn ready for the kill.

Then, inevitably, came the time for me to leave the house. I got married to the nicest guy I could have dreamed of, and yet for days after my wedding, I was depressed. My in-laws would try to cheer me up thinking that I was having a hard time trying to adjust; my husband would take me out to change my mood and even took me on nice romantic holidays, but nothing pulled me out of my blue funk.

Every night I would remember the mad times I shared with my sister; our pillow fights, midnight bingeing on ice creams, our rows over territorial issues be it the bed or the cupboard or the desk. It was so odd, because the person I hated the most was the one I was yearning for. Stranger still was the fact that I didn't remember any of the fights, just the good times spent together. The way we stood by each other when one was in trouble. The way we secretly cried when the other got a shouting from either of the parents. The way we flirted with the same guy and vied for his attention. Suddenly my life seemed so dull without her.

Unknown to me, she was also in the same state of despondency and it was only when my parents called up my husband and mentioned it to him did he understand why I was so melancholic all the time. He happily took me to Mumbai and we all had a good laugh about it.

Poonam and I share a beautiful bond now. We may not talk every day but I know she is there for me and vice versa. I love her and when she is hurting I can feel her pain.

Today I have two daughters and they don't fight, they wage wars! At times I have had to come back from the airport — missing my flight in the process — to settle their scraps. Very often I despair that they are missing out on the beautiful moments that only sisters can share, if only they'd make an effort to get along.

One day after umpiring one of their brawls, I was overcome by feelings of self-pity and helplessness. I called Poonam and we remembered our noisy quarrels and the plight of our poor mother who wouldn't know how to handle the situation. We laughed till our stomachs ached; and after that conversation, I realised that, in time, my kids too would be just fine.

Shashi Agarwal

Voices

When your kid sister is only a year younger than you, sibling rivalry is not uncommon. Yes, we were such a set of rivals. She got all the attention because she was the baby of the family. Plus, she was prettier than me, smarter than me, and (in a few departments) luckier than me.

We had a few things in common, though: parents who loved us both, a house where we shared a room where we shared a bed, and loads of toys with which we played girlish games. But the loveliest thing that we shared was something no one had given us and something no one could take away from us: our voices.

Actually ... not our voices, our voice. Singular.

I'm calling it a voice because I myself couldn't tell my voice from hers. Oh, it was a magical thing, our voice. From silly boyfriends to not-so-silly husbands, we'd fool them all with our little phone tricks.

But the real magic would happen when we'd sing. Neither of us could play a musical instrument or anything fancy like that, but our throats made up for that. We'd sing all the time.

Be it while helping with the dishes, while plaiting each other's hair, or while walking to school, we'd always have a song on our lips.

We weren't brilliant in any sense of the word. We never sat down and practised. We didn't know any of the complicated Sanskrit terms that they talk about on *Indian Idol*. We sang old Hindi film songs because their lyrics were beautiful and easy to remember. We always sang together. We didn't go into solos and duets and interplays. We felt lonely if we did that.

We opened our mouths, words came out and the world sat still and listened.

***

I still remember the time my 'kid' sister, by then married and with children, had her throat slit open. I didn't know what the medical term for it was and I didn't dare Google it, but we were given a rather brusque explanation at the time: she had a growth on her thyroid gland. The operation would remove it. Simple.

Five-and-a-half hours it took them. For five-and-a-half hours they had my darling sister slit open. For five-and-a-half hours I paced up and down the waiting room, avoiding glances from the relatives who had filled it to capacity. Five-and-a-half hours I prayed non-stop.

The surgery went well. The growth had been non-malignant. The gods had to be thanked.

But surgery always has its drawbacks. In my sister's case, it was that she would be required to be mute for the next week. The week turned into a fortnight and the fortnight turned into a month. The vow of silence unofficially changed from a doctor's order into a patient's nightmare. It changed from voluntary to involuntary.

Finally, a test showed us the worst: a vocal cord had been damaged during surgery.

Loss is a strange thing, you know. No matter how close you are to someone, you can never understand their loss or feel their pain. You can only truly feel it when the pain is yours too.

It was strange, then, that I felt so strongly about my sister's loss. I loved my sister, yes, but there was no logical reason for me to feel this way. I got high fever. I went into depression. My sister had been struck, but I felt stricken. My sister could not voice her frustrations, so I voiced her frustrations compounded with mine.

It took me a while, but I finally realised why it was that I felt what I felt. I'd lost my voice, after all. One half of the voice was as it had always been. But the other half — her half — was soft, husky and rough, with a strange twang to it. My voice could not be left like that, it absolutely could not.

Again, doctors were consulted, while the rest of us ... well, we prayed. This was my voice that I had lost. Though it was she who was facing the brunt of the operation, it was I who was going dumb. Though I could still sing and sing alone, my voice had lost its volume. I hated it. I prayed hard. Nothing else mattered, only that my voice and I had to be heard again.

It was then, when our hopes were at their lowest, that a light came shining through the murky waters of despair. Her best friend came calling from Chennai. She insisted that my sister come with her to Chennai and stay at her place while receiving treatment from the world-renowned Dr Mohan Kameshwaram, whom she had discovered on the Internet.

And so, for the next two months, our hopes rose, as she took speech therapy treatments in Chennai.

Then, one evening, the entire family was given the most pleasant surprise ever. All of us were huddled around the phone, which was on loudspeaker, with Dr Kameshwaram on the line. 'Listen to your mother!' he said, addressing my stunned nephews. And then, in the most beautiful voice ever, my sister sang the song, *'Kabhi kabhi, mere dil mein...'*, breaking into sobs now and then. I joined in. For the first time ever, our voices sounded different.

Nonetheless, it was just like before. We opened our mouths, words came out and the world sat still and listened.

Sheetal Bagaria

Leave All Your Tears for Me

'*Khush raho, har khushi hai tumhare liye; chod do aasuon ko hamare liye...*' (I wish you only joy, every happiness is for you to claim; leave all your tears for me...) My sister, who is three years older than me, always sang this for me when we were in our teens, and I used to find it a little embarrassing in front of my friends. I didn't ever express my feelings for her, because I hadn't truly realised them then. But she loved me like a mother, and despite my failure to reciprocate, she would consistently express her love for me. She would save her pocket money to buy me gifts, she would cover up for me with the family, she would give me her share of chocolates, she would protect me from bullies in school, she would cry more than me if I got hurt, and above all she would take all my rudeness with a smile. I never understood the blessings which God had bestowed upon me in her form, until that horrible day when I almost lost her.

That evening, when she came back from work, I was to hand over her three-year-old daughter to her and leave her in the empty childhood home of ours to join my husband for dinner.

She asked me to stay back that night, but I evaded her request by moaning and cribbing about my own problems. I just didn't feel ready for the responsibility of being an emotional support to her in her most vulnerable hour of need; at a time when she was trying to cope with the fact that the husband whom she had loved totally and ardently had abandoned her and their daughter to marry her friend. Her world had completely shattered. I could not read the warning of what was to come in her eyes that night. She had a stone-like expression and I made a mental note to call our parents, who lived in New York, first thing in the morning. I was sure that Mom would come back to take care of her.

As I prepared to leave the house, I saw her hunched over the dining table and my niece, who was crying to be picked up, was at her feet. I rushed over to check on her, and as I pulled her face up I saw her eyes had rolled back ... her tears had dried up on her cheeks and her body was cool to the touch. I shook her and slapped her several times to bring her back to consciousness but nothing seemed to work. I screamed and my niece started crying. My world was crashing down around me.

We were three people in a traumatic situation and I was the captain of the sinking ship ... for a moment I was at my wit's end, but then I got my act together and splashed water on my sister's pallid face. She was drifting in and out of consciousness and I asked her what she had taken. I heard her whispering, 'Twenty-five ... sleeping ... pills.' I was shell-shocked, but I realised I had to keep talking to her and try to keep her from slipping into unconsciousness. I settled my niece in the other room with her favourite DVD and quickly made some black coffee which I forced down my sister's throat and then called a few of her close friends of whom only one came by to help. My husband rushed to be by our side, but our family doctor refused to help as this was a suicide case. It pierced my soul and I could not believe that that was indeed what it was — a suicide case! I shook with pain and screamed at my sister, 'I will not let you die like a coward; I will not let you die! I am holding on and not letting you go! Don't die, *fight*!' She wasn't responding and I kept shaking her. I hugged her several times and kept telling her that her life meant a lot to her daughter, to Mom and Dad and for the first time in a long time I told her that she meant the world to me and that I loved her. And yet, even then my words were failing to revive her.

I was getting tense and the situation grew worse with every passing moment. She wasn't responding to anything and the coffee I was pouring into her mouth was trickling down from the corners of her lips. Just then my husband came with an obliging doctor who administered a few injections that took almost immediate effect. She started throwing up and I kept cleaning and praying, memories playing havoc in my mind: her cheerful laughter, her songs, her affection and her many expressions of love floated in front of my blurred eyes. After a few hours had passed, with the doctor's consent, we let her sleep.

I knew that when she woke up, it would be a new day for her. Yes, she would regret this act of weakness but it would help her emerge as a stronger person.

I 'woke up' that day as well. I realised how much I loved my sister. I realised how much I still needed her in my life. I realised how much she desperately needed me too. I also realised that

I needed to step back from myself and to pay attention to the lives of my loved ones.

Today is my niece's eleventh birthday; we have come a long way from those dark days. Didi has accomplished a lot in her life and is now a successful person. She is also at peace with herself and helps others who have given up on the journey of life. She pampers me more than ever now.

And it is my turn to take the stage as I dedicate a song to her, declaring my love for her without any inhibitions and embarrassment. I see her smile with contentment and pride as my song, or rather our song, fills the room and our hearts, *'Muskurane ke din hain,na aahen bharo; mere hote na khud ko pareshaan karo. Khush raho, har khushi hai tumhare liye; chod do aasuon ko hamare liye...'* (The days are now to smile and be happy, not for sighing; why trouble yourself when I am here. I wish you only joy, every happiness is for you to claim; leave all your tears for me...)

Shreeja Mohatta Jhawar

Watching Out

My sister Trupti and I are three years apart. When we were growing up, our relationship was the usual love-hate kind with a lot of ribbing, but also a lot of caring and loving.

She was always sick, the first few years of her life. She used to have prolonged bouts of asthma and had to be kept indoors most of the time. When we were home, I resented being the responsible one, but when we were outside, I couldn't stand it if someone tried to pick on her. I would become aggressive and lash out at the offender.

But one day, in a small but significant way, the roles were reversed...

We lived in a colony, and every evening all the kids would come out to play; everyone, that is, except Trupti. So, when I got ready to go out and play, my mother would change her clothes and dress her up too. And then she would take her regular position by the window. The windows were grilled and so my mother would leave her there and prepare dinner. Trupti would stand by the window, holding the grills the entire time that I was playing outside, watching me.

One time we were playing catch and the boy who was chasing ran up to me and grabbed me. I tried to run away, and he pushed me and I fell down. In the heat of the game, I still wanted to escape and he tried to stop me by almost sitting on me. I was around six years old then, and my sister, three. She started screaming, 'Leave my sister! Don't do anything to my sister!' She was so angry, she was holding the window rails, gnashing her teeth, screaming non-stop, until my mother finally had to come and take her away from there and pacify her.

After that, whenever we had a fight, my mom used to remind us of this episode and we would promptly stop fighting and make up. Even now, when I think of it, I can't stop grinning at the memory of that little girl, all dressed up with nowhere to go, but my faithful guardian nevertheless.

Now we are older and living in different countries, and appreciate each other more, but some things don't change. We fight, we criticise each other, but she is still the first one to jump to my defence, if someone else says even one negative thing about me. I am the older one, but she is the one who watches out for me.

Trishna Pillai

Confessions of a Sister

It was close to midnight. I had put my toddler to sleep and my sisters and I headed out for a coffee. The TV in the café screamed for attention from people who were there to enjoy coffee and conversation. The coffee-maker churned out beverages that looked more like dollops of ice cream and chocolate rather than coffee. The aroma of hot muffins and puffs made our mouths water and we decided to order some.

We had never actually done this before. Pihu, Chikki, and I. We had been busy living different lives, in different cities. But that night, there we were, together, chatting about everything under the sun — make-up, brands, latest fashion, boyfriends, cooking, Chikki's new Roman sandals, relatives, work, married life, kids. Everything. It reminded me of the pyjama parties with my friends where we sat in someone's house, stocked up on chips and chocolates, gossiped and giggled and slept in the wee hours of the morning.

We licked the chocolate off our steel spoons to make them shine like silver, just like we did when we were little girls, and our mother was making cake. We were hanging out like friends. And then it dawned on me that this was probably the first time we were all on the same page as equals. As friends. Not just sisters with huge age gaps between them. I watched them chatting, laughing, giving each other high fives and looking stunning. It suddenly came to me, how much they had grown up, and so fast. I had missed their growing-up years, busy with my school, college, office while they were still learning to walk, talk, and greet the world.

It was only twenty years ago that we had a newborn in the house, whom we called Chikki. At the age of eleven, nothing seemed more important to me than looking after my four-year-old and four-day-old sisters. I used to come back from school and give them food. Take Chikki for immunisation shots in the nearby clinic. Cradle her to sleep. Sing her songs that my parents sang to me. Change nappies and everything that a mother does. Yes, before I was a friend, I was a mother.

Then when were we sisters?

And I was expected only to be that way. Take care. Lead by example. Always be Miss Goody-Two-Shoes. Watch what I say. Never do anything unconventional that could threaten to teach my sisters something they should not be doing. Like boycotting family functions. Like going for movies with friends. Like wearing miniskirts and sleeveless tops.

I did it like it was something that all elder sisters must do by default.

But I want to build those doll houses together. I want to make sand castles on the beach. I want to shake hands with them in the sand tunnels and hold hands and stand by the shore, waiting for the waves to caress our feet. I want to make rotis with clay dough and act like we are feeding each other. I want to make paper boats with them during the monsoon and drop them into puddles from our room window. I want to hug them like soft toys and go to sleep. I want to see them transition from being giggly girls to women. I want to do so much with them!

But it was too late for all of that.

We decided to leave the café after the manager glared at us for the umpteenth time. Pihu was in the driver's seat. She suddenly screeched to a halt in the middle of the road.

'I think I forgot something at the café!' she exclaimed, holding the wheel tight and staring at us.

'The owner must be sleeping at home now. What have you forgotten?' I asked.

She said nothing. She just drove back to the café.

'Get down both of you,' Pihu ordered us out of the car. 'Now stand in front of the gate.'

As both of us stood in front the gate, she requested a passer-by to take a picture of the three of us on her phone.

'Okay, now we can go back home.'

On the way home, Chikki suddenly said, 'We look up to you Didi. Ever since we were kids, we wanted to be like you and still wish the same!'

I didn't say anything. Somewhere the feeling of guilt still lurks inside me that things could've been different.

But I love them. And I hope that we will always be the best of friends.

I like it better that way.

Vaishali Shroff

My Sister, My Soulmate

She was there when I goofed up.
Thanks to her, I was let off the hook.

She was there when I played pranks.
Thanks to her, I had a partner in crime.

She was there when I petitioned the elders.
Thanks to her, I had a pillar of support.

She was there when I felt bullied.
Thanks to her, I stood up for myself.

She was there when I was rebuked.
Thanks to her, I had a shoulder to cry on.

She was there when I needed her.
Thanks to her, I never felt alone.

She was there when I felt lost.
Thanks to her, I found my direction in life.

She was there when I doubted myself.

Thanks to her, I knew nothing was impossible.

She was there when I was down and out.
Thanks to her, I bounced right back.

She was there when my heart was broken.
Thanks to her, I could move on.

She was there when things appeared bleak.
Thanks to her, I spotted the silver lining.

She was there when I failed miserably.
Thanks to her, I found the strength to fight back.

She was there when I hurt myself.
Thanks to her, I healed pretty quick.

She was there when all seemed lost.
Thanks to her, I could hope once again.

She was there when Lady Luck smiled.
Thanks to her, I didn't get too big for my boots.

She was there when my dream came true.
Thanks to her, I attributed it to God's grace.

She was there when I felt pure joy.
Thanks to her, I had someone to share it with.

She was there when I prayed to God
Thanks to her, I felt all my prayers answered.

Vibha Batra

4

BROTHERLY BONDINGS

Sometimes being a brother is even better than being a superhero.

–Marc Brown

Never Apart

Seventeen. That's how old I was. And that's how long the two of us had been together before circumstances brought in the distance factor. Being raised in a typical Indian family, emotions, however deeply felt, were never expressed. Not overtly anyway. There were gestures, gifts, a glance, but never were they put in words. Within this subtle world, where hugs hid under a blanket of unease, love rested behind sealed lips and tears rolled out only in the solitude of a bathroom, the following story is about the definitive moment when this inertia was broken between my brother and me.

My brother and I have had many fights. Shared many happy moments. But never once did those incidents sink in. Because brothers take each other for granted. Being the younger one, I never truly understood the impact he had on my life.

No birthday passed without him gifting me something. Every accomplishment of mine got sweeter with the box of sweets he got. Music sounded better when he shared his collection. The mirror smiled back in appreciation when I donned his clothes. My friend circle got wider when he introduced me to his friends.

I used to share my day with him. Even the tiniest of details. And to every story I had, there was always a pair of patient ears waiting back home; waiting to add to my laughter; to improve my ideas; to add to my joy. And to every idea implemented, those same two ears awaited me every evening, often with eager eyes and a wicked grin.

I still remember my prank that day. Roy, the annoying college brat, was late as usual. I was early, waiting to pull a fast one on him. Roy walked in with his usual incessant banter, pushing other kids, cracking jokes at the girls seated on the front benches. He never really looked at his bench before he sat down. Therein lay the opportunity. As his sorry butt rested on the bench, it was greeted by three sticky chewing gums. The entire class let out a stifled laugh. Glaring at everyone, he got up to shut them up. The sight of overstretched threads of chewing gum dangling from his trousers caused the giggles to give way to roaring laughter.

I rushed back home early to tell my brother about my prank. I did not realise he was my only confidant until that summer evening.

He wasn't home that day. I eagerly waited for evening to come. Patience was never my virtue, and this time, it was testing me. When my patience gave in, I asked my mom when Dada would return. She called my father and they sat me down. 'Beta,' my mother said, 'your brother has landed an excellent opportunity in hotel management and has left for Goa. We did not want you to know as you had just joined college. He'll call in the night, talk to him then.'

I was angry. And my ego simply would not let me talk to him. Days went by, but my anger refused to subside. And one dreaded evening it happened. An alien emotion stirred inside and then tears started trickling down my cheeks. I could not stop them. I missed him so much. Silence had taken over my life. There was a void which could not be filled. Impulsively, I took a piece of paper and penned down this letter:

Dear Dada,

Why didn't you tell me, Dada, about your course? What is this hotel management? I came home to tell you about that chewing gum prank on Roy, but you were gone. Whom will I tell all my secrets to now? I feel lonely. No one to share masti with. Who will I come home to? You are not around when I need you. I really miss you. I always wanted to tell you this. I love you.

Your naughty brother

Rambo

That letter sparked off many conversations. With every interaction, our relationship grew stronger. We exchanged letters, books, music, dreams, secrets, opinions, and above all, we exchanged emotions. And in those moments, all inhibitions left the window.

Ashirwad Mhatre

Like Brother Like Brother

Fardeen finished his workout with his best friend Ritesh and then headed towards the changing room because Ritesh said he wanted to do an additional half hour of cardio. When he reached the locker, he found Sabah on a call. Lost in his own thoughts, Fardeen was fiddling with his phone aimlessly when Sabah asked, 'Why the slight smile on your face, bro?'

'It's Kidz,' said Fardeen.

'What has he now done?' asked Sabah with interest.

'Nothing really,' replied Fardeen casually.

Sabah looked at Fardeen enquiringly.

'You know how my baby brother is at times, right,' said Fardeen, extracting his shampoo and shower gel from his toiletry case.

'Bro, he's too much at times,' said Sabah.

Fardeen turned to him knowing that it was more than just a statement. Sabah leaned forward and said, 'We were renovating our house last year and had moved into an apartment close by. One evening, your Kidz called and told me that he was in the vicinity and wanted to visit. I had forgotten to take the key to the main door with me and was waiting outside for my parents who said they were on their way back home. When they arrived, I noticed that my mother was holding some grocery bags in her arms. Your baby brother rushed to her, reached out and requested my mother to let him carry them for her. My mother was telling him that it was fine, but you know your Kidz, he insisted that he carry all of them. I told my mother that there was no point in resisting him. She gave him the bags and he carried them into the kitchen and even asked her where he could arrange the contents ... and I was like — what? Is this guy from this planet or someplace else?'

Fardeen smiled, 'I know what you mean.'

'But sometimes he makes us feel like we need to be so much better, bro,' said Sabah. 'One evening after football, Ritesh, Rahul, Kidz and I were on the way to a friend's house on Lavelle Road. While passing through St Mark's Road, Kidz suddenly requested Ritesh to stop the car the first chance he got. Ritesh pulled over to the side in front of The Egg Factory and killed the engine. Before we could ask him anything, this boy flung the door open and got out of the car. We saw him dashing up to a blind man and helping him to the other side of the road.'

Fardeen nodded.

'We were quiet when he got back inside the car, except your brother — he thanked us a million times for having stopped the car in time. And, bro,' Sabah paused, holding his head, 'he thanks you so much when you do something for him that you actually begin to feel embarrassed at the end of it all.'

Fardeen laughed.

'Not to forget his apologies. "Aeh, I'm so sorry, man, I

couldn't take your call because I was riding". "Aeh, I'm so sorry, man if I woke you up from sleep". "Aeh, man, I'm so sorry, is it a good time to talk now?" Gosh! Sometimes we all wonder where on earth he has come from!'

Fardeen smiled a little. 'Thank you for putting up with him, Sabah, and I'm sorry if he bothers you this much,' he said gently.

'Dude! Now you don't start,' said Sabah, shaking his head and heading for the showers with a look on his face that clearly indicated that he thought them all a family of lunatics.

'Well, what can I say? He's my Kidz, after all. My baby brother,' thought Fardeen and proceeded to the showers.

Farahdeen Khan

I Love You, Too

To the outside world, my brother and I will always seem to be at loggerheads with each other, what with all the kicks and punches we keep throwing at each other. But what no one will ever understand is that these fights are our way of expressing our affection for each other.

We have lived apart for most of our lives. The first time we separated was when my father, because of his job, was transferred from Ahmedabad to Lucknow, and in the process changed our lives. I was in the second grade and Aswin was still in playschool. The five year gap between us helped, because when I was taken to Delhi to live with my grandma, and Aswin went to Lucknow to live with our parents, we didn't even notice the change. My mom said, years later, that it was the hardest decision she ever had to make, but it had to be done for my own good. 'We didn't want to interrupt your studies,' she said.

It was only when I went to the eighth grade that my mom decided I should come live with them. A lot had changed in the years gone by. My brother and I had obviously changed quite a bit; the love was still there, just not visible on the surface. We would have crazy fights; similar to those shown on WWE, the ones where they use chairs, jump from ringsides, and finish their opponent with their signature moves. I gave him bruises, bumps and fractures, and he in turn ratted me out, and later rolled with laughter at the sight of my red bum, like a langoor's, from the caning my dad gave me.

No one thought we had an iota of love for each other. But it wasn't true. I remember once my dad had punished me and I couldn't stop crying. I'd covered my face with my bed sheet, trying to be as inconspicuous as possible. My brother was lying next to me. I definitely didn't want him to see my tears for it would probably be used against me later; *'Oh yeah? At least I didn't cry like a little girl ... like someone here did. I'm of course not talking about you, just generally speaking.'* I could almost picture his smug face. But instead, I heard sobs. It was my brother. I felt awkward about turning around to ask him what the matter was, but I didn't have to. Within seconds, I felt his arm across my chest, and my brother whispering through sobs, 'I love you. I always will, no matter what.' I still didn't turn around, but I couldn't help crying, for a different reason now. I still cherish that memory, like the first 'V. Good' remark I got from my second grade teacher in a spelling test.

That little boy, bursting with tears and love for me is now all grown-up and married. He lives and works in New York with a big IT firm. Because of the distance and time difference we don't get to talk much. I miss him often, and when I do, I go back to the summers and winters I spent with him in Lucknow. Like how he and I, on afternoons when the sky would be overcast, would make kites out of plastic bags by tying a piece of thread around its ears and then I'd run around the terrace till it bloated up and made ruffling sounds. If the breeze was really good, we'd run around a bit longer and then let go of the bag, watching it float over the houses, over the treetops, the buffaloes and the little shops selling cigarettes and betel leaves, till it finally disappeared.

And how when it rained, we would go out on the terrace in nothing but our underwear and dance around like sunflowers on a sunny day. We'd then block the drain outlet and wait for the water to reach our ankles. When it did, we made paper boats and held boating races, hooting and cheering our boats to victory.

On Diwali we bought fake guns along with strips of tikli and played chor-sipahi, I, the thief (mostly) and my brother, the cop. I let him be thief too sometimes, on the condition that he'd let me win.

Yes, I love my brother. I'll perhaps never admit this in front of him. But he knows that I do and that's enough for me.

Kailash Srinivasan

A Letter to My Boys

My darling sons,

Today I really lost it with the both of you. And over schoolwork!

First Born (FB), your grades were appalling and even though I have said to myself over and over again that I would never let grades, marks and percentages be benchmarks in how I judged you, I was crazy letdown by the marks you came home with. What really got me furious was that you knew *everything* ... but you made careless spelling mistakes and couldn't finish.

Second Born (SB), you just, you just ... gosh, I don't even know where to begin!

After a lot of screaming and crying (oh yes, I cried too, big bucketfuls of tears I wept!) I went out of your room to calm down and to get us some chocolate — yes, yes, for me too.

As I left the room, I banged the door shut but something made me stop and look through the crack. FB, you were sitting at the table doing your homework, SB, you were sitting on the carpet clutching your class work in your hands. What I saw next, made my knees give way...

FB, you turned around on your swivel chair, SB you looked up at your big brother; next, you held out your arms to each other, clasped them tightly for a few seconds in silent solidarity ... and then quickly looked away for fear that the harridan would storm into your lives yet again and wreak havoc with her insane fury.

Your wordless comfort to each other shattered my heart into a million little pieces. Yes, it shamed me into feeling like something worthy of being flushed down the toilet, but it also comforted me in a strange way.

That one little gesture just reaffirmed, all over again, that the SB was the best possible thing that I could do for you, FB. I gave you to each other and even though you are as different as Jupiter is from Neptune, you are both bonded to each other forever. By blood, of course, but as you grow older, also by shared experiences and moments. I want you both to love each other because you just do and not because you have to; and often, because you are so different from each other, I worry about your own love growing. But there are moments like these to reassure me that maybe I worry needlessly.

Like last week at your friend's birthday party in McDonald's, FB. You boys were playing a rather fast and furious game of musical chairs, with the SB being somewhere towards the bottom of the age chain. The first time the music stopped, FB, you managed to sit down and with one hand you 'saved' a seat for your cousin and with your other, you grabbed the SB, pulled him to you and made him sit along with you on your chair. Okay, technically I knew that wasn't allowed, but I just had to let it pass, because I thought it was the sweetest thing. The music began and the next round started ... this time, you managed to save the SB but not your cousin. By round four, just as you managed to pull the SB onto your lap, a much bigger, taller and very obviously stronger classmate of yours called you out on what you were doing. You tried to shout him down, but when he tried to drag your brother off the chair, you lost it! You put an arm around the SB's shoulders and wagged your finger vigorously under your friend's nose, screaming, 'Don't you dare touch him! Don't you dare touch my younger brother!' You, SB, had your arms around your brother's waist and had snuggled your head into his chest all the while. FB, you were amazing.

My darling boy, you could have easily been beaten into FB-jam by this much bigger boy, but that thought didn't enter your mind at all as you donned your mantle of a big brother looking out for his younger sibling.

Of course, in the interest of fairness, I did have to pull you, SB, out of the game and you were both upset with me about it. Sigh....

I guess if nothing else, you'll both bond over the 'Mamma-was-so-horrible-to-us-and-that's-why-we're-so-screwed-up' stories when you're in your teens.

Just remember, even when you're both hating me, I gave you each other.

And also, that I love you both more than you can even begin to imagine.

Forever and always yours,
Mamma

Baisali Chatterjee Dutt

Big Brother Calling

When my paternal grandfather died, my grandmother was left with four young boys to raise on her own. She was a young widow, and money was limited; the challenges immense. Needless to say, the four brothers grew up amidst severe financial constraints. They remember having to use discarded pencil stubs because they didn't have enough money to buy new ones. They made their own kites and even sold them because it meant having extra money. They eventually moved from their village Bhadarwa to Ahmedabad and worked very hard to find their footing and place in the world.

But in those years of struggle, a beautiful bond was formed. As they grew up and settled down with their respective families, that bond continued to be strong. They looked out for each other, even when they moved on to being in their sixties and seventies. If they had their differences, they never let them come in the way of being brothers.

My father is the youngest of the four. He has always had the love and pampering that is reserved for the youngest one, and he never tires of telling everyone how his brothers ensured that he could pursue medicine even when the money was tight and it would have made more sense for him to start on a job than study further. He remembers his brothers (one of them is no more) in various little ways, but these days, one of his favourite stories is about 'Tirupati and the phone call'.

If you were to talk to him, he would tell you that a couple of years ago, he made a trip to Bangalore where one of his brothers, the one just older than him, had flown down from Dar-e-salaam for treatment at a hospital there. Hasmukhkaka was in Bangalore with his son and my father joined him for a few weeks. During his stay there, my father decided to visit the temple in Tirupati.

The journey to Tirupati, by bus, was to take some six to seven hours. My father was to stay there for the night and make the seven-hour journey back to Bangalore the next day. A simple one, really. My father is rather old fashioned and at that time, he didn't own a mobile. My uncle, who owned one, wanted my father to take his. He gave him his mobile with the following instructions: 'Give me a call as soon as the bus reaches Tirupati and give me a call again when you board the bus for Bangalore.'

My father agreed. But as he reached the temple-town, he didn't immediately make the call. Some ten or fifteen minutes must have passed from when he arrived in Tirupati. The phone rang.

It was my uncle. As soon as my father picked it up, a concerned and worried Hasmukhkaka told him off for not making the call earlier: 'I had told you to call me as soon as you reach. Why didn't you do so? Don't you realise it would worry me? How would I know if you were safe in a new place?' My father apologised for the delay but he was both surprised and pleased that his brother cared so much; that his brother continued to be the elder brother that he remembered, looking out for him just like he had when they were children.

My father never failed to remind his audience that he wasn't a child, a teenager, a young adult, or even a man in his late forties when the incident took place. He was well over sixty. He knew that the bond that was formed in the dusty by-lanes of the village that he and his brothers grew up in would always last. He knew that even as he marched into the twilight of his life, the memories of his childhood and the love of his brothers would walk with him.

Whenever I hear him speak of his brothers, or see them together, I know what it must be like to have a sibling. Those years of growing up together, the recollections of a shared childhood, the comfort of having each other as one navigates life. When my father used to tell me one of the hundreds of stories of the four of them growing up together, I could picture four, brown boys in their school uniforms, their satchels on their backs, running down a dirt-track road, holding hands, their knees dusty and scarred, their faces breaking into a smile. The band of brothers, the bond that never faded away — that's the story I would like to share when I have an audience.

As fate would have it, my father died three days (December 23, 2010) after I returned from London after completing my second Master's degree. Two months exactly after my father's death, Hasmukhkaka died as well. Their bond continued in death as it was in life. My sister-in-law was to later tell me that my uncle cried copiously, like a little child, when he heard of my father's death and one of the last things that he would ever say as he was being taken to the hospital, was about looking after the family of his much loved, now dead little brother.

Prerna Shah

The Shirt off His Back

We could not have been more different. He is a Water sign, and I, Fire. He liked superhero comics, and I, Disney. He was less than two years older than me, and he got to have all the fun. 'If we were not brothers,' I liked telling my friends, 'we wouldn't even be friends.' Same schools, same address, same parents, same room and yet we were poles apart.

What started as a 'but obviously', started to hurt very soon. But obviously he got the new books for school and I got his used ones. But obviously he got the new clothes while I got the ones he had outgrown. It was unfair, I felt. Why couldn't I get new school books and clothes too? Of course I always got new clothes on special occasions, such as my birthday and Diwali, but I didn't feel those counted.

As we grew older, our list of dissimilarities grew longer and what we each liked showed no possibility of converging. He liked George Michael, I liked Prince. He liked Anil Kapoor, I Mithun. He liked whiskey, I liked rum. He saw me as a reason he had to be well-behaved everywhere — at school, in social gatherings, when playing with friends — yes, everywhere!

Otherwise, I would tell our parents. Yes, I carried tales; I was a weasel, like that. It was my way of getting even I guess.

We ended up, despite our best efforts, in the same college, and due to my father's insistence, with the same subjects. Only now, he had his own motorcycle that I could use whenever he didn't need it, which was hardly ever! Of course, I could hitch a ride to go to college or wherever he was headed to, but it was never really any place that I wanted to go.

I was happy in anticipation of finally getting my own wardrobe, but alas, it was not to be! My parents insisted that, being the same size, we should (or rather must) share our wardrobe as it only made sense — except that it made no sense to me! Every stitch of new clothing that I got, he would wear too; and, mostly because of my frantic attention to them, would damage them in one way or another. If it wasn't a missing button then it would be a stain, and all on my favourite shirts, and just on the days I would need them!

My breakthrough moment came when he moved to another city for work. I could finally have the room to myself! And at long last, my wardrobe and everything in it — my t-shirts and my jeans — were finally all mine! However, this bubble of proud ownership and happiness did not last that long, as I soon moved to US for work, leaving behind for long, and then longer intervals, all the footprints, memories and unacknowledged love and care of family. The first year was great; I had enough money and freedom to get whatever I wanted: clothes, a car, a PDA, new watch, and everything was only for me. But then, like a bad habit, this very thing started to bother me.

I missed my home, family, and also, surprisingly, my brother. His beating up guys to help me in fights at school; his covering up for me when I lied at home about spending time and money with my girlfriend; his laugh, his stories and his attention to mine. The rumpled shirts were now only rumpled by me, the lost buttons were all lost by me, and the stains were my doing as well, there was no one to blame anymore, no one to fall back on.

The first time I went back home, I took several shirts for him. He liked them, and in his usual style, damaged each in some or other way. I winced — but it was fine now because his clothes were finally, irreversibly, forever, for good, his, and mine were mine, I thought. But when I returned to the US, I took one of his shirts with me. The one he was tired of.

Since then, every time I go back home, I leave a few of my shirts with him and bring one of his old shirts back with me. I feel safe wearing his shirts now; it feels like home. He thinks I'm a lunatic, I think he's juvenile. We were never alike, my brother and I.

Rishi Chhibber

Multan — 1947, a Story Retold

Today, we enjoy what we do because of what our forefathers believed in and fought for more than sixty years ago. But there are so many heartrending stories one hears of the time of the India-Pakistan partition. My father always has a lot of pain in his eyes when he remembers Partition and his escape from the place that was once his home. He lived in Multan, in what is now Pakistan, with his parents and three brothers. He was the youngest, fourteen years old, at that time, and only his eldest brother was married.

It was the time when riots had engulfed the entire city. He and every member of the family were strictly instructed to remain indoors and not attract any unnecessary attention. Those were scary times, as even neighbours turned out to be foes. It was one fateful day that a brick changed the destiny of all the family members.

There were loud protests, chaos and shouting in the streets. Unable to control her curiosity, the eighteen-year-old wife of my father's eldest brother rushed to the terrace to get a glimpse of what was happening. Having been confined in the house for so many days, a quick look of what was going on outside won't hurt, she thought innocently. The procession was shouting slogans and the raging protestors were spewing fire, she saw in shock. Just as she leaned over a bit more for a clearer view, a loose brick from the terrace fell down and unfortunately fell on one of the protestors who started to bleed. The shouting suddenly stopped and all the attention was on the injured protestor and then on the balcony. Too traumatised to move, she stood there, not knowing what to do next.

Soon the word spread that my father's family were enemies. The family was left with no choice; fearing an attack, they decided that at least my eldest uncle and his wife should leave immediately for India. They had to leave the very same day. There was no time for tears; they couldn't even mourn the thought of leaving their roots possibly forever. Survival was topmost on everyone's minds. The rest of the family was unsure if they would meet them ever again.

In a few days, it was clear that it was dangerous for the rest of the family to continue to live there. They had to decide to leave their home, everything that was familiar and every asset they had accumulated, and head for the unknown. It was decided that my grandparents would leave for Delhi, hoping that they could come back to Multan to their home and the two sons.

As my grandparents left, my father and his brother were left in a hostile environment that only turned worse with each passing day. Now it was up to the young boys to either keep waiting there, perhaps only to get killed, or to try and unite with their parents. They decided to flee and started to collect whatever they thought would be of value and use to them. They decided to leave on the next train bound for Delhi.

It was an unbelievable scene at the station. There were people weeping, there were people in pain and people who were pushing and trampling each other just to get some space in the train. Both the brothers tried hard but unfortunately, neither could squeeze into the train. So they decided to try the airplane instead. They rushed to the airport. It was their last hope. It was no better there. There were no stairs to board the airplane and the only way people were getting onboard was far too dangerous. They came to the heartbreaking conclusion that one of them would have to climb onto the back of the other to get into the plane. Which meant that one brother would be left behind. The only question was, who? They had to decide fast or both would be left behind. My father, claiming to be physically stronger, volunteered to stay back and lend his back to his brother, promising that he would board the next train to Delhi. Time was ticking ... after many moments spent convincing him, his brother reluctantly agreed to board the plane. Once safely inside, my uncle stretched out his hand towards my father and they held on, not knowing when — or if — they would ever be able to hold each other's hands again.

At fourteen, an age when boys today are busy with their PlayStations or hanging out at mutiplexes, my father was left all alone to make it over the border to Delhi. Day after day, without a tear in his eyes, he waited in the city that was once his home for the train that would help him unite with his family. Finally, his patience paid off and he was able to board a Delhi-bound train. But the ordeal was not over yet. On reaching Delhi, he had to start searching in the many refugee camps scattered all over the city, to find his parents and brothers. It took a few days of searching and wandering, but finally he was reunited with all of them.

He and his family were lucky to have survived the ordeal. History tells us that hundreds and thousands were not so lucky.

Every time he shares his experiences with us, or whenever I have shared these stories with others, I can't help but wonder at everything these families had to go through at the time of Partition ... so many tales of pain and devastation. But also, thankfully, stories of hope and joyous reunions.

Like my father's.

It's true. I still get goose bumps whenever I picture two frightened little boys clutching onto each other's hands as they say goodbye.

Sushma Malhotra

Of Monkeys and Best Men

It was 17 May 2008. We had flown from Delhi to Champaign in Illinois, where my elder son Prakrit was marrying his classmate Jennifer Ann Bartlett. Ankit, my younger son, was the best man, and soon after the wedding vows were exchanged it was time for him to give his speech. As he began, I started to get nervous. Images of the two boys punching each other, or engaging in bouts of wrestling flashed before my eyes. I could remember sibling rivalry more than a sibling bond, which was not difficult to understand, since there was just a two-and-a-half year gap between the two.

Ankit, however, took me by surprise. He began his speech by saying, 'In a way, Prakrit saved my life.' His words took me back to the events that had taken place seventeen years ago.

It was 1991. I was deputy commissioner of Churachandpur district in Manipur and had come to the state capital Imphal for election training as the General Elections were due to be held that year. I had brought with me my sons Prakrit, aged eight, and Ankit, aged five-and-a-half, along with my domestic help, Parshuram and driver Jamte. 'In case they get bored sitting in the guest house, you can take them out, but be careful,' I had instructed the two, referring to the candy store or the toy shop around the corner. I do not know what madness possessed them to take the children to the Imphal Zoo which was on the outskirts of the town and where we had never gone before.

When I returned from the training workshop to the state guest house where we were staying for the night, I found Ankit sitting quietly on the sofa. But Prakrit was jumping up and down in excitement. 'Mummy, Mummy,' he blurted out, the moment I entered the room, 'Ankit has been bitten by a monkey.' My entire world started to spin. Manipur had always seemed to me to be the back of beyond, strife-ridden and insurgency-prone. How could I ensure the best medical care for Ankit in Manipur? I saw the long gash on Ankit's neck along with a number of scratch marks and looked questioningly at Prakrit. His words came out in a rush as he told me the entire story.

Parshuram and Jamte had decided to take the children to the zoo, since they knew that I would be away at work the entire day. They had bought peanuts to feed the monkeys. After some time, Ankit's packet of nuts was over. The langur he was feeding then stretched out his paw and got hold of Ankit's neck. My five-and-a-half-year old son had the wisdom to fall to the ground, forcing the langur to loosen his grip. While Parshuram and Jamte froze in horror at the scene unfolding before them and did nothing at all to help Ankit, a schoolmaster who had arrived with a contingent of children lent Ankit a handkerchief to stop the flow of blood. Then, a conspiracy of silence had begun. Parshuram was too scared to tell me what had happened. He knew that the responsibility for the incident would be laid squarely at his door. He feared that he would lose his job, so he made the children promise to not say anything to me when I returned. Ankit, traumatised as he was by the incident, agreed to keep quiet and so did Prakrit, but the moment I returned he just couldn't contain himself and blurted out everything.

I immediately went to our former neighbour and family physician Dr Rabei Singh who was an authority on rabies. I was frantic with worry and almost hysterical by the time I reached him. He calmed me down, arranged for a nurse and the Rabipur vaccine, wrote out the schedule in which the six vaccines had to be injected and told me not to worry too much. Over the next few weeks, I travelled from Churachandpur to Imphal for a fresh dose of vaccine, carrying it in an icebox to ensure its efficacy. Every day I prayed that the vaccine be effective and that I wouldn't lose my son to rabies.

'Prakrit was always a bit of a sneak,' Ankit concluded his speech jokingly, 'and that's why he told Mom about the whole monkey business, but honestly, if he hadn't, perhaps it would have been someone else standing here as his best man, toasting him and talking to you all today. But thanks to him, it isn't.' Ankit ended his speech amidst wild applause, but I couldn't help the tears that rushed from my eyes as I saw that, despite their rambunctious childhood, innumerable brawls and a sense of rivalry, there existed between them a treasure trove of happy memories and an unbreakable sibling bond.

Vandana Jena

5

COOL COUSINS

Cousins are different beautiful flowers in the same garden.

–Anonymous

When Little Brothers Grow Up

Riddhi was just seven years old at the time, thirteen years younger than me. He was the first boy born in the family after two generations. Riddhi, my aunt's son, my first cousin, my brother.

It was a family picnic that included a few close members from our extended families as well. One of those was my aunt's sister-in-law's family. Adhiraj was the son of my aunt's sister-in-law.

While my parents were busy socialising with the adults, Adhiraj began to make unwanted advances towards me.

'This is my kitchen. How do you like it?'

'I really couldn't care less,' I thought as he showed me yet another picture of his luxurious flat in Singapore. I wasn't interested in anything related to him, but then he was from my aunt's family, so I nodded and reluctantly said, 'It's lovely.'

There wasn't anyone of my age at the picnic. The only one I could look to for some company was my little cousin who was more interested in the chocolates, cold drinks, and the new cricket kit that Adhiraj, who was after all his cousin, had got for him.

'Bhai, come here. Sit with me. I will read you a story,' I called him trying to get away from Mr Singapore.

'No, no story. Stories are for girls. Will you play cricket with me?' he demanded.

I didn't take a second to submit to his request. All I wanted was to get away from Adhiraj and Riddhi's innocent demand was a perfect excuse.

'Hey, that's not the way you hold the bat. Wait let me show you how to do it.'

'There comes another unwanted interruption from the "dude" in town,' I thought to myself. I had never held a bat before; obviously, I was no Sachin Tendulkar, and I had no desire to be one. I certainly didn't need this haughty guy coaching me.

'Didibhai, you can't bat. You do fielding. I will bat. Adhi bhaiya, you do balling,' commanded by little cousin in seven-year-old cricket-speak, just as Adhiraj came up to teach me 'how to hold a bat'. My little brother had no idea that he had saved me from a potentially embarrassing and uncomfortable situation.

'I am new to this place. But I am really fond of sparsely populated suburbs like these. Would you come with me for a little drive after lunch and show me the locality?' he asked later, when no one was around.

Riddhi was hitting the wickets with the bat to ground them, or else I would have made better use of it! I remained quiet though.

We had a lavish lunch, the only good thing at the picnic for me. Unfortunately, the food didn't seem to have suited Riddhi. He started crying and demanded to be taken home as he wanted to go the toilet. Riddhi could never use any other loo except for the one at his home, the one at our grandpa's place or his school. I volunteered to take Riddhi home.

To my utter shock, the kid who had been crying all the way back home, entered the house and started jumping up and down. Quite obviously, in the absence of elders, he was free to mess around without being reprimanded.

'Hurry up Bhai and go to the loo!' I said, trying to be a strict sister as he rushed towards the TV remote.

'Loo?' he asked in a manner which suggested that he had heard the word for the first time in his life.

'Yes, the loo! You had a stomach ache half an hour ago, remember?'

'No ... I didn't.'

'What?' I exclaimed.

'You didn't want to go for that drive with Adhi bhaiya, no,' said my little rescuer, giving me a sly yet innocent smile.

'Didibhai, chalo! Let's have some more gulab jamuns from the fridge. No one is at home.'

We ate up all the gulab jamuns while watching Cartoon Network. And then we attacked the chocolate cookies and namkeen. So little Riddhi managed to upset his stomach after all, and rushed to the washroom for a total of seven times that evening! I remember the number so accurately, because I had to help him clean up all seven times myself! My little brother was old enough to protect his sister from an uncomfortable situation, but too little to clean himself properly after using the loo.

Avantika Debnath

Right from School

Most of my friends and classmates hated going to school. Whether it was due to the pressures of the A-B-C's or the 1-2-3's, or the fact that you had to leave the safe haven of your mother's arms for a few hours, or whether it was because of the fear of getting scolded by a teacher, they all had their reasons. Yes, most of my peer group hated school. But not me.

I was an exception. I loved going to school! And my reason was quite simple — I had someone special to go with me. Annu, my dad's sister's son, was a few months younger to me and hence we ended up in the same class in kindergarten. Initially, we would go to school clutching each other's hands as tightly as possible, sit through class all day, still holding each other's hands, and then come back the same way! Our mothers would find our hands sweating all the time … no mystery there! The thing is, holding onto each other like that, we felt safe and secure. And we didn't walk to school, we marched; like soldiers in an army, ready to take on the challenges of school — it was in togetherness that we found strength! If one of us was ill and missed school, the other was absent too. Our mothers couldn't do anything about it!

If by any chance a teacher would make us sit on separate benches ... well, was she asking for trouble and noise pollution! The whole period would see the assistants trying to get the both of us to stop crying! Finally the teachers realised that it was easier — and quieter — to just let us sit together!

When I turned five, my family moved to Pune. That was the first time Annu and I were separated and when the new academic year arrived and it was time for us to go to school again, neither of us would budge! In fact, I vividly remember telling my mother to go get Annu so that we could go to school together. And my aunt later said that Annu had said the same thing to her!

Annu and I are twenty-five today; and even though we eventually and obviously did make it through our school days without each other, there is no way that we could have made it without one another in life. We are still as connected to each other as a pair of souls that share a profound connection.

Kavita Chandrashekhar

Oh My! Homai!

I can safely say that there is no one in my family who knows how to put me in place better than my cousin Homai. And after four years of repeated blows to my queen-sized ego, I have given up trying to cut her down to size. It's no use. Homai is one-third my size and height, and is nine years old. The other day, rather proud of an article I had written on gourmet cooking, I bragged about it to Homai. She looked at me and said matter of factly, 'That's good, but don't you think you should learn to cook first.' She had a valid point; I couldn't argue with that. Plus she practises what she preaches — she makes the best caramel custard I have tasted and that too, all on her own.

I confess I have or rather had one bad habit: I am a late riser. I tried everything from warm milk, soothing music and different wall colours to get to bed early, but I just couldn't qualify for 'the early to bed and early to rise' category. When Homai took it upon herself to break my sleeping in habit, I was in trouble, serious trouble. The first day she took me to the garden much against my wishes (in my defence it was 5.50 a.m.!) and looked around to see that we were not being heard. Then she gestured to me to come closer and muttered, 'I am going to tell you a secret that only I know. It is top secret.' I sprung to alertness as my anticipation soared. She then led me to a corner of the garden and this time I enthusiastically followed her, almost tripping on a skipping rope left outside. Homai stopped and pointed, 'Here it is ... our very first white jamun flower. It is so pretty, right?' Yes, I love nature too, but the timing was way off. My imagination had taken me to family skeletons tumbling out of a closet or plans to ship out an obnoxious relative on a spiritual sojourn. As I tried not to yell at her, she smiled and said, 'Now if you want you can go back to sleep but I will wake you up in half an hour as I would like you to see me off to my school bus.'

The next day she dragged me out of bed again and told me that I was now going to meet the newest member of our family. This time I was cautious, my aunt surely didn't want another Homai on her hands did she? Thankfully it wasn't a new baby, it was a mixed breed dog that Homai insisted I must introduce myself to. She had adopted him. After his initial growl and seeing his huge fangs, I backed off. 'His name is Timmy,' said Homai as she patted him.

The third day it was homework, the fourth day she got me to make her tiffin, the fifth day she decided that I must watch her dance practice, the sixth day she came up with a game that she had invented. By the seventh day, I got up on my own. That was the end of my late mornings and I thereafter referred to Homai as the cure for my insomnia much to her happiness.

Jokes apart, I couldn't help but wonder at her tenacity to help me out and her dedication to me as a project.

Truly, sometimes it's the youngest members of our family who are possessed of a wisdom and patience beyond their years.

Khursheed Dinshaw

Three's Company

Dilys and Helen have been around for as long as I can remember. In fact, they were living with my parents before I was born. They are my cousins. My aunt (Dad's sister) had two daughters who were still very young when she was diagnosed with terminal cancer and her husband with muscular dystrophy, so my parents took care of the family before my uncle and aunt passed away. During that traumatic time, Dilys and Helen started living with my parents and my aunt made my parents promise to look after them after she passed away.

I arrived on the scene a few months before my aunt died. By then, Helen and Dilys already had a firm hold in my parents' hearts. The day my mother went into labour, she was sent off to hospital with cries of, 'It had better be a girl', from Helen, 'Try and have twins', from Dilys, and so on. When I was born, they ran around telling all their friends, 'It's a girl! Aunty and Uncle have *another* girl and we have a baby sister!!'

My earliest memories are of playing 'house' with them. We would join two chairs together, with a sheet as a canopy roof, and play under this 'house' for hours. I so looked forward to the weekends because we could play all we wanted without worrying about school the next day. The years passed and we moved from simple childish games to little skits. Dilys would be the director/musician and could be heard exhorting us, 'Melanie (that's me), sing louder, you can't be heard', and, 'Helen! (who took the part of both mother and villain), stop prancing around like a horse, you are supposed to be brandishing a sword!' I was always the little baby of course, and I played this role to perfection, both on stage and off!

And all the while, the bond between us grew stronger and stronger. Despite the many disagreements and quarrels, a deep abiding love held us together. The huge age difference between us may have played a small role in this. Time passed, we finished with school, went to college, moved away from home. Thanks to the good old postal system (snail mail in today's jargon), the Internet with the added advantage of Skype, and mobile phones, all of which redefined distance, the ties we shared were always strong. We fell in love, shared our heartbreaks, fell in love again, changed jobs, and in short, grew up. Although Helen immigrated to another country, the bond we share remains unchanged. I remember, once, the three of us were going through a rough time and they looked at me and said, 'Don't forget, no matter what happens, we will always love you and you will always be our baby sister.' I'm proud to say we share a closeness I've seldom seen between siblings.

I have always been so grateful for my two older sisters, I could never ever think of them as cousins. I always think of Dilys' son as my first baby, her daughter, my second. It is wonderful to see the same closeness in the next generation as well. We can reach out to each other (and do) at any time of the day or night, wherever we may be. In fact, my parents often say that we still gang up together and keep secrets from them! When I met the man I was to marry, advice from both of them poured in. Helen, the most practical of the three of us, asked, 'Are you sure you love him, and most importantly, does he truly love you?' Her next words were, 'Don't rush into marriage. Remember this is a lifelong commitment.' My husband was, and still is, quiet and reserved and both Dilys and Helen wondered how I would adjust to someone who is the complete opposite of me. Helen arrived from Canada for my big day as did Dilys and family. And I looked with wonder at this unfamiliar ethereal image in the mirror — my two sisters standing on either side of me. It brought into sharp focus the fact that they have always been there for me.

Looking back now I know why I have never felt like an only child — it's because I never was one.

Melanie Lobo

A Monsoon Gift

I remember the rainy day when he was born. The little, wrinkled, pink face; the green bed sheets in the small nursing-home room; his mother's tired face next to his. I remember thinking, 'Gosh, he's so tiny!' As I was leaving, a relative teasingly asked me: 'Do you want to take Unni home?' ('Unni' means 'baby boy' in my mother tongue.)

No way, I thought uncharitably. All of two years, and the only thing that I could think of was how this wrinkled little ball would be squealing away in the house, shattering my peace. Now who needed that?

Time moved on, sometimes speeding like a snake-boat, sometimes drifting like a hyacinth on a lake. We lived about 200 kilometres away from each other and met about five or six times a year; his sister and he, my brother and me, connected by a strong, organic bond of friendship and kinship.

And then, the big event happened: they moved to the same city as us. Finally, the family was together! Uncle had an official, imported station-wagon, a waterfront bungalow with timber flooring, a private jetty — and joy of joys, a wooden boat with brass funnels, called *Dorothea*. Often, we would huddle near the quay; four young cousins talking softly, looking at the dark, rippling sea, a lone star watching over us from the monsoon sky. Suddenly, a silent, dark ghost of a dredger would loom up and startle us. One eminently unforgettable evening, we crossed the backwaters and arrived like royalty to watch a PC Sorcar show.

If there was one strong quality my cousin-and-best-buddy-for-life showed right from a young age, it was his presence of mind. There was this one time when we had parked his dad's brand-new Ambassador and had gotten out of the car to stretch our limbs. Suddenly, the most eerie thing happened: the headlights came on, the horn started blaring and the car jerked forward. As all the grown-ups just froze, he, then just a gangly twelve-year-old boy, yanked the door open, jumped in, pulled out a few wires and stopped the vehicle.

So many other memories come flooding to mind.... I remember his wedding, steeped in the monsoon showers. As we were getting ready, he suddenly came looking for me, panicking, 'My belt's too loose, I need an extra hole!' I calmed him down, assuring him that I would take care of it. Soon enough, armed with a hammer and nail, I busied myself, poking a crude hole into the leather. Soon after the wedding, he and his bride spent two whole months with us in Bangalore, where he was researching for his post-graduation project. What a blast we had, catching up in the evenings as we revisited our childhood; bike-rides on our old Yamahas; walks on the terrace; and watching our spouses become friends. And that spine-chilling incident when he slipped into the narrow well in our yard and held on for dear life — until my wife, heavily pregnant with our child, set all caution aside and pulled him out.

Growing up in the monsoons, you tend to think of the years as fast-moving rain droplets, barely visible in the wind. Now, it all seems like a blur: my cousins' migration to the Middle East; his sister's yearly visits with her girls, while he and family remained on the fringes with occasional but heartfelt reminders that he was always there. Like his one-line e-mail saying how proud he was to have a brother like me, when I launched my first exhibition of photographs. And then his reassuring phone call to the hospital where I had been admitted, to treat a disease with no known cure, saying, 'Man! Don't worry! You'll dance on all our graves before you go.'

It was again during the monsoons when he called my convalescing father one morning; 'Uncle, shall I come down?' he asked seriously, his voice full of love and concern. My father had quipped, 'Now I can go peacefully; my sons are doing fine, and your aunt is well provided for.'

The same evening, I had to call and break the news. Dad had passed away quietly, characteristically; sitting next to Mom, he simply fell into her lap and died. The phone trembled in my hand as I told him; I heard him sob quietly. It was as if everything was conspiring against him. The planes were full; nothing was available through Bombay or Delhi, or Calicut, and so, finally, my elder brother and I laid our father to rest, while he sat, broken, in his Abu Dhabi apartment.

Yes, the years have sped by. His dental practice took firm root (!) and his love for sport and adventure introduced him to tennis, and later on, to raiding the desert in an SUV. He even found occasion to indulge in an old passion of his — writing.

And combined with his wonderful sense of humour, the results were quite awesome.

Last year, his wife and sons finally made it to our home, for a few days. Watching our children play together, fighting and chasing each other over Beyblades and CDs, and then making up the very next minute with generous hugs, my childhood came flooding back.

A month ago, a phone call from Abu Dhabi scythed through the peace of our quiet Bangalore home. A mentally deranged patient had attacked him in his clinic, with a seven-inch chopper. The man had sat in the patient's chair, taking him unawares with a lightning move.

An attack that could have led to sadder consequences, however, left him with just sixteen stitches on his hand and back. He had stopped the knife with his bare hand, overpowered the assailant, and even tied him with bleeding hands and called the police. His old asset — his presence of mind — had saved him.

As I walked home from the phone booth the next day, after speaking to him and listening to his jokes about doing extractions with a bandaged hand, I felt the anxiety and shock slowly leave me. As I lay down to sleep that night, however, I realised one thing: that I was immensely thankful for that rainy morning forty years ago, when a little baby boy came home.

Pramod Shankar

Ryan

Gulbarga is my maternal grandmother's hometown, and every vacation, chaos would ensue in her home. The reason? Well, fifteen energetic cousins from all over the country would meet up for one whole month. Granny would have mangoes delivered from the neighbouring orchard; our favourite meals would be prepared; and we would run riot all over town.

I was seven and learning to ride my bike. Unfortunately, I took a rather nasty fall and hurt myself pretty badly, the wound was deep and the slightest touch resulted in a stinging pain. I was petrified and the fear of falling again was so intense that I just couldn't muster up enough courage to try and ride my bike again. While the rest of my cousins would peddle away with absolute abandon, having races and enjoying themselves, I would stay behind. Tears would slide down my cheeks because I longed to be with them, but the fear of falling was crippling.

Ryan was the eldest cousin, six years older than me, and I hero-worshipped him. After all, he was taller and stronger than the rest of us. Ryan watched me mope in a corner and finally after four days of my self-wrought misery, he decided to take matters into his own hands. That evening a herd of buffaloes was crossing the adjoining road. Ryan threw caution to the winds, jumped on the biggest one and enjoyed the ride, sitting a-top the huge black beauty. I was aghast. When he'd gotten down, he calmly walked over to me, looked me in the eye and remarked, 'That buffalo weighs more than your bicycle. I was also scared when I jumped on him but then fear would have taken over and won. Don't ever let your fears rule your life. You will only look back in regret, then.'

The next morning, armed with Ryan's words of wisdom and a new sense of purpose I got on my bike again. I fell repeatedly, and each time it stung like crazy, but Ryan's words in the back of my mind didn't let me give up. I eventually mastered the art of riding my bicycle. The sense of finally being able to ride, and be a part of all my cousins' bicycling expeditions made me feel proud. Ryan simply winked at me and said, 'Good going.'

Even now, whenever I feel afraid or hesitant to undertake a new challenge, I recall my wise cousin's words, 'Don't let fear rule your life', and I am motivated to forge ahead once more.

Sanaea Patel

Never Too Far

We keep each other sane, which is why as soon as I was permitted to use my mobile phone in the hospital, I called her. I knew she would be a mess, sitting so far away in San Francisco and imagining the worst. Once we had spoken and cried and laughed, we both felt a lot better. Of course my brothers and sisters and friends who had spent sleepless nights nursing me were foxed and upset. To be honest, both P and I were used to these reactions. The truth is, P and I are much closer than we are to our real siblings ... something none of them can quite come to terms with. Technically, we are cousins with a two-year age difference. Our mothers were friends before they became sisters-in-law when my aunt suggested my mom marry her brother, thus keeping her friend in the family!

P and I used to meet up at our grandparents' home during the vacations. We understood each other thoroughly, from gestures to expressions to body language; we had our own code and private jokes, made up devious plans and played pranks on the rest of the clan.

As fate would have it, when we were in high school, she lost her parents and had to move in with an aunt of hers in a town that was a mere two hours away from ours. We met practically every weekend. We saw each other through crushes and heartaches; plotted and planned together into making the right impression; discussed dreams, ambitions, fantasies. Summer vacations were always spent together, as were birthdays and festivals. She moved in with us while studying in college, and stayed on when she started her first job. It was such fun, and we honestly didn't need friends ... though we each had them by the truckload!

We covered up for each other and to date nobody knows the number of times we sneaked out at night or what the code words meant! We shared a bedroom and had to take turns sleeping on the one bed in the room. It was a huge bargaining chip when one wanted to borrow a new bag, dupatta or just hard cash. Of course we fought and sulked but if someone else dared to say a word against the other, daggers were drawn immediately. At twenty and twenty-two, we thought this is how life would be; we would get married and move a few blocks away from each other and still meet for lazy Sunday lunches.

Things didn't pan out as planned; they never do, right? P fell in love with a dear friend, got married and they moved to the US. We both felt lost; the pain, almost like a break-up. We spoke on the phone often since she was homesick, and mailed each other twice a day. That became a habit and soon, with Skype and Facebook, we didn't feel that far from each other at all. It's how we saw each other through new jobs, work pressures, my wedding, moving cities, her babies, my mother passing away ... we were together every single day. Supporting each other. Just knowing that she is a mouse click or a phone call away means a lot.

We still have our code words and share secrets that each of us will carry to the grave. Who knows; maybe if we lived in the same city and didn't have time to meet, grudges might have crept in. Maybe if we expected one to drop everything and rush to the other, it wouldn't always have been possible. Who knows? But like this, when we know that there is a limited but necessary interaction on a daily basis, it works wonderfully. It is an addiction we both love.

We meet once in about two years and instantaneously pick up from where we left off. We demand all the gifts for birthdays gone by and bets won or lost! Actually we help each other go back in time when we were young and pretty and uncomplicated and not torn between so many roles.

We can be candid with each other and yet wickedly deceitful and say the right things to cheer up the other! Close yet far ... oh, the joys of technology! My most recent promise to her is to try and stay away from hospitals so that we can get our daily dose of each other without any interruption!

Shifa Maitra

Your Brother, I'll Always Be

I am an only child, so I grew up alone. Actually, I wasn't the first born. I lost an elder sister even before I got the chance to know her. There were times I would miss having her in my life, especially during the festival of Rakhi. The colourful rakhis tied on wrists seemed to jeer at my empty one. It would always pinch me, making me incredibly jealous, and I wished I had a sister too. I remember sometimes my mother would tie a rakhi on my wrist to make me feel better, and truly speaking it worked, but still....

Time passed and I joined college. By that time I'd totally gotten over my feelings of missing a sister in my life. In fact I was very happy that I was the only child and that I got to enjoy my privacy. In college, one doesn't think much about one's family, friends being paramount to one's existence. I was no exception — my friends were everything to me! When we weren't in college, we would hang out in my room where no one would disturb us; both my parents worked, and none of the domestic help came to my room unless asked.

However, the happiness was short-lived. One day, my

cousin, Swati, came to stay with us. Six older than me, she hailed from a small town near Kolkata, and had secured a job in the city just after her post-graduation. Her entrance in my life didn't bother me much until my father declared that she would stay in my room and that I would have to shift to the small cubby-hole next to my parents' room.

I was devastated. That meant friends couldn't come over as freely anymore, and that I wouldn't have my privacy either. I hated her and wouldn't accept her as part of my family. I was often rude to her, for which my father once slapped me in front of everyone. That made me even angrier and so I made her life difficult. She would mostly keep to herself, reading in her room, or helping my mother about the house. She hardly ever went out anywhere; it was just office and home. I often used to tease her, saying, 'What's the use of earning so much money when you don't spend it on yourself? You girls and your savings ... huh!' But she would never react and never once showed me even a hint of anger; on the contrary, she was always caring and nice to me and that pinched me somewhere deep inside.

Once, my parents went out of town for a week. Before they left, my mother said she was leaving the house in Swati's responsibility. I was waiting for them to leave so that I could break free for a while — it had been so long! As soon as my parents left I made plans with my friends for a night out. I wasn't allowed to drive my father's car, especially at night, but all those rules were the last thing on my mind. Swati obviously tried to stop me, but I was in no mood to listen. I went out anyway.

While I was returning from the party at some really late

hour, I met with an accident. Everything after that is a little hazy to me, but I remember someone picking me up and taking me to a nearby nursing home. Someone called a few numbers on my phone. I was expecting my friends to arrive but after a while I saw Swati didi rushing towards me and then I lost consciousness.

I opened my eyes the next morning and felt a sharp pain in my head. I looked around and it took me a while to realise that I was in a hospital. Then I remembered the previous night's incident. I panicked thinking about my father's car. He would kill me. Just then Swati didi entered my hospital room, put the medicines on the table and noticed that I was awake. She came and sat next to me, and I thought to myself, 'Here it comes, the scolding and the lecture.' I was afraid that she had already informed Dad about the car. But she gently touched my cheeks and said, 'How are you feeling now? The doctor said there's nothing to worry about, thank god. It's just a small cut on your forehead. They'll let you go really soon.' Then she got up to give me my medicines and continued talking, 'I gave the car to the mechanic; there's a dent in the bonnet and the headlights are broken but they can fix everything by tomorrow. Your Dad doesn't have to know if you promise not to repeat the mistake again.'

I didn't know what to say ... all I could ask her was, 'Where did you get the money from to take care of all of this?' She smiled and said, 'Oh, well, you know girls and their savings!'

On the way back from hospital, I wondered, isn't this what I'd wanted all my life? And now that I'd finally got it, how come I didn't appreciate it? Not a single friend came to help me, but this cousin of mine, who I had always been so mean and petty towards, had come running to me when I needed someone the most. My eyes filled with tears; I looked at her, she was looking out the taxi window. Hesitantly I said, 'Didi…' She turned towards me. I couldn't find the right words, but she understood and said, 'Don't mention it. I am sure you would have done the same for me. After all you are my *little* brother.'

Her little brother. How beautiful those words sounded to me that day. Yes, I'll always be her *little* brother.

Often we look far away for the things that are already so close to us. I know I'll never make that mistake again.

Shoumik De

A Big Girl Now

Anand could see Renu was angry from the way she rearranged the cushions with unnecessary gusto and how she rebuffed all his attempts at small talk. Better to have it out now rather than prolong the agony. He took the plunge.

'Why are you angry, Renu? What did I do?'

His acceptance of guilt seemed to thaw the ice.

'Nothing,' she said and began to surf channels.

'Come on, tell me.' He took the remote from her and switched off the TV.

'It is nothing really ... but ... I get so angry when I see you with that Jaya! You have so much to say to each other! I feel totally left out... And yesterday, the way you laughed! What do you both have to laugh about so much?' It all came out in a rush.

Anand sighed. His cousin Jaya and her kids had visited them the previous day. He knew that Renu hadn't found her bearings in his extended family even after five years of matrimony. She had never understood his special relationship with Jaya, seven years older than him.

He sat down next to her and asked, 'Do you remember when we started laughing?'

'That was what was strange about it … I asked Jaya how old Ruku is and when she replied, both of you looked at each other and burst out laughing!'

'What did she say?'

'She said Ruku is thirteen.'

'No, do you recall her exact words?'

'Mmm … she said, "Ruku is thirteen, she is a *big girl* now".'

Smiling, Anand put his arm around her shoulders and said, 'Let me tell you a little story. I have told you about the old house where I was born, haven't I? My grandfather's house? The place where we all lived till it was sold? Well, in that house, there were two people who were the centre of my universe. One was Amma. The other was Jaya.

She took charge of me the moment I started turning over by myself, I think. If I wasn't in Amma's arms, I was in Jaya's. She would carry me around the garden and sing songs to me when I was cranky. If Amma was too busy, she would give me a bath. When it was mealtime, I would fight to sit near Jaya.

It was Jaya who taught me how to search for the best fruits from the badaam tree in the compound, how to crack them open and get at the tasty nuts inside. We played all sorts of games: hide and seek (she would hide in the most obvious places when it was my turn to seek), seven stones (I was permitted to throw the ball from point blank range), and house. House was our favourite game. Jaya would be Amma and I would be her little boy. She would make dishes — rice, sambhar, idlis, dosas — from sand and pebbles and serve me in plates made of jackfruit leaves, and I would pretend to eat everything with great relish.

In school, Jaya was my guardian angel, extending her protective role at home to the newer, tougher environment. Our teachers didn't mind. She was a good student and got even better by teaching me what she had learnt. Every evening at four, she would hold my hand to walk me down the narrow lane back home.

And then one day, after school, I waited and waited at the school gate and Jaya did not come. It was the ayah who told me that Jaya had gone home early.

At home, I threw my bag down and struggled out of my uniform. All I wanted was to find Jaya and ask what happened. Amma stopped me as I hurried to the room where she and her parents stayed.

"Don't disturb Jaya, *mone*, she is a *big girl* now."

"So what, I am a *big boy*!" I shouted over my shoulder as I raced down the corridor.

The door was locked. I knocked and banged on it, calling for Jaya. Her mother opened the door and didn't move aside when I breathlessly told her that Jaya had come home early from school without waiting for me

"You can see Jaya later, *mone*. She is not well," Renjini Valliamma said.

"What is wrong with her, Valliamma?" I shouted, frantically.

"Nothing, nothing ... she is a *big girl* now," she said as she firmly shut the door.

I couldn't figure it out. What did all this mean? Jaya had always been bigger than me. What was so special about her being a big girl? And why did they all say it in that strange tone of voice?

The next morning Jaya didn't come to school. Amma told

me to be a good boy and not to bother her ("She is a *big girl* now, Anand, she can't be with you all the time from now on").

When I came back home that evening, there was a big crowd in the sitting room. All our neighbours and distant relatives were there. Trays of sweets were being passed around. Jaya was seated on a chair in the middle of the room in a sari. I had never seen her in a sari before.

Someone gave me a piece of Mysore pak. I bit into it. Strangely, it felt absolutely tasteless. Everything was happening in a blur.

"Anand, now what will you do? Jaya is not going to play any more games with you, she is a *big girl* now!" Remani Auntie from next door said, tweaking me on the chin as she passed by with a big plate of kesari.

I began to cry. The tears streamed out of my eyes like they would never stop. At first I wept silently, but soon my sorrow began to assume substance and shape and exhibited itself in wails. Everyone stopped whatever they were doing and stared at me.

Amma started to pull me out so that the party could go on in peace. But I struggled and shrieked and wouldn't go. I could see Jaya looking at me, her eyes wide open. She didn't come to me.

Renjini Valliamma came to my mother's assistance and tried to sooth me, "What is it, *mone*? Why are you crying?"

I ceased my sobbing long enough to ask, "What is the matter with Jaya?"

"Nothing at all, what gave you that idea?" she said, wiping my face with the end of her sari.

"Nothing at all? Then why does everyone say she can't play with me anymore? Why does everyone say she can't do anything? So what if she is a *big girl* now?" I shouted at the top of my voice.

For a moment, everyone was silent. Then they all started laughing.

My father got up from his chair and held out his hand to me. I grabbed his finger and went out of the room with what dignity I could muster.

Out in the garden, he told me a few things about life.

...and so when you asked Jaya how old Ruku was and she said she is a *big girl* now.... Come on, Renu, stop laughing!'

Srinath Girish

Growing Up

I have a brother. He's my baby brother. Well, actually, he's my aunt's son. Our mothers are sisters and our families are very close. In fact, we grew up like siblings and I can't think of him as a cousin anymore. He is the youngest in the family and the only brother to three sisters. So, he has been pampered a lot and all three of us claim to be his other mothers.

My first memory of my baby brother is that of a naughty toddler. Somehow I don't remember him sleeping much as babies do, or rather, as supposed to do. I loved carting him around. I was nearly nine and loved giving him baths, feeding him and taking care of him in every which way. We met every year for three months and I never noticed that he was growing. In my adoring eyes, he was always the baby of the family.

When I was sixteen, I went to stay at my aunt's place for an extended period and that's when I realised that my baby brother was turning into a protective brother. When we went out for a walk, he was on the watch for eve-teasers or rowdy neighbourhood boys and would always caution us. Yet, when we were at home, he was back to being the baby, revelling in the attention and affection we readily showered on him.

I got married at twenty-three; he was sixteen then. I was visiting my aunt and we received news of a cousin's death. She had committed suicide. The entire family was shocked. We couldn't help but think, 'What could have prompted her to take this step? Surely, she could have confided in someone — why didn't she? Was there really no one with whom she could share her worries? Were there really no opportunities for her to speak out?' These were the thoughts voiced.

As we sat talking, trying to find answers, baby bro came up to me, held my hand and looked me in the eye and said, 'Di, whatever happens, remember you can always talk to me. And no matter what, I will always be there for you.' I was touched beyond measure. I controlled my emotions, looked into his worried eyes and said, 'I know,' and squeezed his hand. Without breaking eye contact, he continued, 'You promise?' I said, 'Yes.'

That was the moment that I realised that my baby brother had indeed grown up. He was no longer just the baby of the family — he was a young, sensitive man with a sense of duty, responsibility and dependability. God bless you, baby bro!

Trishna Pillai

6

BONDED BY THE HEART

*F*riends are the family we choose for ourselves.
                                                    –Edna Buchanan

Incredible Life-Force

It's past midnight and I'm still wide awake, sitting in my balcony, watching the rain drops falling on the trees. Suddenly a message on Facebook reminds me that it's Rakhi today. Immediately my thoughts turn to my two best friends from college, Ramesh and Vikram. Fifteen years of friendship, defined by selfless love and giving. We shared so much in common that I often rued the fact that we were not real siblings. But despite the fact that we did not share the same set of parents, we were never anything less, with me being the pampered, protected younger sister.

I was the first one in our group to get engaged in 1997, an absolutely unexpected incident. All my friends took a backseat as I switched my allegiance to the person with whom I was about to spend my whole life. I remember how I hung up on Ramesh, who was the first caller on my birthday that year, as I was anticipating my fiancé's call.

I got married, and suddenly the rest of the world became unimportant. Time flew and I was swimming in the sea of marital vows. But destiny had something else planned for me. My world shattered after my daughter's birth, when I experienced my husband's disinterest in me owing to my post-pregnancy figure. To add salt to my already grave wounds, I learnt about his affairs.

My family was certainly by my side, but where were my friends? I saw people whom I'd once thought were mine drift away as if I were an alien. And then came these two as my saviours, my life-force.

Now, despite feeling burdened with my decaying marriage, I allowed myself the liberty to laugh and dream once more, with this twosome who appeared time and again to show me that life is indeed to be lived. Both were aware of my situation back home where I was trying to save my marriage and going through mental turmoil.

We would meet once a month without fail and those evenings were stress-busters for all of us. One incident stands out in particular. I was very upset and telling them about the new twists in my life. At one point, I became so overwhelmed that I got up and ran to the ladies room, tears streaming down my face. I took a little longer than usual and Vikram got worried so he came into the ladies washroom, uncaring about what the world would think. Even today, whenever we meet at that coffee shop, we can't help but laugh over this. But of course, it's also one of the sweetest things anybody has ever done for me.

While Vikram was busy doing his CA and M.Com, Ramesh and I decided to enrol for an MBA. Ramesh and I did our MBA from different schools. In fact, he did his from another city and I only got to see him when he came down for vacations twice a year.

Times were tough and I often felt disconnected from my two pillars, but thanks in part to technology and in part to our will to never be separated, we stayed connected via phone calls and emails. I would call them at odd hours to sob and pour my heart out without bothering to ask them how they were doing and they never complained, they just listened — patiently, quietly. I remember one night, while talking to Ramesh, I heard a loud thud followed by a pause. I stopped crying and asked him what that noise was. He reassured me that it was nothing and continued to console me. Later, I learnt that he had been perched on the first floor window of his hostel dormitory while talking to me and had lost his balance, falling down on the ground and hurting himself quite badly. However, since I was so tense and upset, he did not want to say anything to stop me from talking.

We completed our MBA and started our careers; he had his set of emotional traumas too. He had a nasty break-up with his first love and was devastated. This time, our roles were reversed and I took it upon myself to bring him out of his quagmire of depression. Time passed and he found his way out too.

I remember the day I got my divorce petition, and in a traumatised state gave Ramesh a call, not knowing what to do. And he arranged for me to go to his father's office and thus my legal battle started.

Now, ten years have gone by, with all the accompanying ups and downs. We lived and rejoiced our bonding in our own ways, sometimes connecting daily and other times less often, occupied in the business of life but always present at times of stress or happiness, setbacks or triumphs. We all have matured in our dealings with life, but with each other we continue to be as candid as mirrors. Ramesh and Vikram are now married and have successful careers. I am a mother of a ten-year-old daughter, contentedly settled in my profession and living life to the fullest.

Even though we are not connected by blood, we are by our heart-strings, and a few hours later, for Rakhi, I will meet my two life-lines to celebrate this special feeling of oneness that we share; where I will, once again, tell them without too many words, 'I cherish you and am grateful that you are in my life'.

Anushree Karnani

The Stranger on My Way

Coming from an army background, I have grown up with people from various communities. In Hyderabad, where I began my career as a journalist, most of my friends belonged to the Islamic community. How I used to relish the biryani and halim made during the festive season!

Now I have always been very conscious of my skin's well-being and have tried almost every available sunscreen brand there is to save myself from tans and sunburns. My search for the perfect sunblock ended during my stay in Hyderabad. My friends Shaheen and Firdaus used to tie a stole around their faces like a purdah as they were not allowed to expose their faces while out on the streets. Another friend, Rukhsar, gifted me a similar stole and I started tying it around my face — it was the perfect sunblock! We used to roam around together, exploring the streets of Hyderabad. People thought that I was a Muslim too and greeted me with 'salam walekum'.

Once Shaheen and I had to cover a sangeet sammelan at the Bhartiya Vidya Bhavan. We didn't take the office transportation as we had plans to visit Rukhsar after the event. Due to some emergency, Shaheen left by 8, and I covered the sammelan alone. It ended at 10 p.m. Having stayed in Hyderabad for only a month, I simply could not figure out the way to either my paying guest accommodation or Rukhsar's place. I tried calling Shaheen but her cell phone was switched off. Being from a well-to-do family, Rukhsar never took public transport and had no clue about which bus or auto could take me where. It was 10.10 and I was lost in an unknown city.

Because I had entered the bhavan premises in the afternoon with the stole around my face, people had assumed that I was a Muslim lady. Even though the sun had long since set, I kept the stole around my face as I didn't want to cause any disrespect or harm by insulting their beliefs and practices.

'Any problem, Aapa?' I heard a voice. I turned around and saw a thin boy.

'Beta, I am not able to find my way to Madhapur. Can you help me?'

'Yes Aapa. Just take the left turn and you will find an auto stand. You can take an auto to Mehendipattanam; from there you can easily get many buses to Madhapur.'

I thanked him profusely and quickly followed the boy's directions. It was 10.20 p.m. by the time I found myself sitting in an auto. However, the place where the autowallah dropped me off was definitely not Mehendipattanam. By the time I realised that, it was 10.35. I had no idea which part of Hyderabad I was in. For a while I couldn't hear anything that was going on around me as my heart was beating louder than all the drums on earth. And the moment I tried to hear beyond that sound, a roar of laughter that literally curdled my blood struck my ears.

I turned around and found four young boys, probably in their early twenties, leering at me.

'I bet there is a beautiful face under that scarf,' one of those boys said to his friends.

'I won't bet. I am sure she is pretty,' returned his mate.

Now while I was a bold journalist during the day, as those boys advanced towards me, my watch showing it to be a quarter to 11, I was nothing but a helpless woman alone. I just prayed to all the gods whose names I could recall while trying to swallow my fear.

'So Madamji, what is your name? Salma?' asked one of them. I took a step backward.

'I'm warning you, I am a journalist, so don't try to mess with me kids,' I somehow tried to sum up my courage. And just as I was trying to whip out my ID card, a bike stopped nearby. It was an old Kinetic with chipped red paint. The person riding the bike had an unshaven face and oily hair. Whoever he was, a John Abraham he certainly was not.

'What's up with you'll, huh? It's late. Go home.' He tried to help me get rid of them, but they didn't pay him any attention. He got down from his bike and said, 'Go home. Your mothers must be wondering where you are now. Don't force me to do anything that would make them really worried about you. Ramzan is going on.' Though he said everything very calmly, there was a slight edge in his voice which made the guys disappear.

'Do you have to go somewhere, Aapajaan?' he turned towards me, after making sure that the boys had left.

'I have lost my way. I want to go to Madhapur,' I replied.

'I am going towards Konadapur. I can drop you there.'

I had no reason to trust him, but then again, my options

were limited. I could stay on at that unknown place for the rest of the night and risk being accosted by those devils again, or I could take a chance and go with him. I decided on the latter.

'Where do you stay in Madhapur, Aapajaan?'

I told him. In twenty minutes we reached my destination.

'Why do you stay in a PG, Aapa?'

'My family is in Kolkata.'

'Oh, you are a Bengali, like Rani Mukherjee? I like her a lot, my Aapajan used to look exactly like her.'

'Where is your Aapajan? Is she married?'

'No,' he said, and after a couple of seconds, continued, 'She died during the Gujarat riots. It's good that I have met you during Ramzan. My mother will be glad to see you. Come home someday.'

Then he pointed at a street nearby and gave me directions to his home.

I felt guilty of camouflaging myself as a Muslim.

'Bhai, I can't come to your place.'

'Why not?'

'I am a Hindu.'

'Yes, I know that you are a Hindu. Though you were wearing this scarf, when I stopped my bike near you, I noticed the locket of Shivji dangling at your neck and the red temple threads on your wrist.'

'And yet you helped me?'

'Why shouldn't I? My sister was killed because nobody helped her; I make sure that my presence saves other people's sisters. Better that your brother and I share a sister, rather than end up having no sisters at all.'

He took my cell phone from my hand.

'I have saved my number. Call me up whenever you feel like. My name is Kareem.'

Being an only child, I had always envied my friends who tied rakhis on their brothers on Rakshabandhan. The Almighty must have been smiling all this while thinking that he did in fact have a brother in store for me. He had to give me a surprise gift just when I needed him the most. And while his name might be Kareem, that night, he was no less than Lord Krishna saving Draupadi from a heinous crime, centuries ago.

Avantika Debnath

My Soul Sister

'How do people make it through life without a soul sister?'
                                              –Sara Corpening

Sometimes, it's strange how you can meet someone just once and feel that you've known the person all your life. It makes you believe that there are some relationships which go beyond blood ties, beyond family, and perhaps beyond time also.

Though never a big fan of Facebook, I used it to keep in touch with friends who had moved away from Kolkata. I did not know then that one day this site would bring into my life Mansi.

It all started with my creating a work group on the site and inviting friends and friends of friends to be a part of it. It was the easiest way to promote the online lending library that I had just started. Mansi left me a message saying that she was keen to donate books. I left her a message asking for her number. Our first call was a little formal as Mansi is a reserved person. She did not talk much, just gave me her address, a time to collect the books and hung up. I was overwhelmed when she donated 118 books and wanted to thank her in some way, so I invited her for coffee. I suspected she might refuse my invitation, but to my surprise, she accepted.

It was sometime in August when we first met. I picked her up from her home, where, much to my disappointment, she made me wait for a good ten minutes. Even now, when I think about that time, I just smile. She was as nervous as I was, because both of us are complete introverts. In fact, our first words when we met each other, was a just a meek little 'Hi'.

Together we walked to a nearby café talking about the weather and general stuff. It was only when we started talking about books did we get extremely comfortable. Suddenly, the ice was broken. We went on and on, discussing books that we were reading, our favourite books, our respective book collections, my online library and a whole lot of other things. And after that, our conversation seemed to shift naturally to our personal life. I found myself pouring my heart out to Mansi about the fertility treatment I was undergoing at that moment and she started talking about her struggles in her marriage which ultimately led to her divorce. By the end of the conversation, we both had tears in our eyes; sharing such private thoughts with a complete stranger had been extremely cathartic and somehow secured us to one another.

That day, when we left the coffee shop, Mansi and I knew that in each other, we had found our soul sisters.

Within days we grew so close that it was hard to believe that we had just met a few days before. We shared everything with each other, right from the moment we got up. She is a psychotherapist, and her words, wisdom and tips helped me maintain a positive attitude throughout my treatment, and my cheerful and positive attitude about marriage gave her the courage to dream of a future she was too scared to even think about. We complemented each other perfectly, just like real sisters do. She had my back and I had hers. I could not thank my lucky stars enough for giving me a soul sister who not only lived in the same city but also stayed just two blocks away from my house.

Within a month of our first meeting, Mansi had to return to the US to complete her course in psychotherapy. She promised to keep in touch, and she did. She would send me long emails every day and I, too, would share everything with her. There were times when I faltered and broke down because of my fertility treatment and Mansi gave me the courage to fight and not give up. There were times when she would e-mail me and voice her fears about her future and her relationship with her boyfriend. There were times when she would just cry and cry and I would soothe her through my emails and words. We both remained strong for each other. We didn't really need words to tell each other how much we cared; our actions spoke volumes ... and sometimes, even our silences.

Time moved on and Mansi shifted back to Kolkata to set up her practice here. Once again we could meet and chat for hours. We would land up meeting in the parlour where she had to wait for long hours for her hair treatment. We would sit in a secluded room, oblivious to the fact that it was a beauty parlour and people all around were watching us. I still remember the day I told her of my fear of dogs. Within a few days, she got a pup home and encouraged me to come and play with it every day. Today, whatever little fear of dogs I have overcome, is all thanks to Mansi.

I firmly believe that every person comes into your life for a reason, to teach you something valuable. I had always longed for a sister all my life, and when God sent Mansi, I knew that my prayers had been answered.

Bali D. Sanghvi

Sister Act

I grew up bereft of hugs. Neither Baba nor Ma was the cuddly type, really. Hugs generally made me feel awkward. Just before my seventh birthday, when I was big enough to understand things, my father married again, splitting my whole world into three: the material, non-material and the immaterial. This sudden change in our lives disrupted everything, leaving a strange bitter feeling, never to heal. Baba moved to a new house with his new-found love, my stepmother and her daughter from her previous marriage. We felt cheated. I wondered if Baba even loved or cared for us anymore. Little worldly pleasures of the past were robbed. The garage was empty; there were no more weekend outings, movie trips or fancy meals. The smell of fresh linen in unfamiliar, exotic hotels of long summer holidays also seemed a distant dream. Ma was now a single parent working doubly hard. Relatives and neighbours gradually distanced themselves. In school, deflecting unwanted questions became a ritual. The joys which once filled our home were no more.

My custody rested with Ma. Legal bindings meant that

Baba had the right to see me and that I could visit him. I was ripped between two households. Weekends at Baba's were cold and unfriendly. When I did go at all, I actually counted the hours till I could get back home. Each stay culminated in an uncomfortable peck on my check as Baba said goodbye — a moment I cringed at the thought of for hours in advance. My indifferent stepmother and Baba's old-fashioned stiff, upper lip meant we never got close. Moreover, Baba's pretext of work and household duties widened our distance.

Yet, in all those visits, there was someone who stared at me with haunting eyes as if to say, 'Can't we be friends?' This was my stepsister, a bubbly girl of nine with an enchanting smile. The vibe she gave off made me feel as if she had lots to share and only longed for a chance to open up. What a welcome respite she was in that otherwise unfriendly house! In the months that followed, the ice broke, and we found our way to each other's hearts. Of course, there were several subtle undercurrents, but one factor helped us bond intrinsically: we both felt cheated; as if we'd been painfully implanted in an alien setting only to fulfil someone else's interests.

Meanwhile, I also sensed that Ma was seeing another man — her boss at work who had helped us through many trying times. This development certainly did not happen overnight. Ma had been busier than usual in office, was working overtime with client meetings stretching to unearthly hours and had monthly tours to undertake. Reasons which in the past seemed sensible for her late hours were now mere excuses. At fourteen, I was now mature enough to understand and overlook this consciously. It was for my peace of mind and hers. After all, unlike Baba who had walked away with someone he fancied,

Ma was still holding on and I was scared to let this go. Life by now had taught me that every relationship I valued was fragile, demanding deft handling. Moreover, my first cruel blow had cushioned me to take things in my stride by being a little indifferent. Over time, my dependency on Ma reduced.

It was during these times that my stepsister and I grew closer. We had so much to share that the Net, phone and weekly meetings seemed insufficient. As our relationship blossomed, it was a strange revelation for me to increasingly appreciate how one relationship was gradually waning to make space for another.

A month after my twentieth birthday, my stepsister underwent surgery for a congenital heart defect. Despite a successful incision, a severe infection followed, raising serious concern. Days later as she slowly gained some strength she told me how much she loved me and through tears I admitted that I loved her too. I started planning ways to make her happy as soon as she was fit to be out of hospital: shopping for books and trinkets; looking up plays and movies to catch up on; recipes to try out; partying with friends...

In what was supposed to be my last visit before her discharge, my stepsister grabbed and hugged me so hard that I had to push with all my might to keep from pressing down on her newly-stitched torso. And just when that hugs sent shivers down my body, she died, ever so peacefully. I watched those fingers gradually transform to a stony white; that told me she was no more, not the bleeping of monitors or the bustling of nursing staff. Standing at her bedside, I felt like a little girl again, unable to talk. All my life, I had wondered if there was someone who really loved me selflessly, and just when I had finally found that person, she passed away. Her last hug changed my life though. It replaced the loss I felt for all those hugs which I had never been given before. She had extended herself in loving me; she had transcended all barriers of blood by feelings of her heart. She was no more my 'other sister', but a true soul sister.

To a child, a hug says many things. It tells you that a person hugging you loves you and cares for you. A hug also confirms what you are a lovable being. As time passed, my grief and anger over my sister's untimely death began to recede. I began to appreciate that her affirmation of me from her deathbed had filled a gaping hole of insecurity that I had carried all these years. I realised with a jolt that the lack of hugs said more about Baba than me. Once I digested this insight, my feelings changed from those of a needy child to a proud daughter. Looking at Baba more objectively allowed me to view him more clearly and, ironically, to begin feeling closer to him now than ever before. I was a lot less cynical about my stepmother who had previously been my adversary in this perpetual tug-of-war. With Ma, how could I not be anything but forgiving? With my newfound wisdom, came the freedom of giving up trying so very hard to gain the affections of others, but to seek my own self. That last hug carried me gently from childhood to adulthood. At last I became my own woman.

Ilika Chakravarty

My Eye Flu Sister

I was ten then and visiting my maternal aunt's place in Kolkata. Kamala lived next door. Her big joint family ran a traditional business and they lived in a large, old mansion. Kamala was around three years older than me and I remember her as a lanky girl with long legs, dishevelled tresses, pale eyes, and always dressed in oversized frocks. She took a shine to me right from the first day we met. She would come straight to my aunt's house first thing in the morning, sometimes with her toothbrush dangling from her mouth. She would stay through the day, vanishing only for short spells, like to take a bath or to have a meal at her home.

Kamala was full of new ideas and every day we would try out one or the other. Our favourite game was to enact rituals. We would often collect flowers, burn incense sticks, tie red threads on each other's wrists and perform ceremonies like dolls' weddings, tree worshipping, purification of toys with holy water, exorcising ghosts from dark corners, going on pilgrimages around the house with Kamala leading the way reciting strange chants which she might have learnt from her ancient and shrivelled grandmother. I was thoroughly impressed with her and became her ardent fan and follower.

One day we performed the ceremony of 'becoming sisters'. Kamala put a vermillion dot on my forehead, showered marigold petals on me and we tied 'sisterhood' threads yellowed with turmeric on each other's wrists. 'We are sisters now,' Kamala declared solemnly, 'and we have to share each other's pains and sufferings henceforth.' I nodded in agreement.

The testing time came soon after as I was struck with a very bad spell of eye flu, with swollen eyelids, intense pain and irritation in my blood-red eyes. I was isolated and put in confinement and Kamala was not allowed into my room. But she sneaked into my room the second day and told me, 'Remember, we are sisters, so I am bound to share your pain. I know a mantra that I will recite and then you will become free of the disease. Though this disease will not vanish — it will get transferred from you onto me. Do you agree?' I thought for a while and suggested that maybe we could transfer the flu to my uncle or my aunt or somebody else from the neighbourhood instead. Perhaps even the dog. 'No,' she said, 'only god-sisters can share the suffering.' Then she waved a red hibiscus flower on my head three times, sprinkled some water on me, chanted a mantra and went away to throw the flower in the well.

Next day when I woke up, the pain was gone and my eyes were clearer. I was cured! After a while, Kamala was back with a broad grin that reached her red, swollen eyes. The simple fact that I was cured because the flu had run its course and that she had contracted it from me were beyond my comprehension, so I was awed by her 'magic'.

I never met Kamala after that visit. When I visited my aunt next after six-seven years, Kamala was already married and living in her in-laws' house. Then my aunt relocated and I never went back, but each eye flu season brings back fond memories of Kamala who gave a new meaning to the sanctity of sisterhood ties by taking my pestilence on herself so selflessly.

Jayanti Dutta Roy

The One You Don't Know About

A few weeks ago, I celebrated twenty glorious years in the fashion industry. When I took my first fledging steps in 1991, I never thought that one day my name would become synonymous with men's designer wear in India, or that I would get the accolades that have been heaped on me. As I look back on this beautifully creative and intensely rewarding journey, I know that there is someone who deserves my heartfelt thanks, loyalty and gratitude; someone who gently pushed me into this world; someone whom the rest of the world does not know about; someone without whom this wonderful life-adventure would never have happened — my sister-in-law, Rita.

I was born into a culturally vibrant family. My father was a well-known poet and our home was the hub of many a creative and artistic get-together, with eminent personalities from the world of art, literature and music always in attendance. I immersed myself in the joys of the literary and artistic world and consider myself very lucky to have had the kind of exposure that I did.

I got married at a very young age; while I was still in college!

And my husband was one of ten siblings! Along with looking after my in-laws, household chores, studying for my exams, having a baby and even completing my MA, I also helped with my husband's textile business; more specifically with the designing of the saris.

Somewhere around this time, along came Rita. She married my husband's younger brother and we formed a strong bond. We weren't that far apart in age, we had married into the same family and we had a lot in common. It was Rita who was most fascinated by my artistic skills. She would always seek out my help for drawing alponas (Bengali-style rangolis), for doodling in cards and also writing in them using calligraphy, for decorating wedding trousseaus, for wrapping presents and even making them. It was when I made an unusual map for her grandfather's birthday which was greatly appreciated by her family that she really decided it was high time I did something more with my life and talents.

Rita pushed me to do an exhibition. It was all her idea and she was the catalyst. I was very unsure about that first step, but her excitement and gentle encouragement soon had me thinking about what I could do that would be different. Since embroidery was a passion and I had noticed that there was a dearth of artistic ethnic wear for men, I decided that I would embroider kurtas and dhotis for men. I also wanted to try something different and out of the ordinary, so I also embroidered dupattas for men and made coloured dhotis as well.

Rita was beside me every step of the way. She had invitation cards made in her name and sent them out. And so, in 1991, I had my very first exhibition at the Conclave Gallery. I was still very hesitant and didn't call the media, but it was a marvellous experience. My embroidery was greatly appreciated and except for the coloured dhotis, everything was sold out.

Rita was thrilled by the success of this first exhibition and pushed me to go even bigger. Realising that we would need a loan to do that, Rita secured it for me — from her mother! She went out and bought me the silks that I would need to design and embroider. She knew I treated the fabric as my canvas and she left me alone to create as she handled everything else.

This time, the media was there and the rest, as they say is history.

Twenty years is a long time and I know that there are still miles to go. And this has all been possible thanks to the person who pushed me to take my first steps — Rita, my friend, my sister-in-law, my family.

Sharbari Datta
As told to Baisali Chatterjee Dutt

The Golden Chain of Love

Munni was her name. She was my dai-ma, ayah, and everything that a mother could be. That's how I remember her. Overweight though I was, she carried me in her arms whenever my small legs got tired. She would pamper me, console me if I was hurt, both physically and emotionally; and give me nice things from the kitchen when I threw a tantrum.

She had a daughter, almost of my age. Being the only child in the family, I looked upon her as my sister. In fact, until I was three, I did not realise that she was Dai-ma's daughter. Then, I grew up and was sent away to boarding school. But I was homesick. More than anything else, I remembered Dai-ma's fresh food which she would keep ready for me when I came home from school on cold, wintry afternoons. I also remembered her warm hugs with which she would greet me. I missed her as much as I missed my parents.

Whenever I visited home, she would always have that special smile for me, special delicacies made for me and some special stories to share with me. As children often do, I too thought that this would go on forever. A year later, when I had an accident and my mother decided to move to the city where I studied, she asked Munni to accompany her. But she could not leave her husband and small kids to go away to another city ... there was a disagreement, I suppose, and she stopped working at my house.

When I heard all this, it broke my heart. I tried to reason with my parents, but to no avail. They felt that she had been disloyal and that was that. Who listens to the plaintive cries of a youngster when adult issues are at stake? My stay at boarding school ended the next year, and I was back home.

Today, I am in a dilemma. Dai-ma's daughter is getting married. I remember the sister she had been to me in my lonely childhood. Looking out at the sunlit terrace, I remember how I would chase her, but could never catch her. She was nimble-footed and would tiptoe into my room and take my pens to write with. She had a fascination for pens and that's why, every Rakshabandhan, I would gift her a pen. I remember the sparkle of excitement in her eyes as she opened the wrapping paper. I also remember the sparkle of unshed tears in her eyes when I went away to boarding school. I had promised her then that I would be back for her wedding, a childish promise, but intense and sincere.

Today, as these thoughts flit across my mind, I realise with a pang that neither would my parents go to the wedding, nor would they allow me to attend it. Should I listen to the intense longing in my heart and let the fragrance of childhood memories guide my way, or would it be truly wrong to disobey my parents? There are no words to express the pent-up feelings inside.

I make up my mind. After all, there has been no loosening

of the bond between Dai-ma and me. Another thought fills me with dismay. What can I give as a wedding gift? Why did I squander my savings on that PlayStation last month? A crazy thought crosses my mind, as I sit thinking, fingering the gold chain that I received from my grandmother on my last birthday. I can give her that. Maybe it's not such a crazy idea after all. My granny would not have minded; she was always telling me to be sensitive to others around me. The problem was that she passed away a few months back and so I could not ask her. Perhaps this was her way of helping me out of my problem. The thought lifts my spirits.

I take out an old Parker pen box, smiling at the symbolic significance of putting the chain in it, line it with cotton and wrap it with bright paper. I can imagine the sparkle in my sister's eyes as she opens the box and sees the chain nestling inside. Sure, my mother will rant and rave when she hears about the chain and Dad will probably punish me in some way or the other.

Or maybe they will understand.

As told to Monika Pant

A Two-Man Baraat

The girl and the boy were deeply in love with each other. The boy worked with a well-known MNC and the girl was well-educated and pursuing her own career. They wanted to get married. The girl's family had already accepted the relationship, but it was the boy's parents who were not ready to accept the marriage for reasons best known to them. The couple tried to convince them several times but to no avail.

One evening, over several beers, the boy told two of his colleagues his story. The colleagues, both young men brought up on a steady diet of Hindi movies, failed to understand why the two weren't going ahead with the marriage. They offered their full support. They offered to get the girl to the registry office. They also offered monetary support if the two decided to elope. Instead, the boy later surprised them with an invitation for his wedding. The two colleagues agreed to attend, thinking they would be one of many friends.

The wedding was to be held in Ludhiana. The groom turned up for a Punjabi wedding with a two-man baraat. The three friends had hired a white mare and a band. They had the mandatory car follow with the booze in its dickey. The two-man baraat danced the streets of Ludhiana with gay abandon as they celebrated their friend's wedding to the girl he loved. That night, they were more than just friends and colleagues to a buddy at work; they were his brothers, his entire family. They ate, drank and made merry and ensured that the girl's family did not feel cheated of not having been able to give their daughter a proper wedding. They performed the rituals and duties required of the boy's side with sincerity and dedication. They cheered up their 'brother' when he missed his family and ensured that he did indeed have a wedding that he would remember; and that too not for the wrong reasons.

My husband, one of those friends who danced the streets that night, said it was one of the best weddings he ever went to in his life and would do it again in a heartbeat. And why not? He was, after all, a brother in love!

Supriya Maulick Mahajan

Sent by God

It was raining cats and dogs for the third day in a row. She was in her monsoon gear, but the only thing missing was a protective helmet. It was rush hour and she was caught in a bad traffic jam. She was approaching a traffic signal to turn right on to another main road. As she readied to speed up, the signal changed to amber from green and so she slowed down instead. The truck behind her didn't.

In a fraction of second, she heard a thud and was thrown off the scooter, falling in the line of a speeding motorbike to her left. Her head struck a protruding part of the bike as well as a sharp metal part that caused a deep gash in her forehead.

The truck driver sped away. The bike rider screeched to a stop. A traffic policeman rushed towards the scene. While there were many bystanders looking at the injured lady, no one came forward to help.

Amar Singh had parked his taxi along the sidewalk. As soon as he saw the lady fall from her scooter, he immediately started towards the spot. He sank to one knee and tried to talk to her, noting with horror the deep head wound which was bleeding dangerously.

Amar found that she was somewhat conscious, but could hardly speak. He said as loudly as possible, 'Madam, you are bleeding too much. I will take you to hospital.' It was obvious that she was in terrible pain, but in between her cries, she had the presence of mind to mumble her blood group, cell-phone and office numbers. He saw that the contents from her handbag were strewn around her damaged scooter. He gathered everything together and stuffed it into her handbag. From her identity card, he saw that the lady's name was Arthi. The bike rider offered to take care of her scooter and give a statement to the traffic policeman. They exchanged their phone numbers and a couple of numbers from Arthi's cell phone.

Amar lifted Arthi, carried her to his cab and put her on the back seat. Taking his own turban, he tied it around her head wound to try and contain the bleeding. After bandaging her head as quickly yet gently as he could, he closed the rear doors and sped to the nearest hospital.

Sensing from his blood-stained attire that it could be a police case, the hospital staff refused to admit Arthi unless a police complaint was made. He pleaded with the staff and doctor on duty who eventually admitted the lady for immediate investigation and treatment. He informed the doctor on duty that her blood group was AB negative and then proceeded to make the phone calls.

He dialled her office number and the voice at the other end informed him that he was now connected to a bank. After explaining the situation, someone from the bank told him Arthi's home telephone number and with that help, he could speak to the lady's younger brother. While Arthi was in the emergency ward, her younger brother, office colleagues and relatives arrived one by one at the hospital.

A staff nurse called for someone who could do the registration/payment formalities. Sensing that the brother was too young and the others were hesitant to make an advance payment, Amar offered to pay the amount. He went ahead in fulfilling the admission formalities and put down an advance.

In the admission register under the column 'Relationship', he wrote, 'Brother'.

About an hour later, a doctor came and told them that Arthi needed a blood transfusion, and despite their best efforts, the hospital could not get supplies of blood matching her group as AB was a rare type. He wanted to know if any of her relatives could come forward to donate. No one could remember their blood group.

Amar remembered that his blood group was rare. Yes! He was AB negative. He told the doctor his blood group and said that he was ready to donate. He was taken into the lab, a drop of blood was taken and tested. It was a match. The transfusion was arranged and completed successfully. Sometime later that night, Arthi gradually became conscious. When she was told of all that had passed, she wanted to meet Amar, the Good Samaritan. Everyone started searching for him but he had gone. And he never came back.

Several years have gone by since the accident. Arthi maintains that Amar was truly sent by God to help give her a second lease of life. Her daily prayer includes a wish that God help her find Amar, wherever he may be, so that she can finally meet her brother.

As told to V. Thyagaraj

Lighting Up My Life

When Ajay walked into our house one sunny afternoon, booming a loud, 'Mummy, Mummy', at the doorstep, I did not realise that knowing him would enrich my life so deeply. His mother walked in sheepishly, holding his hand, and made the introductions. 'Jijiya,' he said respectfully, in his loud voice, which reminded me of drums beating, as he bent down and touched my feet. I drew back at that gesture, for Ajay, thick black glasses firmly in place, looked at least five years older than me.

Realising that he had come looking for a reader, I shrugged resignedly. My mother, a reader in Daulat Ram College University and erstwhile In-charge of the National Service Scheme, was a born social worker. Ajay was studying Law while I was doing my Master's in Political Science. As I opened the large volume he had been carrying, and began reading out to him, I found his attention beginning to waver. It would be difficult, I decided, to read out to him, or to teach him anything. I soon realised that he may not be a model student, but he was a great teacher.

He taught me to take adversity with equanimity. I learnt that he had lost his eyesight at the age of two when his mother had put hot ash on his eyelids in order to cure an eye ailment. I was stunned at the revelation, but he only smiled and said, 'As a result I am the most educated person in my family. I am a graduate, now doing LLB, while my brothers have not studied beyond matriculation!'

One Sunday when he walked into our drawing room he requested if he could watch the serial, *Ramayana*. 'But you can't see,' the words were out of my mouth before I realised it. 'So what?' he responded, 'I can hear the dialogues and imagine the scenes ... isn't that what we do when we hear the cricket commentary on the radio?' I thought about it for a minute and knew that he was right.

He taught me how to take life sportingly and make a game out of adversity. On my twenty-first birthday, when I cut the cake and arranged a plate of food for him and handed it over, I began to list it out for him, 'Here is a piece of cake...' But before I could go any further, he commanded, 'Don't tell me, let me guess.

'A sandwich,' he said, running his hand over it, 'a samosa, a rasogulla, a slice of cake, a pakora...' and then, a moment later he conceded defeat. 'Khaman dhokla,' I said triumphantly and suddenly his guessing game of, 'What's on my plate', seemed more interesting than any regular party game.

His disability became his strength when he had to return to his hostel late at night. 'It's late,' I would say, 'and your hostel is far away, shall I ask someone to drop you home?' 'Night time may scare you,' he would retort, 'but for me there is no difference between day and night.'

I only realised his vulnerability when his marriage negotiations were on and he asked me to accompany him for his shopping trips. 'I can't see Jijiya,' he confided, 'and I do not want to be taken advantage of and cheated. What if I'm given a suit length of an undesirable colour?' Even though for him the entire world was dark, he knew that others could see, and he cared about their opinion.

On my wedding day, he gifted me half a dozen apple-shaped candles which he had made himself. He knew that his world was dark, but he wanted my world to be bright.

Ajay is now married to a visually-challenged woman who is a teacher in a school in Mumbai. They have two children, a girl and a boy, both with normal eyesight. Ajay works as a receptionist in the Delhi Development Authority and it was he who took me by my hand, from door to door, to help me get the registered sale deed and documentation done for my DDA flat. He was surprised and a little hurt when the Officer-in-Charge refused to let him sign as witness on the document fearing that his signatures would go awry.

Every year, one day before Rakshabandhan, I get a call from him and hear his booming voice, 'Jijiya are you home? It is Rakshabandhan tomorrow and I want to come and meet you.' Whenever I am in Delhi and he does come, I keep the rakhi and sweets ready, and I make puri chole, dahi bara, paneer matar and all his other favourites. And then when he sits down to eat, we play the guessing game all over again.

Vandana Jena

7
GOLDEN TIMES

To the outside world we all grow old. But not to brothers and sisters. We know each other as we always were. We know each other's hearts. We share private family jokes. We remember family feuds and secrets, family griefs and joys. We live outside the touch of time.

–Clara Ortega

My 'Cuty' Younger Brother

As I sat cleaning out an old folder, I found two birthday cards. A smile spread on my face as old memories came rushing back.

The envelopes were covered with the usual 'Happy B'day!' and 'Open With A Smile On Your Face!' in the calligraphy that my brother always used when writing his wishes for me. On one card was a big heart drawn in red ink, on the other he had written 'Happy B'day Dida!' and drawn a cake and a long set of teeth which he associated with my big smile.

Inside the first card, I found a long letter written in his childish handwriting. A small brown bucket filled with little red hearts spilling over the sides was drawn on the left side of the card, symbolising, I knew, his unending love for me. He had signed off as, 'From Dholu, cuty Akshun'.

Those birthday cards had been given to me by my brother when I was in college and he was still in school. He is six years younger than me, but in spite of this age difference, we were always very close. He possessed a rare maturity and sense of understanding that made me tell him everything that was going on in my life.

My friends never understood this and in fact they were aghast! 'How can you tell your brother these things? Brothers at his age are not supposed to be trusted. They tell our parents all our secrets.' At this I would smile and say, 'Not my brother. He's my friend.' When our gang of four girls used to meet at my place, my brother would always let us have our space, unlike my friends' brothers who used to sneak in and eavesdrop. My brother's attitude always surprised them.

Those cards brought back memories of the day that bound me and my brother deeply. It was a day when my brother had silently communicated his affection for me to the deepest threads of my whole being, which in turn marked the beginning of a bond nurtured through weekly phone calls, occasional letters and week-long vacations twice a year. It was the day when I was leaving home for college.

My parents were coming with me to help me settle in. Unfortunately, my brother couldn't accompany us because his school was in session. As I got things ready for life in a hostel, he stood by, silently observing all the preparations. He was sad because his best friend and pillar of strength was going away. I was sad too, but at the same time, very excited at the prospect of starting a new life. The loss and sadness of separation were not yet completely in sync.

As the time for our departure arrived, I hugged my grandparents and my brother, sat in the car and rolled the window down for a final goodbye. My brother immediately ran towards the car and stood outside my window. He looked at me with tears in his eyes, wanting to say, 'Didi, please don't go'. The car started and tears were running down his cheeks, as he silently pleaded with me to come back, knowing that I couldn't, but hoping with all his heart that I just might change my mind. But that never happened and we kept on looking at each other, crying silently, till the car took a turn around the corner and we were out of each other's sight.

College brought new experiences every day; experiences that I wanted to share with him but could not. There were so many moments when I missed my brother a lot, moments when I needed some advice, moments when I needed a friend, moments which I wanted to laugh with him. I had many friends in the college hostel, but I sorely missed his companionship. That's why my vacation time was precious; in those few, measured days we would fill the gap created by my five-month absence, visiting our favourite haunts, hanging out and chatting away, late into the night.

Things change as we grow up and relationships become distant, siblings move apart and start their own lives which may not necessarily include their brother or sister. But not so for my brother and me! Today, even after I have started a new life with my husband, my brother and I are as close as ever. We still share things, understand each other's problems and are always a part of each other's happiness.

He is and always will be, my 'Dholu, Cuty Akshun'.

Akanksha Agarwal Puprediwar

No Matter What

'What are these?' asked the little girl with pigtails, her round eyes growing rounder as I took out a colourful mesh of entangled threads from a crushed newspaper packet. I separated each thread from the other and placed them neatly on the bed. 'Didi, tell me na!' she said, while trying to pick out the one that caught her eye. I tapped her hand lightly, asking her not to touch. But that was torture for her. The threads had gold tassels and were bright in colour with discs of sequined gold foil in the middle of each thread. Some even had huge flowers made of foil. For my five-year-old sister, Atu, they were manna from heaven.

'They are rakhis,' I finally said after seeing that she was on the verge of crying, frustrated by my all-knowing smile.

'Why can't I touch them?'

'Because they are delicate.'

'I want one…'

'You can't have them. They are for Ma.'

'Why?'

'Tomorrow is Rakhi and she will tie them on all her brothers.'

'She has only one brother and that is Mama.'

'But she has cousins too, na?'

'Why will she tie the rakhis on them?'

'Don't you know the story of Rakhi?'

'No, please tell me, Didi...'

At thirteen, I loved the way Atu looked up to me, as if I was someone who knew it all, making me feel all grown-up. So, that day, as she pleaded with me to tell her the story, I picked her up and made her sit on my lap. Her eyes glittered with eagerness as she took in my words. I told her the story of Lord Yama and his sister Yamuna.

'Yamuna tied a rakhi on Yama's wrist on the day of the full moon in the month of Sravan, the Bengali month of rain, and blessed him with protection and everlasting life. Ever since then, all over the world, sisters tie beautiful rakhis on their brothers' wrists on that holy day in the hope of giving their brothers long life, good health and wealth. Understand?' I asked her. She nodded her head before asking, 'What happens to the sisters?' She wouldn't have understood if I'd told her that in ancient patriarchal India, the benefits were mostly reaped by men. I tried to satisfy her with a more contemporary reply. 'The brothers give gifts to the sisters. Like last year Mama gave Ma that beautiful blue sari that she wore for your birthday party,' I said. She nodded, as if trying to find logic in the entire thing. 'If rakhis are for brothers only, I am no one's brother. Won't anyone give me long life, good health and wealth?' asked my baby sister, her face carrying a rather poignant expression. Her little brain seemed troubled.

Now, usually when she seemed bewildered by something, I would take advantage of the situation and tease her endlessly. Like when I wanted her undying loyalty and allegiance to me, I had told her once that though my parents loved her, she was actually a child who had been found in the dumpster and who had been saved from being eaten by stray dogs because of me, because I had so badly wanted a sister. So my parents had taken pity on her and had brought her home. Thus, if she didn't listen to me, I would throw her back in the dumpster and she would be eaten by dogs. For about an entire month she believed it and did whatever I asked her to do, till one day she told our parents about my story. Of course they had scolded me for my antics then, but now, years later we all laugh about it.

But that day, sitting on my lap, with a perplexed and anxious look in her eyes, she seemed like a cherub whom I couldn't possibly hurt, even for the sake of a good laugh. 'I will protect you all my life, no matter what...' I said out loud for the first time in five years, though it had actually been the first thought that had come to my mind when I had seen her in the nursing home, extending her miniscule hands out of the pink blanket she was wrapped in.

I squeezed her cheeks and gave her a loud, sloppy kiss before starting to tickle her. She burst into shrieks of squeals and laughter. The situation forgotten, she squirmed on my lap like a tadpole. 'I am the tickling monster, I shall tickle the life out of you,' I screamed, loosening my grip on her purposely so that she could squirm off my lap and run, expecting me to chase her. After she left the room I quickly removed the rakhis from her sight before running after her. When I managed to catch her, I lifted her and threw her up in the air. She didn't bat an eyelid and kept on laughing; she trusted me and knew her

Didi would catch her. Amidst all the tickling and giggling and hullabaloo, she forgot all about her questions and troubles.

Atu is seventeen now and we still fight at times. I still like to tease her. I still like to sit her down on my lap. I still treat her like a baby. She keeps on telling me, 'Please take me seriously, Didi. I have grown up! Let me make my own mistakes!' But I still tell her, 'I will protect you, no matter what.' However, over the years I have added some more lines to it. I also say, 'My hands shall always be there for you to grab hold of when you need them. I respect you and I won't grab your hand, till you are drowning. So you can safely make your own mistakes.' She nods her head and says with a smile, 'Didi, you are hopeless!' That's the cue for me to start tickling her. She still breaks into squeals of that delightful laughter that I so love to hear.

Joie Bose Chatterjee

My Little Brother

I remember the joy
of being told
that I was going to have a baby brother

My ten-year-old heart jumped in glee
Ecstasy danced merrily
I could tie rakhi to someone now!

I held him in my arms
And watched him fluttering his eyelids
Peeping at a brave new world
When suddenly he held my index finger
And caught it with a quiver

I took him in my lap
And putting his little face
On my shoulder
Patted him rhythmically...

He smiled mystically
As if his whole world
Rested upon me at that moment...

My little baby brother
Has grown up
So handsome and tall now
He no longer needs my lap for his comfort
But seeing him expand his horizons
With every new day
I smile
And put the imaginary little baby
On my shoulders once again....

Neelam Chandra

Too Much Love

I was barely two, when my cousin was born. I loved the little soul; loved to touch him, to feel his tender skin and kiss his rosy pink cheeks. I yearned to pick him up and cradle him, just like the adults did. But trusting the small little arms of a two-year-old is not easy! I was allowed to play with him only when he was in the cradle or on the bed.

Days passed and I started yearning for a sibling of my very own, on whom I could lavish my affections. I prayed for a little brother, whom I could pamper, kiss, hug and play with … a little one whom I possessed, totally.

Two years later, those innocent dreams came true. I had a baby brother, all my own. Nobody could ask me not to touch him, or not to play with him ... he was mine, completely mine. I would hug him, kiss him, take him in my arms, sing to him and pamper him in every way known to me. Soon, my mother could trust me to look out for my little angel. She would ask me to keep an eye on him whenever she hopped into the kitchen. She was always back within a few minutes, but I revelled in the trust she placed in me.

And then, one day, while Mom was in the kitchen and we were busy playing, something happened and my brother started crying. Not wanting to call my mother unnecessarily, I took it upon myself to calm him down. I sang to him, danced, patted him and did everything else that I could think of, but nothing could stop him from crying. Finally, I took a small stone and placed it in his mouth thinking that it would stop him from crying ... and it did! I was so happy! But within seconds my happiness turned to horror when he started throwing up. This time I panicked. I rushed to my mother and told her that the baby was vomiting. She ran back to the room and found the stone. When she asked, I told her that I'd used it to make the baby stop crying. Of course she was taken aback, but she didn't get angry; I was barely five years old after all! She just took me in her arms and explained what could have happened and what I should do if ever the baby cried again and she was not in the room.

She didn't need to tell me twice! I was very careful with my little brother every moment after that. We grew up to be twin souls, despite the age difference. Not just my parents, but over the years my little brother could trust and depend on me for anything. Whether it was another boy in the class troubling him, or a teacher in the school getting angry at him, he would trust only me with his feelings. Family members still laugh at memories of incidents when my little baby brother would argue, nay, fight with anyone, even his teachers in school, regarding anything that I taught him. He would hold my arguments above all else, and try to convince the others that even though they may not be completely wrong, his big sister was totally right! One of his teachers even complained to my parents that it was very difficult to convince my brother about most things as he always had these pre-fixed theories and notions thanks to me!

And even when it came to family or friends, no one, absolutely no one, could hurt his feelings or give him even the slightest bit of heartache, because he had a big sister who knew how to protect him and keep him safe from the evil eyes of the world.

After all, that's what big sisters are for, right?

Neha Sinha

The Musketeers

I was just a pesky four-year old. Trying desperately to tag along with my sisters wherever they went. They were eight and nine — a huge gap at that age. I tried to sneak into their room while they gossiped and giggled, but was always discovered and banished. I sat on the table when they studied, swinging my legs, upsetting ink on precious homework till wails of, *'Maaaa...'* sent me scuttling off to my refuge — the broad window ledge looking on to the backyard. There I learnt a lot about the secret lives of cats and mice and crows. Or I lay on the carpet building fantastic stories around my large collection of Binaca charms.

Cuffe Parade in Mumbai in the Fifties was a magical place. We lived on the ground floor of an old house. All the houses were like ours, stately two- or three-storey buildings with large flats and lots of greenery. Every afternoon, when my father was away at work, Ma was resting and the ayah had gone off to her room, the three of us would tiptoe out of the back door. We'd sneak up to the third floor and slide all the way down the beautifully polished old teak banisters.

At that age I had no idea I actually suffered from vertigo! Or we would go to the beach. There were but a few cars that trundled down the road that lay between our house and the sea, so we nipped across with impunity. We clambered down jagged rocks, surefooted as mountain goats, and played on the narrow beach which was revealed at low tide. We built sand castles or caught hapless tiny fish in the rock pools and brought them lovingly home to their death in a freshwater bathtub. This was our kingdom. Or we were joined by our friends and played cops and robbers, chasing each other up and down Cuffe Parade. I say we, but I was generally made to hide behind the spider lilies in our compound and no-one ever found me because they were far away. I was too little to keep up. But I did have my uses as we had to get back in the house before Ma woke up. I was hoisted up and easily slid though the gap in the window below the mesh. I then crept up to the back door and unlocked it for my sisters.

Not that my sisters were always friends. I often watched solemnly from the doorway as they fought tooth and nail — in absolute silence. My mother, fed up with their spats and yowling, had said she would wallop them both if she heard so much as a squeak from either of them! And so we carried on, sometimes friends, sometimes sworn enemies, till She arrived.

We came home from school one day as usual, with scuffed shoes, mud-stained uniforms and hair standing on end to find Her sitting on an extra bed that had been put into my sisters' room. She wore tight black jeans and a red shirt. Her thick plait just went on and on, all the way down below her knees. Her shiny red nails matched her shiny red stiletto heels and her shiny red lipstick. We skidded to a halt. She just looked down her nose at us and said not a word. Discarding school bags and kicking off shoes we went in search of Ma. 'What? Who?' 'Shhh…' said Ma, 'That's Her, my cousin's daughter.' Ma had told us about her. Her father was some fat cat in the movie industry in Kolkata. She was going to be in Bombay for about a month, and staying with us. But we had not expected this apparition.

She did nothing to endear herself to us. She never so much as smiled at us or made any attempts at conversation. Her numerous suitcases — not to mention the red vanity bag — had encroached into our 'stage' where we used to perform gymnastics on the clothes horse or enact highly melodramatic plays that my sisters had written, and for which all our friends were hauled in either to perform or to watch. She turned up her nose at Ma's cooking. While we used to do it ourselves quite often, we flew to Ma's defence at this attack from an outsider. The large black clunky telephone was a very valuable thing in those days, specially for my sisters and their friends, and we did not like the fact that she monopolised it all day. We hid behind the door and shamelessly eavesdropped as she whispered and simpered with a string of Bollywood heroes. And then she started bossing us around. Do this; do that; fetch this; take this away…. We were too afraid of Ma's wrath to not do her bidding. But it finally got to us.

She had brought with her about twenty pairs of shoes in every colour and design. They were stacked up against the wall in all their beauty. One afternoon a swanky silver Merc came to the house and took her away for a while. Quick as a flash the three of us fell upon the shoes. My sisters handed them to me and I crawled on my little belly under the big double bed and shoved them right to the back. Then we high-tailed it to play Kings with the neighbourhood boys. We were not there when She got back, but when we returned we had to face Ma who looked like thunder and ordered us to pull out all the shoes from where we had hidden them.

The next evening my parents had to go out and we were left alone with Her. Outside the house we had a very old and large banyan tree. As dusk descended my sister started the attack by telling Her that we had a resident ghost in the tree. My sisters then decided to swap ghost stories while, much to their delight, She grew paler and paler. The windows in the house had wooden shutters. That night after the lights had been switched off and all three were in bed, a wind picked up over the sea and blew straight into my sisters' room. The loose shutter went click-clickety-click. She was by now cowering under the sheets. 'Wh – what's that noise?' She asked. 'Oh that,' said my wicked sister gleefully, 'that's the ghost. He's trying to come in.'

When we came home from school the next day the shoes were gone. All the multi-coloured sticks and tubes and jars and bottles had vanished from the dressing table. Ma looked perplexed. 'I don't know what happened. She was on the phone a long while this morning. I think She was crying. Then She packed all her belongings and a car arrived and She just said goodbye and left. No explanations.'

We tried to look suitably wide-eyed and innocent before we ran off to my sisters' room to celebrate our victory. And for once I was one of the gang.

Rajyashree Dutt

Three to Tango

Being the baby of the family was no fun at all. My sister (older than me by five years) and my brother (older by three) always got all the new toys, books and clothes. I was offered the hand-me-downs. If that wasn't bad enough, there were always the teachers at school who raved about my brother and sister and complained about how different I was from them.

In short, there were many days when I wished I was a single kid. However, all the seniors in school made a big deal of me, as I was their classmate's kid brother. I did not realise it at that time, but when a senior, especially a pretty girl, comes and talks to you in front of all the other guys in your class and puts her hand on your shoulder or pulls your cheek, you do go up a bit in your friends' esteem and get treated a bit differently. Okay, you're treated like a big stud!

Looking back now, I can say that we were good kids, but there were days when we fought and would be ready to kill each other. My mother, who had the patience of a saint, would have been willing to donate the three of us to charity at such times. I think she would even have been willing to pay money to the gullible person who was willing to take us.

Typically, it was my sister and I who fought. My brother would always support my sister. But older sisters are always the kind-hearted ones. She would realise that the fight was too one-sided, so she would switch to my side! We would then gang up against my brother! When it came to an outsider however, we stuck together even firmer than the new product from Dr Fixit. It was as if someone was challenging the combined force of three big devils and there was no way one could let that pass. We had to ensure that the person rued the day he took on our combined might. When someone picked a fight with me, my sister and brother picked up cudgels on my behalf; those were the times I enjoyed being the youngest in the family.

I remember that day in school so clearly. The boys from the other section had this game wherein they would cover the head of a passing child with a cloth, and then one of the boys would pin your arms together and the rest would rain blows on your head. Everyone would disappear after that and one didn't know who or what had hit you. Unfortunately I was one of the few who went through that experience. I found myself pinned down, head covered and beaten up before you could say Jack Robinson. When you are in class seven, such things affect you quite a bit. Not only did my head hurt, my ego got battered that day. I quietly went back to class, and in spite of not wanting to, shed a few tears. Luckily it was towards the end of the day so I could escape home. Once I reached home, I told my mother what had happened and burst into tears again. My parents wanted to come to the school the next day but I

said a firm no since it would seem like I was a cry baby. Also, I was scared I would get picked on more if they did come to school and complain. Boys at that age are like that; you needed to appear manly to your peers.

My sister and brother said they would handle this and told me I was not to go to school. Delighted at the unexpected turn of events, I sat at home and watched TV and ate some great home-cooked food. My sister, who was in class twelve then, gathered all her classmates and told them that I'd been mercilessly beaten up, which kind of instilled the motherly and sisterly instincts in all the girls of her class. The boys, of course, wanting to curry favours with the girls, were not willing to be left behind and all of them decided to take the matter in their hands. For one full period, all the boys who'd beaten me were called out by the senior batches, shouted at by all of them and then made to kneel in the playground.

After that, my brother's class came and gave them a similar treatment. To cap it all, when the teachers got to know about it, they too did their bit based on Chinese whispers that I was near-mortally wounded with potential head injuries, and if my brain got damaged then the whole class may get rusticated from the school and potentially picked up by the police too.

After the overdose at school the previous day, it would have seemed a bit silly if I landed up fit as a fiddle the next day, so as a bonus I got to stay at home for a few more days. When I finally landed up in school, I was treated with kid gloves, people would come and ask me how I was feeling and hoped I would get better soon. With a brave, straight face I told everyone that things were a little better and that I was somehow on the road to recovery. The teachers too

smiled and made a fuss over me, a couple of the girls in my
class copied the notes that I had missed and I was offered
bites from everyone's tiffin; so all in all it was a complete
win for me. That was also the day I realised that having
brothers and sisters was not all that bad — not that I was
foolish enough to tell my siblings that.

Satish Shenoy

The Brotherly Bond

I've always wondered what life without a sibling would be. Incomplete, probably. Even my earliest memories include my younger brother, because by the time I figured out the world and my surroundings, he had already arrived. I wouldn't go so far as to say I welcomed his entry into my life; I've always been a bit of a limelight hogger. But I do know that I accepted it as a fait accompli. An oft-repeated anecdote chez nous, is of me holding forth on something or the other at the age of fourteen months; my parents have it on record (literally) so that I cannot deny it. At this point baby Tambi began to cry and I am heard loudly proclaiming: 'Shut up Tambi, no one calling.' So no, I can't say I was madly in love with the latest addition to the family. He was a necessary evil. A part of the family, and I made my peace with him.

The problem, however, is that to know Tambi, is to love Tambi. I say this not as a doting elder sister, but as an impartial observer. I was the life of the household, noisy, mischievous and full of ideas that were bound to rock the foundations. But little Tambi slowly stole every single heart, including mine, and thirty years later, while I might still be the life of the house, he is undoubtedly the soul of our home. Honest on principle, generous to a fault and always willing to see your point of view, he's grown into a man I am proud to call my brother.

And this loyalty, this consideration, is instinctive. Another gem dug up from the family annals is about the time I fell into the fish pond in the garden. The family was busy, we'd been warned to stay away and were left to play. A splash and much noise alerted the family to the disaster. Out they came running and fished me out none too gently, all the while 'telling-me-so'. The only one concerned about my hurt feelings was the two-year-old Tambi. 'I kick the fishies,' he vowed. 'The naughty fishies, they bited Sriti.' And so it was that his chivalrous act ended in another noisy splash even while I was still being dried off and read the riot act.

I wish I could say we were partners in crime. But we weren't. I was the criminal while he was merely my sidekick. A sweet little sidekick who kept telling me that Mama would be very angry if she found out we were clambering up the larder shelves at midnight to help ourselves to some biscuits. The commonsensical sidekick who reminded me of Mama's wrath while letting ourselves out of our hotel room in a strange city to go for a midnight stroll. A mother today, I feel my heart skip a beat at the thought of two little children wandering strange roads at midnight just for the thrill of it.

We're both in our thirties now and it seems like only yesterday that we got into street fights side by side. Either with the street urchins who threw stones at the mango trees in our gardens or with any fool who made the mistake of eve-teasing me when I was out with him. It took them only ten minutes to figure out that the wiry young boy hadn't got his blue belt merely for showing up at taekwondo classes. He was good and he was that rare fighter — he used his brains when he was outnumbered. Men I dated soon learnt that it was not my father they had to live up to, but my baby brother. It takes a strong man to deal with that.

I never did mean this to be a paean to the little boy who made my childhood the beautiful dream it was or the man who I still call up at midnight with my troubles and woes. I really hoped it would be a bunch of fun anecdotes. But it only took two minutes of finger tapping to realise that there is no way I can separate the fun we've had from the love we shared and continue to share.

He is soon to be a father and I can't imagine a luckier child, being born to a father who is all that is gentle, loving, patient and wise. Sharing blood is a strange thing. It ties you up in ways you never imagined. I'd never thought I could love a child as much as I love my own children. And yet as I anticipate the little one's arrival I feel a lump in my throat similar to the one I felt when my own arrived. This little baby, my beloved baby brother's little baby, may not be coming from my tummy. But he sure is coming from my heart.

Smriti Lamech

8

SAYING
GOODBYE

Perhaps they are not the stars, but rather openings in Heaven where the love of our lost ones pours through and shines down upon us to let us know they are happy.

–Author Unknown

Oh Brother, My Brother

Brother
Is what we always called you
The relationship became your name
For me, eleven years your junior,
And our sister, two years my senior.
Two bratty little sisters
For whom you were god,
a teasable, wheedlable, jump-uponable god
who fascinated us wholly and entirely.
Your teenage sketch book was, for us,
Full of masterpieces.

Grabbing hold of one small hand and one small foot
And whirling me round and round
An 'airplane' ride that both thrilled and terrified me!
Being thrown over your shoulder
In a 'fireman's lift' was great fun, too….

We'd threaten to tell on you when our parents were out

and you'd be playing tennis against the sitting room wall
(Before they put up the new wall paper),
testing our little powers against your might,
probably to no avail!

But then
You went away
Distance added to the myths surrounding you,
The recipient of the first letters I ever wrote
On Noddy writing paper given to me on my sixth birthday.

And I grew up, in a country far away
From you, the blue aerogrammes eagerly awaited by us all.
And Mummy's threats to complain about me to you
When I'd been wicked really worked
I promise I'll be good, Mummy —
Please don't tell Brother.

Did you know you were god for me, back then?
We actually had so little time together …
But we knew you well, Sis and I.
When all our cousins were 'seeing' girls with a view to
matrimony
And having arranged marriages,
We knew that Brother wouldn't do anything so mundane
Or boring, or so 'not him'.

And he came, before his wedding, for parental consent
And blessings, and he practised tying a saree

(imagine him, bearded and hairy!)
so that he could show Carole Bhabhi how it was done!

Pulling trousers over his pyjamas on cold Delhi winter mornings,
down to the paan shop for an early morning fag,
letting me light his cigarettes, just for the thrill of it!
Our pockets full of unshelled, roasted peanuts on long
after-dinner walks round the Met Office....
And Mummy struggling to say meteorological!
(And Bhabhi loving the sohan halwa from the Karachi wala halwai)
And each visit with the boys,
first chubby little Raoul, and then Jared too, a while later....
and Jared's parrot green and blue sweater with a hood,
which my sons have worn, and the Fisher Price dump truck,
and cash register
and toy record player, which they've played with and
handed down yet again.

Wearing Brother's charcoal grey sweater to college,
and wearing it for years (and letting my husband wear it too)
Till it finally got lost on a flight.

The memories don't end....
Till now I could manage several days at a time
Without thinking of you at all,
Secure in the knowledge that you were living your life

In your part of the world, and I in mine
And now, the knowledge of your absence is a gnawing pain
Unearthing memories of long ago....

Be at peace, Brother, wherever you are...
We will learn to live without you
We will remember you with joy,
Thankful for the richness of your life,
 praying for the peace of your soul.

Dipali Taneja

Unworshipped Idols

The dawn breaks to an auspicious day in every Bengali household across the township. As the conch shells blow in the melody of spring and the flowers make the air giddy, somewhere Sumi's heart too stirs.

As they do every year, they've made their own arrangements for the puja by the courtyard, their mother's crisply washed saree serving as the colourful backdrop against which a small, smiling idol of the Saraswati sits.

Two days back, Sumi and her brother Soham had chatted till late into the night, making plans for this day. It was only after their father threatened not to allow the puja to take place at all unless they went to sleep did they leave each other's side and go to bed.

Sumi was still sleeping when she heard her mother whimper in a corner of the courtyard. She looked out and saw her father sitting with his head bowed. She looked around for her ally, her best friend and confidant, her brother, but he was nowhere to be seen. She mentally cursed him for leaving her behind and going to the riverside — his usual holiday haunt — with his friends.

At seven, Sumi thought of her brother, older by five years,

as the perfect hero. For her, Soham was more an idol than a big brother. He was the one who would pamper her silly, like a father-figure, cover up for all her mistakes, and yet at times play childish pranks to irritate her. She never thought it possible that there could be a world that he wasn't a part of.

Yet where was he today, when the entire household looked gloomy and needed his sunshine smile to brighten things up on such an auspicious day?

Sumi had last seen Soham the previous evening, when he had returned from the market, his arms laden with the idol and the fruits which now lay unattended. He had hugged her and rushed out with his friends, not allowing Sumi to follow despite her endless pleas to accompany him. It was as if he knew that she wasn't to go where he was going. But where did he go, wondered Sumi. Why wasn't he home when the puja was about to start?

No one answered her questions the entire day. Her father, who would normally have grown tired of her incessant chatter and tell her to hush, didn't once look up from the floor. Her mother's moans muffled her words and the people who gathered around her house wouldn't tell her anything.

Sumi cursed Soham again as she picked up a few flowers to make a garland. Had he been around, she would have fought with him over who was doing more work, just to show off that she was the more efficient one; but then what was the fun of taking credit when he wasn't there to fight with her?

Soham had never been a heavy sleeper and Sumi loved to tickle him awake. But today he continued to sleep so peacefully while the world around him wailed. Sumi couldn't understand it. She was scared to go near him, with his head and face bandaged, he looked like an alien.

They carried him away, still sleeping. Sumi didn't know why they wouldn't wake him up and ask him to walk with them. After all, being carried around was for babies — wasn't this what Soham always used to say to her when she asked him to pick her up during their silly games?

Sumi woke at the crack of the dawn the next day and thought that it had all been a bad dream. She ran to her brother's room, but Soham's bed lay empty and there beside it sat her stone-faced mother. The Saraswati idol still sat there unattended; Sumi noticed that the glow on her face was replaced by a strange gloom. She screamed for Soham to return and in her screams she promised never again to fight with him, never to blame him for anything, never ever to indulge in what she loved doing the most — seeing him get into trouble. But the door didn't open and Soham did not rush in.

Between making promises and pacts in her head, the days and months crept by, and many a Saraswati puja passed, but time stood still for Sumi who was now a lady all set to celebrate her first Saraswati puja at her in-laws' place. In reality, her heart still struggled to come to terms with that day when she had left the deity un-worshipped years ago.

As dawn broke, Sumi stepped into the courtyard to pluck fresh flowers. Subconsciously her eyes went towards the door and her heart skipped a beat as she felt Soham standing there with a goofy smile and a small idol in his arms.

A gush of spring air brought her back to reality.

Sometimes time erases every memory one has. Yet, sometimes a particular flashback, no matter how old, makes you sweat in the chill of February.

Dipika Chakraborty

Christmas Grieving

It was *not* jealousy.

I simply felt inadequate and completely overshadowed when she was around.

Averil was all that I was not: brilliant in studies, possessor of a vibrant personality that made a room come alive the minute she entered it, passionate in her love for animals, a loyal friend, and *the* child from among the seven they'd borne that made my parents feel the most proud. She and I were not 'sticky close' but we had a happy friendship. I looked up to her and delighted in the fact that all her well-researched notes and answer papers became mine after she finished with each class. Because of that, I too would get good grades

She was my sister and she was sixteen and I fifteen when she died.

On the eve of Christmas day.

An incomprehensible fact for all who lived in the small town called Ajmer we inhabited. There were so many medicos in the family. My father was with May & Baker, a pharmaceutical company of great repute. My mother was a medical doctor, who'd worked for two decades with French missionary nuns before she set up her own practice and hospital. My eldest sister Charmion was a doctor too.

They had saved the lives of many. How could they have just stood around helplessly while my sister slipped away? To be fair to them, she was not under their treatment ... doctors do not treat their own kin. For over a month, specialists had been coming in from all over the place to investigate and treat Averil. Then on 20 December, they said they wanted to move her to the hospital for essential investigation and tests. By then, Averil was so weak and listless that she did not look at anyone or respond to anything. I did not want her to be taken to the hospital. I have always hated hospitals and would refuse to enter them. Everyone knew that. The doctor treating her said, 'You need not come to the hospital; she will be home in two or three days.'

It was important for me to know that because then, while all the other family members took turns to keep vigil by her bedside, I went ahead with the task of decorating the house for Christmas day. It was a large house and I made it look extra gay and special to cheer Averil up when she returned from the hospital.

Around 10 that night my eldest brother Allan landed up and asked me to immediately accompany him to the hospital.

The private room in Jawaharlal Nehru Hospital was crowded with specialists and interns. My family stood desolately in a corner of the room, the expressions frighteningly forlorn. Averil was unconscious and battling for her life. She sounded as if she was in agony, gasping for breath, but we know from people who have regained consciousness that this is not painful or distressing. It's just the respiratory centre in the brain starting to close down, so breathing becomes uneven and eventually stops.

One minute, Averil was breathing, and the room was filled with the noise of those rasping sounds. The next moment, she exhaled the last lot of air from her lungs. And then, silence. No movement in the chest.

The Big Chill.

The infinite dark.

The absolute silence of death.

Few things we encounter impact us as does the paralysing shock of 'breath-stop'. A specialist beat her heart fast and hard as he performed the cardiopulmonary resuscitation. No use. Averil had passed on.

On Christmas Eve. 2.20 a.m.

Amazing how, within minutes, she stopped having a name and began to be referred to as 'the body'. 'The body needs to be taken to the nuns (of the hospital where my mother worked) to be cleaned and dressed before it can be taken home,' someone said.

Home? I suddenly remembered the flourish of gay decorations I had put up all over the place. I ran as fast as my fat legs would allow me to, and was just about tearing down the last one when 'the body' came home. What terrible pain, what a hole in the heart, would we ever recover? Usually, the churches allow 'the body' to lay in state at home for one last day, so families can get some sort of closure.

That was not possible in these circumstances. The next day was Christmas day. 'We cannot have a funeral on Christmas day,' said the parish priest. So within a few hours, the body was transferred to the semi-permanent resting place in a graveyard on the outskirts of the town; the ghoulish peal of 'dead bells' to cause further torment.

It was a sound that haunted me for the next decade of my life, long after I had left the town and its mournful memories and got a nest of my own under the sun that shines bright and maddeningly cheerful all over mischievous Mumbai. Each year would speed by, victory piling after victory, until the calendar turned to page December. The raw pain intensified and magnified every time Christmas Eve pushed itself into local visibility. It got so bad that I went to counsellor after counsellor, begging to be liberated from the prison of merciless memory, the agonised breathing, decorations being stripped, the sound of the dead bells.

One counsellor suggested I have a couple of 'shots' of brandy to get through the night. Shots? I went home, put the bottle to my mouth and consumed it all, welcoming the unconsciousness of alcoholic stupor.

Only to wake up after a few hours with a sick soul; and the bells continued to haunt and taunt.

Trapped forever?

Two things happened to change it. I got married and had children of my own, and could not quite push Christmas or Christmas Eve away, for their sakes.

More important was the very gift of Christmas. A powerful, spiritual encounter twenty-two years after Averil died revived my faith and renewed my relationship with God. Every time those hurtful moments tried to beckon, I would hear the Lord say firmly, *'Don't go there.'* And in humble obedience, I did not.

Instead I would spend that time remembering what a

talented and popular person my sister had been: she once played a double role to perfection in the school annual play; a few weeks before she took ill, Averil had stunned her college audience with a dramatic performance in a theatrical endeavour. She had loved me, watched out for me, and always been there to encourage me. I had been blessed to have her in my life — no matter how short our time together was. Thank you, Lord, for a sister like her!

The first time I offered God my prayer of thanks, a coin fell in place and a principle took shape. There's one and only one thing that can dull the piercing pain of the loss of a sibling.

The power of heartfelt 'thanksgiving'.

Ingrid Albuquerque-Solomon

Once a Brother Had a Sister

'I once had a sister; she is no more,' is how the forlorn brother put it.

I happened to overhear the tail end of the conversation between my eight-year-old son and my seven-year-old cousin. They had started off by laughing at my daughter's antics and soon veered off innocently, as children do, into heartbreak territory. Hearing him, my heart bled just a little bit more — both for the brother and his sister no longer with us.

The last time my cousin ever saw his sister was on a warm October morning. The rest of the world celebrated that day as Halloween but in Chennai, it was just a regular Friday. She was feeling poorly, and with her history of having fits when weak after a bout of fever, her parents were getting ready to take her to the hospital to get her checked by her doctor, and stay overnight for observations, if necessary. As this had happened before, even the little one wasn't particularly worried at the thought of spending time at the hospital.

'I'll get my medicines and will be back by the time you get home from school. Then we can play together,' were her final words to her adored big brother, who nodded and sped off to school.

By the time he came home, the world as he knew it had changed irrevocably.

A group of people stood around, talking in hushed whispers. They stopped that too, as his school auto came to a halt in front of the wide open gates and watched him looking around in puzzlement. Some had fresh tears in their eyes upon seeing him. Even when he walked in to see his parents crying their heart out, to see his sister lying rigidly in their grandmother's lap, with the living room impossibly crowded, he didn't understand what was happening.

He was only five, after all.

But instinctively, he knew something had happened. Something very, very bad. He had never seen his sister lie so still. Their nap times were much later, after they had eaten their lunch together and played a while. She couldn't wait to go to school herself, and would eagerly lap up tales of whatever happened at his school that day. She'd make up stories, make-believe situations for herself, the next day, based on whatever he told her. If he said something about his teacher Miss A, tomorrow she would be in Miss B's class.

She was, of course, much braver than him. Even though younger than him by two whole years, she was never afraid of the dark. If the ball rolled into the unlit bedroom, all he had to do was call out to her and she'd run in to retrieve it.

Did he understand that he would have to face his fear of the dark by himself now? Did he know that his sister had gone beyond everything, now?

Did he realise that the person who had called him 'Anna', big brother, a hundred times a day, would never do so again?

Did that mean he was not a big brother anymore?

I don't know the answers to these questions. I don't think my cousin does. I know he misses the little girl that made him a brother. Though she was his sister for less than three years, I don't think he will ever not remember the bright girl who laughed with him, held onto his hands and had dreams of becoming a doctor one day.

Wherever she is, I hope she knows that he isn't scared of the dark anymore.

Lavanya Asokan

My Brother Saurabh

Tears rolled down my cheeks. Even trying to control them was a waste of effort as their power was far greater than my will. Twenty years and their power hasn't diminished even one iota. What is it that people say about Time healing all wounds? What a lie! Not a day has passed when I've not thought about him. He is and will always be my brother, no matter how many of his death anniversaries go by.

Death fossilised his soul, but it could not dent our relationship. I still am and will always remain the little sister of a loving brother. I find it tough to use the past tense for him, because he is still very much with me. He is still a young boy of twenty-one years, in his final year in IIT Kharagpur, even though I am now the mother of two grown-up kids. He lives in my heart and soul because he lives within us — his siblings, and our parents, whom he left without even saying goodbye.

It seems like life has come full circle. I am reliving my childhood days through my kids. Memories of our childhood overwhelm me, even now. It was full of fun, fights, teasing and endless hugs. I grew up playing what were considered 'boys' games' with him, much to the horror of our mother. But his death brought everything to a screeching halt. I became a responsible daughter overnight, trying hard to comfort our parents. I struggled to fill the void my brother's absence created; I still do.

My brother joined IIT and went to live in the hostel. He wrote me letters every week, without fail. I never missed him, because his letters made me feel like I was right there with him, sharing his trials and tribulations, his adventures and his day-to-day affairs.

When his belongings came from his hostel, after he passed away, I found all my letters, cards and the three rakhis I'd sent him in the box. I was awestruck.

I've never had the heart to celebrate that festival again. Though I relive our childhood celebrations of it over and over again, every year, as I watch my daughter get ready in her traditional attire to tie a rakhi on her brother's wrist, and my son teasingly negotiates with her for her gift.

Yes, I'm living those moments again. I am breathing it again through my kids. It is the same. Only the time has changed; the relationship has not. Brothers and sisters will remain so forever and ever till eternity.

My children, too, fight like we did. They tease each other, like we did. Our games of carom, monopoly, hide-and-seek, and Ludo have been replaced by theirs, of PlayStation, iPad, and multimedia games. We longed to play in the dust and dirt. They love to play in the shade and shelter. My children often argue about who their mother loves the most. Even we waged wars over the same question. We never got an answer then, and my children persist in trying to get one now.

I can see that they share the same bond that we did and feel like I am trapped in a strange time-warp. Have the faces and names somehow gotten entangled? I see myself in my daughter Pakhi when she seeks out her brother every time she's in trouble. I see my brother in my son Anshul, when he teases his sister so much she starts crying, and then cajoles her till she starts laughing. He tricks her into doing his share of chores and she happily does it. I would do the same for my brother. In exchange, he would say, he would buy me gifts from his first salary — a promise he could not keep. I want my son to keep all of his promises and be there for his little sister — now and always.

I've promised myself that I will keep my brother alive in my children's memory. This is the only way I know how to keep him with me — forever and ever. Thereafter he will live in the bed-time stories they will tell their children, because they are growing up listening to their favourite bed-time stories, my favourite all-the-time stories — stories of my brother Saurabh.

Leena Jha

A Star is Gone

'Phoolon ka taaron ka, sab ka kehna hai / Ek hazaaron mein, meri behna hai / Saari umar hame sang rehna hai ...'

As this song blares on FM, my eyes fill up with tears and my heartbeat goes crazy. You never did keep your promise, Bhaiya, the rest of my life lies before me, but you're not there! And yet, every time I hear this song, I feel you never did go away.

He was special, he was a star. He shone on earth for only a short time — just thirty-two years — before he proceeded on that heavenly walk towards the skies. They say it's the elevated souls that come to earth for short periods and with a special purpose; once their work is done, they become one of the jewels that adorn the night sky. My brother took on this difficult life to teach us many things. The sad part is that one learns only after all is lost and the other is gone.

Drug addiction, back then, was a taboo topic. Not treated like a disease, as it should be, but more like a crime. Our understanding, our exposure and yes, our reactions to this frightening reality were all so wrong. He became an addict at the tender age of eighteen and we went through a vast range of emotions, ranging from shock to disgust, from anger to fear. Today, as the mother of a fifteen-year-old, I can see only innocence, confusion and fears in my daughter's eyes as she stands on the threshold of adulthood, and I am instinctively aware of the support she needs from me. When I look at my teenager, I can't help but think about my brother and wonder about the turmoil that he must have been going through. Were we, as a family, able to understand him at all?

Like I said earlier, higher souls choose their difficult journey on this earth not only to reach a higher plane of existence for themselves, but also to teach others by example. He had a difficult life, to say the least, right from childhood, always in trouble with someone or the other. And then the dreaded world of drugs. As his days were interspersed with laughter and lows, pleasure and pain, sheer brilliance and shame, he trudged on year after year for twelve long and difficult years, in and out of rehabs, crying out for love, desperately wanting treatment and help.

There we were, helpless and lost in a country that, at the time, did not provide the right infrastructure and support or the understanding to help him. Had we realised then, that he was suffering from a disease and not perpetrating a crime, that all we needed to do was to come together to pull him out of it, to practise 'tough love' — maybe he would still be alive. We shouted at him for lying to us, punished him for stealing, and screamed at him for slipping back ... over and over again. We did this not realising that it was a chemical disorder, and that all these were mere symptoms of a disease called drug addiction.

His majestic voice still booms in my ears. Being his little sister, I adored him and was his biggest fan. How he loved to sing *Una Paloma Blanca* — and was he a free bird in the sky! No one could take his freedom away. Everyone who knew him said he had a heart of gold, the heart of a king, always reaching out to the needy and the underprivileged. Acting was his forte; sometimes I feel he donned so many personalities in his life — from King Lear to Antonio, from Jim Morrison to Naseer Saheb! Yes he was a great actor. Drama ruled his life, on stage and off. He spent hours in front of the mirror practising lines, dialogues and verses to bring perfection to each and every word, intonation and expression.

After years of fighting the addiction, losing the battle often and more times than we could remember, he finally won the war. He came out of rehab, reborn and a changed man, finally rid of his demons, finally released from the vice-like grip of those chemical fiends, finally free of the haze and horror that clouded his senses. And he stayed clean ... until his sudden death.

Such a beautiful, talented life ... laid to waste by that scourge called drugs.

My one question to the pastor at the prayer service on his death was, 'Why did God take him away when he had been clean for over two years?' His answer was, 'Never question God's timing. He gave him dignity at death.'

While there are days when I can't help but question the reason he had to leave us and go, I also know and believe, without a shred of doubt, that he did indeed have his dignity intact. He died a star.

'Phoolon ka taaron ka, sab ka kehna hai / Ek hazaaron mein , meri behna hai / Saari umar hame sang rehna hai ...'

This iconic number has become the definitive song about the brother-sister relationship. It was certainly representative of the feelings my brother and I had for each other. And I use this song in every Annual Day function at the play-school I run. I find a place for it, develop a theme around it, draw up a little plot especially for it to make it appropriate to the performance; yes, I will do anything to make the song work, because it is a tribute to my brother's memory, my star's memory.

And my star's name, my big brother's name, was Kabir.

Malika Varma

Remembering Rohan

Can you miss a brother you never had? My brother died before I was born, which technically makes me an only child. Or does it? How do you define a relationship that never was? You don't. You just deal with it as you go along.

I grew up an only child. I had no regrets. I wasn't really spoilt rotten, nor was I pampered. My upbringing was sensible, my childhood happy, warm and rich with friends and fun. I replied brightly to everyone who asked, 'Don't you feel lonely?' Many people asked, because my generation had few only children. I hope that the only children of the current generation don't have to field those same questions and comments about what then looked like a dysfunctional set-up to most people.

My answer to the nosy questions was, 'You can't miss what you never knew.' I had never known the company, the competition, the clashes and the relationship, how could I miss what I'd never had? But most people did not understand or accept my reasoning. And now, I don't accept it either. Because at some level, deep down, I always knew that I had had a brother.

As a child, I would occasionally fantasise about having an elder brother, never a younger one, never a sister. In pictures, I often had a niggling sense of something not right. A favourite uncle who looked a toddler, instead of the preschooler he should've been at my mom's baby shower. Constant prying questions from people about why my parents had waited four years to have me. Maybe I wondered about it, but never very seriously or frequently.

At the ripe old age of twenty, I had a dream. I was waiting about by my parents' front gate. My parents' Fiat came down the road, swung into our gate. A young man clambered out. He looked exactly like my father had at a younger age. And I knew this was my brother who had come home, after many years away. I knew also that he was twenty-three.

Still, I didn't give much credence to the dream. Not until two months later, when an aunt blurted out the secret everyone had been keeping from me. They'd wanted to protect me from pain and sadness. Nobody wanted to talk about a dearly beloved five-month-old, the first grandchild of the family, lost to an illness, gone in a few hours, leaving everyone devastated. They all considered me the apple of their eye, a blessing after that tragedy. Why talk about a child who's gone, when God blessed my parents with a healthy baby, who grew up, and is still very much alive and kicking?

Now that I knew, my brother had really come home, in a manner of speaking. For a week after finding out, I was dizzy with shock. I digested the story over the years, went through the stages of grieving very gradually. How do you grieve for someone lost decades ago?

So Rohan has been forgotten by most people. But his sister

remembers. I found a few precious pictures of him; he looked exactly like me albeit a good deal plumper. He had a mild club foot, for which he was under treatment. The poor baby would cry often because the therapy hurt. He was gorgeous, lots of thick black hair, merry black eyes and a cheerful smiling face. His birthday was just two days apart from mine. Coincidences mean a lot.

Rohan would have turned forty at the end of this year. I've lost thirty-six years of having a brother. My kids have lost an uncle, my husband a brother-in-law of almost the same age. My children have lost an aunt too, the woman Rohan might've married; she might've been the sister I never had. There might have been nephews and nieces from my side, first cousins to my children. What my parents have lost is a lot more. To think of them keeping it secret in the face of people's endless curious questioning makes my heart bleed for them and rage against people's insensitivity.

When someone dies young, we lose the future. It becomes about what might've been, what should've been, but never was. It all becomes glorified. Who knows whether I would have had a decent loving relationship with him? Maybe I wouldn't have been on speaking terms with him ... cold comfort to combat the sadness. I look around me and see estrangement, distance and very difficult relationships between some brothers and sisters. And I feel lucky that I will never have to face the pain of being cut off from my brother.

It's difficult to think of the support from my sibling that I might've had as an adult, of the thought that I could have been his baby sister. That aspect of my personality never got a chance to develop; it died before I was even born. My childhood was an ideal one, and I wasn't lying when I emphasised to people that I was not a lonely only child. But as a thirty-six-year-old, the loneliness has finally come to stay. Being an adult only child is not fun.

Rohan lives on in my heart, in my memory. I don't think of him all the time, I don't mourn endlessly. I never knew him; I will never know him, not in this life anyway. Someday we will meet again, either up there in heaven, or in another life.

Meeting someone with the name Rohan always startles me. There have been times when I longed for my brother intensely. I searched for him, wondering if he had been born again, if he would know me, if he's in my life right now, as someone who loves me and whom I love. Maybe he is around and I don't know it.

All the same, I do miss him. And I think I never want to figure out if I'm really an only child, or a sister without a brother. Looking forward is better than looking back, which is why I was very sure that I did not want my daughter to be an only child of an only child. Along came my son. I live vicariously through their sibling relationship. Their fights are as precious as their ganging-up-against-Amma strategies.

If I had never found out about Rohan, I might never have felt anything missing as an only child and my daughter might not have had a brother. I might not have got the courage needed to build my family differently. Sometimes, loss can translate into gain, even if it's a generation later. Fate works in curious ways. Some of Destiny you can't control, but there are choices you can make. I'm satisfied that I made mine well.

Nayantara Mallya

Inner Strength

When our elder sister — mentor and guide, friend and philosopher — was diagnosed with a terminal illness, our family was devastated. Suddenly her life was measurable in weeks, days and hours. And for her ... the picture one had painted — watching your children grow up, growing old with your spouse, caring for an aged parent — that picture is violently redrawn. There is a constant ache as the colour scheme of your life pattern is rearranged, for it is not your choice of colours, it is not your choice of design. It is a vicious paint spill destroying your canvas.

Bhanji, our beloved elder sister, was on a roller-coaster ride, whizzing through the abrupt change in landscape. There were moments of grief, there were moments of self-pity and there was rage and anger too at the turn of events. Sometimes, we four sisters just sat together and cried, each one of us trying to deal with the pain and grief in this suddenly new and unforgiving scenario.

But Bhanji was no ordinary person. She was a hero. This was a woman with a will of steel. This was a lady who understood that, come what may, the show must go on. That come what may, there can be a dignified exit. And that is what she chose for herself.

She was an active participant in all decisions relating to her treatment. She aggressively sought explanations from doctors, searched the Internet for the latest breakthrough in treatments and interacted with people who were suffering like her.

The doctor asked her to take 100% oxygen for an hour every day. She had a habit of reading her prayers for an hour a day. Those days it was not unusual to find the multi-tasking lady of the house with an oxygen pipe leading to her nose, head covered in reverence, praying.

As we sat at the dining table one afternoon, she casually commented that she was more likely to die of heart failure as she grew frail with the illness. That was just like her. No fuss, only facts.

The C-word was not banned from usage. It brought on educated, well-researched discussions. That was her take on other situations that had crept up on her earlier in life too. Face it. Resolve it. Move on. It was no different now.

One evening in her hospital room, she said to me, 'I think I may not be able to walk to the loo. Please get me some adult diapers.' In her presence I was my usual self, but the purchase at the chemist brought on copious tears that were wiped clean before I returned to her room. I could not be weak when I had to be there for her, to share her burden too. The question is, did I?

The day before she passed away, Mama came to visit her, lunch in hand. A couple of days prior to that she had been too weak to feed herself. I had been assisting her. As I opened the tiffin, she stretched out her hand towards me, implying she would eat on her own. This is how she wanted Mom to remember her. Strong, determined and collected.

'This ain't no wilting lily, this daughter of yours, Ma!' I thought I read that in her mind. A display of steely reserve despite the C-cells attacking her innards.

Mom left after lunch and Bhanji took a nap. It had become a routine that I pressed her hands and feet as she slept. It kept the circulation going. Sometimes I would hold her hand just so she would know she was not alone. That afternoon she opened her eyes briefly, squeezed my hand lightly and smiled a weak smile that had the most brilliant sparkle in it. It was Bhanji saying, 'I'm glad you are here!'

As I helped clean her up for cremation, I knew the strength I'd had in the months leading up to her demise was not mine at all. It was she who lent me her inner strength. Her behaviour in such trying times has now become a yardstick for me as I handle the googlies that life throws my way.

She taught me that it is not the cards that life doles out to you that matter. It is how you play the game that defines you as a person.

Niku Sidhu

Inside the Womb

'Those things which are precious are saved only by sacrifice.'

–David Kenyon Webster

Ziya is my beautiful thirty-year-old friend who has always smiled in life, no matter what the situation has been. From her, I've learnt that nothing is impossible. Nothing. This is her story. This is her victory.

Ziya and Dev had been married for eight years and had been trying for a baby for quite some time. I had always known that Ziya was having problems conceiving as she had told me that her hormone levels were messed up and she had a blocked tube. She had been undergoing fertility treatment for the past one year. I could only imagine what life must have been for her, waiting month after month for her blood test report in the hope that, one day, it would read 'positive'. No matter how severe the treatment was, she never gave up. She would howl and cry over the phone with me on the first day of her period, all broken, all vulnerable and then, the very next day, she was ready to fight again.

This was her persistence and she had the will to go as far as life would take to ultimately fulfil her dream.

And then, it happened! Ziya called me on one hot July afternoon saying that her IVF had finally worked and she was expecting. I was elated. I couldn't think of anyone who deserved it more.

I went to visit Ziya immediately. I jumped with joy when she told me that she was carrying triplets. My first reaction was that God had truly listened to her prayers and, despite all the pain and heartbreak, He had now blessed her with triple joy. But something was not right. Ziya did not look happy. And then she started crying. I tried to console her and talk to her. After what seemed like ages, she said, 'I can't carry the triplets to full term because I don't have the structure to sustain three pregnancies. I have to get one … aborted.' With that, she broke down once again. I was too shocked to say anything. What could I have said?

The next month, Ziya started talking to her three children. She named them Aalia, Vedant and Kajal. She would tell me that she could hear what her children were saying. She would tell me they were all inside the womb, together and happy. They felt secure because there were three of them. One was always watching out for the other two. They would share the food amongst themselves and rebel if they didn't like a particular meal. They would hear Dev's voice reading them a story every night. In the ultrasound as well, their actions were so coordinated. For instance, during one of Ziya's initial ultrasounds, when she was still being looked after by the fertility doctor, who, in plain, simple words was super attractive, Ziya was sure that Aalia and Kajal were jumping in excitement at seeing the doctor, whereas Vedant kicked about in irritation. Another time, the child who was in the middle sucked his thumb while the other two frantically shook their little arms to dissuade the middle one from doing so.

Initially, I thought that Ziya was losing her mind. Her depression was extreme. But I could not deny the babies' actions at the ultrasound as I was present there. Our human mind tries to perceive things in its own way, but this was eerie. I understood exactly what Ziya was trying to say, and I actually started believing that the babies had already formed an unbreakable bond inside the womb.

Within three months, Ziya went through the reduction with a heavy heart. Somehow, she could never bring herself to accept the fact that her triplets were being reduced to twins. She would often tell me that one of the babies had sacrificed their life so that her siblings could see the world, and she was so proud of the baby.

In the meanwhile, the pattern of the other two children changed. It was evident that they were missing their third sibling; right after the reduction, when Ziya went for the ultrasound to check whether the other two children were doing fine, they could see that both the babies' heads were facing the third sibling who was now no more. It was almost as if they were refusing to let go; as if they realised that their sibling had given up its life for them. After that, with every ultrasound that Ziya had, the babies somehow looked very quiet. Were they mourning? Could this be true? Can such a strong bond be formed between siblings when they are inside the womb? Maybe I would not have believed it otherwise. But how can I deny what I saw?

Perhaps there are some things that go beyond science. And perhaps the bond between siblings is one such thing.

Kajal

More Chicken Soup?

Share your heart with the rest of the world. If you have a story, poem or article (your own or someone else's) that you feel belongs in a future volume of Chicken Soup for the Indian Soul, please email us at cs.indiansoul@westland-tata.com or send it to:

Westland Ltd
S-35A, 3rd Floor
Green Park Main Market
New Delhi 110 016

We will make sure that you and the author are credited for the contribution. Thank you!

Contributors

Aamrapali Bhogle Sonawane is the owner of NORTH LIGHT — a Mumbai-based interiors and creative design firm. Since her early years, Aamrapali has been actively involved in several social contribution initiatives. She enjoys spiritual ecstasy through photography, creative design and deep silence. She can be reached at: aamrapalibhogle@gmail.com.

Aarti Katoch Pathak is a professor of Economics, freelance writer and a travel enthusiast. She has recently compiled the title *Chicken Soup for the Indian Soul: Teens Talk: Growing Up*. She would love to hear from you at aartikpat@gmail.com.

Abha Atitkar Jain is a hopelessly optimistic person. Tears come easy to her — for good and bad. She loves living her life to the fullest with her beautiful family. She simply cannot live without books and the internet. And love and laughter.

Aishwarya Bharadia is currently in the 11th grade at Mahatma Gandhi International School and enjoys reading, swimming and her sister's company. You can reach her on aishwarya-b@hotmaiil.com.

Akanksha Agarwal took up writing short stories as a hobby when she was in college. Having an aspiration to become a writer, these stories are her initial attempt at professional writing. She has her own blog akanksha-lifeisprecious.blogspot.com where she posts her short stories. You can write to her at akanksha10@gmail.com.

Amrita Rajan is a writer and internet enthusiast. Her brother is big, strong, scary — and absolutely refuses to beat anyone up when she asks.

Anushree Karnani is a business developer in a popular fashion house in Kolkata and mother to a ten-year-old daughter. She has been writing since childhood, winning awards for creative writing in school. Writing is her chosen method of introspection and expression. She has written for two Chicken Soup for Indian Soul titles. She can be reached at anushree76@gmail.com.

Arthur Cardozo heads his own advertising communication and marketing agency, Cardozone Communico. Besides being an adman, he is also an actor, satirist and cartoonist with over 5000 published works to his credit. His out-of-the-box ideation workshops and classes on creative communication and branding for various corporates have received rave reviews. Contact: arthur.cardozo@gmail.com.

With a quirky sense of comprehension and a knack for dabbling in abstract subjects, originality is what drives **Ashirwad Mhatre**. From scripting movies to getting down to writing a book, his hands are full. Professionally, he writes copy for advertisements. You can visit his site, www.ashirwadmhatre.com to know more.

Nourishing the dream to publish her own collection of stories someday, **Avantika Debnath** is your regular girl next door who tries to make extraordinary stories out of her ordinary life, every day. She can be reached at avantika.dg@gmail.com.

Bali D. Sanghvi is passionate about life, her husband, her twins, books, poetry, travelling and writing. An honours graduate in Accountancy, she has always been partial to literary pursuits. She started writing poetry at the age of thirteen and is working on her novel. She co-runs an online library in Kolkata, www.myonlinelibrary.co.in. She can be contacted at cupidrose@rediffmail.com.

Chitra Srikrishna is a classical musician and freelance writer based in Bangalore. A graded artiste of AIR, she performs regularly on stage in India and overseas. She has several music albums to her credit. Her first person essays, middles and travel pieces have appeared in leading newspapers and magazines. She blogs at www.chitrasrikrishna.com.

Deepika is passionate about life, poetry, music, Darjeeling tea, Indian Railways and looking at the changing colours of the sky. She hopes that by some act of miracle, she will have lots of zeroes added to her bank balance. Then she can happily shift to the cool mountains and retire. As that's not happening, she is busy earning a livelihood.

Dipali Taneja is in her mid-fifties, and has a husband and four kids who have all enriched her life immensely. The past few years have found her globe-trotting in both the real and virtual world. Online friends have added new dimensions to her life. Books, music, theatre, films and art are important to her.

Dipika Chakraborty is a homemaker settled in Kolkata. She has quite a few Bengali short story publications to her credit. This is her first attempt at English short story writing. A loving sibling who has always been surrounded by her brothers and sisters, this is a tribute to her favourite one, who left her very early.

Farahdeen Khan is the author of *Heartbeat* and *Inner Voices*. He is currently working on a book on master cinematographers, co-authored by Ravi K. Chandran, award-winning cinematographer. Khan is a partner in 2927 Communications, a business group with a branding and communications division and an art firm. He is a painter and also writes screenplays for leading film studios. Contact: farahdeenkhan@yahoo.com.

Goutam Dutta is an engineer by qualification and he has been working in the field of minerals and metallurgy for the last twenty years. His interests span from soccer to cooking to travelling within India. Writing is a passion that he pursues during his spare time. He can be reached at gdutta17@gmail.com.

Ilika Chakravarty loves the world and all things that make it beautiful — man, landforms and animals. Travelling gives her a high, and as a Taurean, she loves all good things in life. She juggles her time between her daughter, family and work – so far, she hasn't been too bad in the balancing act really.

Ingrid Albuquerque-Solomon has been in the Indian mainstream media for over three decades and been editor of several national publications including *Stardust*, *Savvy* and *Bangalore Times*. She has launched a publishing company and authored several books. Currently, she works for Haggai Institute International which advances leadership skills in Christian professionals. She can be reached at ingridalbuquerque@yahoo.com.

Jayanti Dutta Roy is an academician in Punjab University, Chandigarh. She has a multidisciplinary background with a PhD in Zoology and degrees in fine arts and several languages. She grew up in the quiet town of Chamba, Himachal Pradesh. Her areas of interest are creative writing, education and health. You can reach her at: jayantiduttaroy@yahoo.co.in.

Joie Bose Chatterjee has degrees in Literature from St. Xavier's College, Kolkata and Jawaharlal Nehru University, New Delhi. Previously a freelance journalist and an educator, her creative endeavours have been published in newspapers and anthologies. Settled in Kolkata, she is working on her collection of short stories and can be contacted at joiebose@gmail.com.

Juhi Rai Farmania is an entrepreneur, actor and writer currently building an e-commerce project in India, UK and Iran. Editor of *Chicken Soup for the Indian Soul at Work*, she paints and dances to remain connected to her soul. A believer in miracles, she dreams of creating mainstream movies and large organisations in the future. Contact: juhi.rai@gmail.com.

Jyoti Kalapa is a German translator and interpreter. A mother of fifteen-year-old twins, she lives in Bangalore where she enjoys cooking, reading, writing, music, art, theatre, trekking, running and getting away from the city for holidays. She can be reached at: s_kalapa@hotmail.com.

Kailash Srinivasan has a degree in creative writing from Macquarie University, Sydney. His first book, *What Happened to That Love*, was recently published. His second book will be out soon. His work has also appeared in literary magazines and other titles of Chicken Soup. He can be reached at kailash.srinivasan@gmail.com.

Kajal is a dreamer and optimist; someone, who feels life deeply. A quote which aptly describes her: 'She walks amongst us, but is not one of us'. Words are sacred to her and writing is almost like going to a temple. Mysterious, loyal, compassionate and caring ... she is all that and more.

Kavita Chandrashekhar is a software engineer by profession and a spiritual teacher by choice. She holds a PhD in Metaphysics. Working with all major forms of alternative medicines, she conducts workshops on creating spiritual awareness and co-creating better lives in organisations. Contact: dr.kavitachandrashekhar@gmail.com; www.immortalpresence.com; www.iemanate.com.

Khursheed Dinshaw is a Pune-based freelance writer with more than 800 published articles in major Indian newspapers and magazines. An avid traveller she writes on lifestyle, travel, health, food, trends, people and culture. She has also undertaken editing for publications and can be reached at khursheeddinshaw@hotmail.com.

Lavanya Asokan is a mother of two delightful children and has long held a dream of becoming an author. The written word has always fascinated her and she hopes that one day, her words can fascinate others. In the meantime, she slakes her thirst by writing for a few websites.

Leena Jha is an Ahmedabad-based homemaker and a mother of two sweet kids. She writes when emotions overflow. She has been published in the *Times of India* and *Femina Online*. Currently she is working on a book, *Women in Science*. She gets her ideas from her travels and by observing people. Her email: leenajha.ar@gmail.com.

An ex-student of Loreto House and Loreto College, mother to two daughters and administrator of Kangaroo Kids, a well-known pre-school and kindergarten in Kolkata, **Malika Varma** wears her many hats with aplomb. Actively involved with kantha revival projects like Malika's Katha Collection and SHE (Self Help Enterprise), Malika also works closely with NGOs such as Calcutta Foundation, Child Care Centre, Udayan etc.

Maria Francis is currently day-dreaming about authoring a novel someday. She is either found with her nose buried in a book or on the brink of a new weight-loss regime. She blogs her take on life at wannabauthor. wordpress.com. She can be contacted at maria.francis@gmail.com.

Meera Govan is a consulting professional by day and a blogger by night. She blogs at happyhoursbeginhere.wordpress.com, where she chronicles the fact, fiction and hotchpotch that is her life. She lives in Gurgaon with her uber-bohemian husband, Abhilash. Meera can be reached at govan. meera@gmail.com.

Melanie Lobo is a Pune-based freelance writer. Her husband and son inspire her with new writing material daily. When she isn't spinning articles or battling with her son's homework, Melanie sings soprano with a choir. She writes for Women's Web, a reputed women's website. Write to her at lobomelanie@gmail.com.

Monika Pant has authored several English course books. Her poems have been published in *Fancy Realms* and her micro-fiction in *Twenty20* journal. Her collection of short stories, *Through the Broken Pane,* is about to be published. She is currently writing a couple of novels. She can be reached at mpant65@gmail.com.

Mudra Rawal enjoys writing, be it designing test cases, reporting mails, scribbling poems, travelogues, stories and what not! She staunchly believes that everything and everyone around her has stories to be unearthed. These days she is deeply involved with her new-found love of backpacking trips. She blogs at mudrarawal.blogspot.com and you can drop her mail any time at mudra.rawal@gmail.com.

Nayantara Mallya, a mom of two, feminist, idealist, writer and people-watcher, strongly suspects life challenges to be disguised learning and growing opportunities. When she finally 'grows up', she's going to write a book and be a counsellor. Addicted to the written word, she writes feverishly … anything, all the time, everywhere.

Neelam Chandra is an engineer by profession. About 200 of her stories/poems have been published in various leading magazines and anthologies. She has won various awards in literary field and also has three books published to her credit. She can be reached at: neelamsaxena27@yahoo. com or 0522 2450251.

Neha Sinha is a business analyst for a well-known MNC. Writing is a hobby that she has pursued from an early age. She is what she writes. Read her blog to know more: nehasinha.wordpress.com. E-mail her at: nsinha.0206@gmail.com.

Nida Karim went straight from college to the board room. When she isn't attending meetings, she is secretly working on her first novel. She loves to travel and explore, collecting interesting souvenirs and friends and finding her own adventures along the way. You can mail her at nidakarim@gmail.com.

A service industry veteran with over twenty years of experience and an instructor/trainer for the last five, **Niku Sidhu** is experimenting here with her love for the written word through a sibling fondly remembered. She can be reached at: niksy2@gmail.com.

Palak Surana is a 2nd year engineering student from Coimbatore. Apart from cramming codes and circuits, she enjoys writing, reading and cooking. She lives with her loving parents and sisters who are also loving, yet crazy. She can be reached at: plksurana@yahoo.com.

Poornima Dhiman belongs to Dehradun and lives in Delhi-NCR. She holds a Master's degree in Computer Application and works in a MNC. She loves to write and dreams of getting her own book published one day. She can be contacted at poornima.dhiman@gmail.com.

Pragati Adhikari, a NIFT graduate, is a designer by profession. Based in Bangalore, she is now a stay-at-home mom of two lovely daughters. She is also a painter, poet, writer and counsellor. She strongly believes in the saying, 'Things do not happen, they are made to happen'. She can be contacted at pragatiadhikari@yahoo.co.in.

Pramod Shankar is the author of *From the Terrace* (poetry) and *The Power of Positive Healing*. He is also a photographer and public speaker. An advertising professional, Pramod lives in Bangalore with his wife Lakshmi and two teenage children. Visit shootitifitrhymes.blogspot.com, or e-mail: pramshanks@gmail.com

Prashant Kumar, popularly known as 'Kenya' by his friends, has a postgraduate degree in Telecom management from Symbiosis and is currently working at a global software firm. He loves coffee and cookies. When he is not at office, he spends time reading and watching his favourite soaps. Contact him at: prash1006@gmail.com.

Pratishtha Durga is a fur-hater, animal-lover, part-time dreamer, full-time writer, and a desktop philosopher. She yearns to travel across the world, and live her life out of a suitcase. Her blog, her cooking and her friends make her life a busy one.

Preeti Shenoy is an author and an artist with two national bestsellers. Her third book will be out in February 2012. Her interests are as multifarious and diverse as her several academic degrees, which include an internationally recognised qualification from UK in portraiture. To know more go to preetishenoy.com.

Prerna Shah deeply believes in the magic of a well-told story. For seven and a half years she wrote stories every day, albeit for a newspaper. Then she went on to pursue a second Master's in Creative and Life Writing at Goldsmiths, University of London. If you have an interesting story to share, she would love to hear from you at write2prerna@gmail.com.

Prerna Uppal is a London-based freelance writer who writes for many

Indian publications. She did a BSc in Zoology before choosing the pen over the scalpel. A postgraduate in communication studies, she has reported for the *Week*, *Indian Express* and CNN-IBN and is currently busy raising funds for charity. Reach her at prerna.uppal@gmail.com.

Fifteen-year-old **Priyanjali Maitra** is preparing for the 2012 board exams. She is a voracious reader and enjoys music. Having lived in many cities she feels she already has a rich bank of experiences. She looks forward to an exciting future, travelling around the world and gathering varied experiences that she wants to immortalise through her writing.

Priyanka Goenka is a working professional and mother to her beautiful, little daughter, Sara. She's an MBA from IIM Calcutta, and works in the entertainment and logistics industry. She's vice president of Theatrecian, the most prolific theatre group in Kolkata.

Rajyashree Dutt has been running Write-Arm for over twenty years, writing, editing and publishing primarily for the development sector (www.write-arm.com). She also owns Right Lines, an art gallery in Bangalore (www.right-lines.com). She is also the editor of *Chicken Soup for the Indian Couple's Soul*. Contact: mamadutt@gmail.com.

Raksha Bharadia lives in Ahmedabad with her husband and two daughters. To know more about her, visit her website: rakshabharadia.in.

Raamesh Gowri Raghavan moonlights as a copywriter by day, and daylights as a poet and writer by night. He thinks he writes really funny stuff, but his friends don't seem to agree. His dearest wish is to be remembered with tears a century after his time.

Rasagya Kabra is a Delhi-based writer and blogger. She is graduating in economics from St. Stephen's College, Delhi. Her work has appeared in *Journeys* (an anthology launched at the Birmingham Book Festival, 2010) and the magazine *Reading Hour* (September 2011). Read her work at: rasagya.blogspot.com.

Reeti Roy is from Calcutta. Her work has been published in Indian newspapers and magazines such as the *Statesman*, *Telegraph*, *Times of India*, *Femina* and *Tehelka* and her travel writing has been published by Matador Network. She is currently pursuing a Master's degree in social anthropology at the London School of Economics and Political Science. She can be reached at reeti.roy@gmail.com.

Rehana Ali is a school teacher, a plant geneticist, an environmentalist and an aspiring writer. She delves into her experiences with school children for her stories. Her other interests are trekking, travelling, reading and sewing. She can be contacted at ali.rehana@gmail.com.

Richa Wahi is a creative writing teacher working in a reputed day boarding school in Kolkata. She also works as a trainer with British Council. Her work focuses around introducing children to the joys of writing and honing their skills. She may be reached at wahiricha@gmail. com.

Rishi Chhibber, a software engineer, lives in California with his wife, two kids, and a fish called Jumperoo. When not adding and removing bugs from his software, he enjoys breaking his kids Lego towers, contemplating philosophies of Curious George, and when his family allows, he sketches, reads, writes, photographs, and sometimes sleeps — in random order.

Ritika Mittal Nair runs a textile brand called Mora that takes her to some of the most remote parts of India in search of rare weaves. It was during one of these textile treasure-hunt expeditions that she found this family that she has written about for this title.

Sagarika Chakraborty is a corporate lawyer by profession and a writer by passion. She loves to travel, cook, think, dance and to write about anything that touches her soul. And most importantlym she is the luckiest sister alive. This story is dedicated to the most important person in her life — her elder sister and lifeline Kamalika.

Sanaea Patel is an avid travel and food writer who loves travelling, challenging her palette, listening to music and reading non-fiction. She can be contacted at sanaea.patel@hotmail.com.

Sathya Saran edited *Femina* for 12 years and shot to fame with her 'Me to You' column that she continued in her next magazine, *Me*, for DNA. Sathya has also authored *Night Train and Other Stories*; *10 Years with Guru Dutt: Abrar Alvi's Journey*; and a compilation of her writings, *From Me to You*. Now working on a second film book, she also conducts writing workshops.

Satish Shenoy works in a multinational at a senior management level, and dreams of the time when he sits in his sea-facing mansion, plays his guitar, watches movies and reads books. A devoted dad and a family man, he enjoys writing and pencil sketching. He can be contacted on sats.

shenoy@gmail.com.

Savitri Babulkar is a retired teacher and freelance journalist. Her hobbies include reading, writing, music and dramatics. She can be reached at savitri.babulkar@gmail.com.

Shashi Agarwal is a homemaker and the mother of two daughters. She likes a bit of reading and writing. She can be reached at agarwalsash@gmail.com.

If **Sheetal Bagaria** were a bird, she would be a peacock – colourful, vibrant, and prone to bouts of impromptu dancing. She can eke out a story or poem from any real-life incident. Currently a homemaker living in Calcutta, her dream is to publish a voluminous compilation of her poetry.

Shifa Maitra's combines her passion for storytelling with a high pressure job as a TV channel head ... never easy, but great fun. She writes regularly for the Chicken Soup series, as well as articles and scripts for live events. Contact: shifamaitra@gmail.com.

Shoumik De was an IT Engineer, having worked the industry for 10 years. He decided to quit the cantankerous corporate world to pursue his passion. Writing comes naturally to him as he has always had a vivid imagination since childhood along with a flair for telling tales. Shoumik is a photographer by profession now, and a voracious reader. Contact: shoumikde@gmail.com.

Shreeja Mohatta Jhawar is a graphics and web designer and a social entrepreneur, who organises uplifting workshops globally. She is the co-founder of Think Unlike. A natural writer and a philanthropist, she co-founded Kritagya Foundation an organisation that aims at aiding the destitute. Reach her at shreeja.jhawar@gmail.com.

Smriti Lamech is a writer who lives in and loves Delhi. She also loves her babies, her husband and her life, hot chocolate fudge and reading, in no particular order. She loves dabbling and gardening and on a good day fits 36 hours into the given 24. On a bad day she recommends staying out of her way and corresponding via e-mail to smritilamech@gmail.com.

Sreelekha Chatterjee is a researcher and an editor by profession. She has a postgraduate degree in science from Calcutta University and is also a trained singer with a degree in music (Geeta Bharati). Although her discipline is Plant Physiology with research experience in biotechnology, she considers creative writing to be her true passion.

Srinath Girish is a lawyer, living in Calicut with his wife Rathna, son Bharat and mother Sita. In 2006, he started blogging on sulekha. com. His articles have appeared in the *Indian Express* and the *Khaleej Times*, Dubai. Published by Penguin India in the anthology *BlogPrint*, this is his third Chicken Soup for the Indian Soul story. Contact: srinathgirish@gmail.com.

Sujatha Bagal is a full-time mother and part-time writer whose essays and articles have appeared in various online and mainstream publications. She lives in the suburbs of Washington, D.C.

Sunayana Roy writes for a living, acts for fun and sings for enjoyment. She lives in Calcutta with her son and husband. She can be contacted at sunayanaroy@gmail.com or @sunayanaroy (Twitter).

By day, **Supriya Maulick Mahajan** is a lawyer and by night she dreams of writing her own book one day. She is based in Gurgaon and can be reached atsupriya.maulick@gmail.com.

Sushma Malhotra is a home manager from Delhi with an unconventional mindset. An ex-Dipsite and alumni of Lady Sri Ram College, she likes keeping in touch with all her friends. Blessed with a supportive and loving husband, daughter and son-in-law, she loves taking care of her adorable pet as well. Mail her at malhotrasush@gmail.com.

T.S. Karthik has an MBA from the Indian Institute of Planning and Management, Chennai. He is a voracious reader and an aspiring writer. He has won several prizes in business quizzes. His pastime includes watching movies, plays and listening to music. He believes in inspiring people to achieve their dreams. He can be reached at tskarthik13@yahoo.com.

Tishani Doshi is an award-winning poet and dancer of Welsh-Gujarati descent. Her first novel, *The Pleasure Seekers*, was published to critical acclaim in 2010. A new collection of poems, *Everything Begins Elsewhere*, is forthcoming. She divides her time between Cheyyur, Tamil Nadu, and elsewhere. www.tishanidoshi.com.

Trishna Pillai, stay-at-home mom to two lovely girls, has written many articles and award-winning poetry, since she was 17. She is an avid crafter and blogger, and loves cooking up a feast. She currently resides in Melbourne with her family. Trishna can be contacted at craftymaa@

gmail.com.

V. Thyagarajan was a part of the Defence and Atomic Energy of the Government of India, for over three decades. A voracious reader, he enjoys cooking, listening to Carnatic music and solving Sudoku. He lives with his family and son in a suburb of Chennai. Contact him at: kart1975@gmail.com.

Vaishali Shroff is a freelance writer, editor, columnist, and runs a children's reading club, Eik Thi Rani (eikthirani.wordpress.com). With movie scripts for animation studios, children's stories on smories (smories.com/author/vaishali-shroff//), over twelve short stories in various anthologies, a children's illustrated book contract, and a toddler that is more than an inspiration, she continues to write. Contact: vaishali.shroff@gmail.com.

Vandana Kumari Jena is an IAS officer by profession and a writer by inclination. She has published over 250 middles in leading newspapers. Her short stories have appeared in 11 anthologies, including *Black White and Various Shades of Brown*, *India Smiles*, and *Blogprint*. Her novel *The Dance of Death* was published in 2008. Her e-mail id is: vandana.jena@gmail.com.

Vasudha Iyer is the pen name of Padmaja Ganeshan-Singh. She is a Metallurgical Engineer from JNTU Hyderabad and an MBA from XLRI, Jamshedpur. She currently works in HR for Deloitte. She loves writing, although it had been restricted to school/ college magazines, e-mails and office presentations! She hopes to write a complete novel soon. She can be reached at: padmaja.ganeshan@gmail.com.

Veena Gomes-Patwardhan is an experienced Mumbai-based science journalist and freelance writer, copyeditor and copywriter with national and international credits. She is currently working on her first book. Her life's motto is 'Live and let live'. For more details please visit veenapatwardhan.com and feel free to contact her sat veenagpatwardhan@gmail.com.

Vibha Batra is a copywriter by profession and fiction writer by passion. She is the published author of *Ishaavaasya Upanishad* (a translation of her grandfather's book), *Tongue in Cheek* (a collection of poems) and *A Twist of Lime* (a collection of short stories). She can be reached at vibhy.batra@gmail.com.

Permissions

Quality Time. Reprinted by permission of Chitra Srikrishna. © 2012 Chitra Srikrishna.

Because of This Bond. Reprinted by permission of Baisali Chatterjee Dutt. © 2012 Baisali Chatterjee Dutt.

'We're Getting a Boy Baby!' Reprinted by permission of Nayantara Mallya. © 2012 Nayantara Mallya.

Pilgrimages of Love. Reprinted by permission of Prashant Kumar. © 2012 Prashant Kumar.

The Four of Us. Reprinted by permission of Rehana Ali. © 2012 Rehana Ali.

Same-Same, But Different. Reprinted by permission of Ritika Mittal Nair. © 2012 Ritika Mittal Nair.

Full House … Full of Love. Reprinted by permission of Veena Gomes-Patwardhan. © 2012 Veena Gomes-Patwardhan.

Unity in Adversity. Reprinted by permission of Aamrapali Bhogle Sonawane. © 2012 Aamrapali Bhogle Sonawane.

The Buddy. Reprinted by permission of Aarti Katoch Pathak. © 2012 Aarti Katoch Pathak.

Touching Wood. Reprinted by permission of Abha Atitkar Jain. © 2012 Abha Atitkar Jain.

370   PERMISSIONS

Selected Scenes from 'Memories of a Life'. Reprinted by permission of Sagarika Chakraborty. © 2012 Sagarika Chakraborty.

When Opposites (Finally) Meet. Reprinted by permission of Sathya Saran. © 2012 Sathya Saran.

Waging Wars. Reprinted by permission of Shashi Agarwal. © 2012 Shashi Agarwal.

Voices. Reprinted by permission of Sheetal Bagaria. © 2012 Sheetal Bagaria.

Leave All Your Tears for Me. Reprinted by permission of Shreeja Mohatta Jhawar. © 2012 Shreeja Mohatta Jhawar.

Watching Out. Reprinted by permission of Trishna Pillai. © 2012 Trishna Pillai.

Confessions of a Sister. Reprinted by permission of Vaishali Shroff. © 2012 Vaishali Shroff.

My Sister, My Soulmate. Reprinted by permission of Vibha Batra. © 2012 Vibha Batra.

Never Apart. Reprinted by permission of Ashirwad Mhatre. © 2012 Ashirwad Mhatre.

Like Brother Like Brother. Reprinted by permission of Farahdeen Khan. © 2012 Farahdeen Khan.

I Love You, Too. Reprinted by permission of Kailash Srinivasan. © 2012 Kailash Srinivasan.

A Letter to My Boys. Reprinted by permission of Baisali Chatterjee Dutt. © 2012 Baisali Chatterjee Dutt.

Big Brother Calling. Reprinted by permission of Prerna Shah. © 2012 Prerna Shah.

The Shirt off His Back. Reprinted by permission of Rishi Chhibber. © 2012 Rishi Chibber.

Multan — 1947, a Story Retold. Reprinted by permission of Sushma Malhotra. © 2012 Sushma Malhotra.

Of Monkeys and Best Men. Reprinted by permission of Vandana Jena. © 2012 Vandana Jena.

When Little Brothers Grow Up. Reprinted by permission of Avantika Debnath. © 2012 Avantika Debnath.

A Natural Bond. Reprinted by permission of Savitri Babulkar. © 2012 Swati Babulkar.

A Sense of Sibling Love. Reprinted by permission of Sreelekha Chatterjee. © 2012 Sreelekha Chatterjee.

The Manifold Advantages of a Big Brother. Reprinted by permission of Sujatha Bagal. © 2012 Sujatha Bagel.

The Impromptu Party. Reprinted by permission of Sunayana Roy. © 2012 Sunayana Roy.

Fisherprice Men. Reprinted by permission of Tishani Doshi. © 2012 Tishani Doshi.

Night Duty on Raksha Bandhan. Reprinted by permission of Vandana Jena. © 2012 Vandana Jena.

Big Brother's Got Your Back. Reprinted by permission of Vasudha Iyer. © 2012 Vasudha Iyer.

Of Cars and Cushions. Reprinted by permission of Priyanka Goenka. © 2012 Priyanka Goenka.

A Brother in Need. Reprinted by permission of T.S. Karthik. © 2012 T.S. Karthik.

Through Sobs and Spoonfuls. Reprinted by permission of Aishwarya Bharadia. © 2012 Aishwarya Bharadia.

Of Missed Calls, Plastic Bags and Love. Reprinted by permission of Deepika Sahu. © 2012 Deepika Sahu.

The Gap. Reprinted by permission of Maria Francis. © 2012 Maria Francis.

Always Ahead. Reprinted by permission of Meera Govan. © 2012 Meera Govan.

Some Things Remain the Same. Reprinted by permission of Monika Pant. © 2012 Monika Pant.

A Boon. Reprinted by permission of Pragati Adhikari. © 2012 Pragati Adhikari.

The Best Gift Ever. Reprinted by permission of Priyanjali Maitra. © 2012 Priyanjali Maitra.

Three Sisters in Vienna. Reprinted by permission of Raksha Bharadia. © 2012 Raksha Bharadia.

Sent by God. Reprinted by permission of V. Thyagaraj. © 2012 V. Thyagaraj.

Lighting up My Life. Reprinted by permission of Vandana Jena. © 2012 Vandana Jena.

My 'Cuty' Younger Brother. Reprinted by permission of Akanksha Agarwal Puprediwar © 2012 Akanksha Agarwal Puprediwar..

No Matter What. Reprinted by permission of Joie Bose Chatterjee. © 2012 Joie Bose Chatterjee.

My Little Brother. Reprinted by permission of Neelam Chandra. © 2012 Neelam Chandra.

Too Much Love. Reprinted by permission of Neha Sinha. © 2012 Neha Sinha.

The Musketeers. Reprinted by permission of Rajyashree Dutt. © 2012 Rajyashree Dutt.

Three to Tango. Reprinted by permission of Satish Shenoy. © 2012 Satish Shenoy.

The Brotherly Bond. Reprinted by permission of Smriti Lamech. © 2012 Smriti Lamech.

Oh Brother, My Brother. Reprinted by permission of Dipali Taneja. © 2012 Dipali Taneja.

Unworshipped Idols. Reprinted by permission of Dipika Chakraborty. © 2012 Dipika Chakraborty.

Christmas Grieving. Reprinted by permission of Ingrid Albuquerque-Solomon. © 2012 Ingrid Albuquerque-Solomon.

Once a Brother Had a Sister. Reprinted by permission of Lavanya Asokan. © 2012 Lavanya Asokan.

My Brother Saurabh. Reprinted by permission of Leena Jha. © 2012 Leena Jha.

A Star is Gone. Reprinted by permission of Malika Varma. © 2012 Malika Varma.

Remembering. Reprinted by permission of Rohan Nayantara Mallya. © 2012 Nayantara Mallya.

Inner Strength. Reprinted by permission of Niku Sidhu. © 2012 Niku Sidhu.